T3-AJK-602

BRAZIL SINCE 1930

GARLAND REFERENCE LIBRARY
OF SOCIAL SCIENCE
(VOL. 59)

I.
Reference Works and Research Aids

A. REFERENCE AIDS

1. Reference Works: Statistical Sources

1. Arriaga, Eduardo. *New Life Tables for Latin American Populations in the Nineteenth and Twentieth Centuries.* Berkeley: University of California Press, 1968.

   Summarizes the major Brazilian censuses: 1872, 1890, 1900, 1920, 1940, 1960.

2. Brasil. Conselho de Imigração e Colonização. *Modern Brazil: Resources and Possibilities.* Rio de Janeiro: Immigration & Colonization Council, 1949.

   A statistical almanac for potential immigrants and foreign investors.

3. Brasil. Departamento Nacional de Estatística. *Estatística Intelectual do Brasil (1929).* 2 vols. Rio de Janeiro: Instituto Brasileiro de Bibliografia e Documentação, 1931-1932.

   Contains detailed statistical data on libraries, schools, voluntary associations, newspapers, publishing houses, and theaters on the eve of the 1930 Revolution.

4. Brasil. Diretoria Geral de Estatística. *Anúario estatístico do Brasil. 1936.* Rio de Janeiro: Instituto Brasileiro de Geografia e Estatístico, 1937.

   Contains tabular data on population, agriculture, industry, revenue, cultural facilities, education, and a host of other subjects.

5. Brasil. Diretoria Geral de Saúde Pública. *Boletim de estatística demógrafo-sanitária da cidade do Rio de Janeiro.* Rio de Janeiro: Departamento de Saúde Público, 1900-1930.

A monthly bulletin containing statistics on demographic and hygienic conditions for the former federal capital, with information also on mortality, public health, sanitary services as well as births, deaths, and marriages.

6. *Brasil em dados 75*. Rio de Janeiro: Rio Gráfica Editôres, 1975.

   Contains extensive statistical data about productivity, economic growth, and natural resources. Designed to impress foreign readers with Brazil's vast potential.

7. Brasil. Instituto Brasileiro de Geografia e Estatística. *Anuário estatístico do Brasil. Ano V, 1939-40*. Rio de Janeiro: I.B.G.E., 1941.

   A major statistical source. Includes not only detailed information on revenue, taxation, demography, mortality, education, shipping, commerce and banking, but provides retrospective information for earlier periods.

8. Brasil. Instituto Brasileiro de Geografia e Estatística. *Estudos sôbre a composição da população do Brasil segundo a côr*. Rio de Janeiro: Serviço Gráfico do Instituto Brasileiro de Geografia e Estatística, 1950.

   A series of statistical analyses compiled from national censuses from 1872 to 1940 on racial composition. Corrects earlier misleading data.

9. Brasil. Instituto Brasileiro de Geografia e Estatística. *Sinopse estatística do Brasil, 1971*. Rio de Janeiro: Instituto Brasileiro do Geografia e Estatístico, 1971.

   Contains tables on economic and social data for the period through the 1970 census.

10. Brasil. Ministério da Fazenda. *Economical Data about Brazil, 1910-1928*. Rio de Janeiro: Imprensa Nacional, 1929.

    Amasses detailed statistical data in tabular form about fiscal resources, trade, production, agriculture, mining, shipping, and government revenue.

11. Brasil. Ministério da Fazenda. *Quadros estatísticos do Brasil, 1928-1935*. Rio de Janeiro: Diretoria de Estatística Economômica e Financeira, 1936.

    Contains tabular data on dozens of statistical categories for Brazil since the First World War.

12. Brasil. Ministério da Fazenda. *Quadros estatísticos do Brasil, 1932-1939*. Rio de Janeiro: Imprensa Nacional, 1940.

    Continues the series initiated in the previous entry.

13. Brasil. Secretária de Planejamento. *Índice do Brasil, 1977-78*. Brasília: Secretária de Planejamento, 1977.

    A bi-lingual index of economic statistics published by the Ministry of Planning.

14. Brazil. Ministry of Foreign Affairs. *Brazil: 1933*. Rio de Janeiro: Commercial Service of the Ministry of Foreign Affairs, 1933.

    Contains hundred of tables summarizing Brazil's agricultural output, tax revenues, imports and exports, mineral production, industrial output, and related statistics.

15. Collver, O. Andrew. *Birth Rates in Latin America: New Estimates of Historical Trends and Fluctuations*. Berkeley: University of California Press, 1965.

    Uses published censuses, statistical tables and other data to construct a comprehensive synthesis of known population trends for the region.

16. Gonçalves, Carlos Alberto Stoll. *Brasil*. Rio de Janeiro: Litotipografia Fluminense, 1930.

    Offers a wealth of statistical data on subjects ranging from commerce to extractive industry (mining) to education. Some series deal with the 1920's; others span from the early colonial period.

17. Hasselmann, Sérgio, et al., eds. *Situação social da América Latina*. Rio de Janeiro: Centro Latino Americano de Pesquisas em Ciências Sociais, 1965.

    One of the first comparative statistical studies of social conditions throughout Latin America produced in Brazil. The authors examine data relative to demography, education, health conditions, poverty, work conditions, and social structure.

18. Nascimento Brito, José do. *Economia e finanças do Brasil, 1822-1940*. Rio de Janeiro: Freitas Bastos, 1945.

    Offers a statistically-based retrospective of Brazil's economic evolution based principally on the pre-census 1939 *Anuário estatístico* and on nineteenth-century works.

19. São Paulo. British Chamber of Commerce. *Facts about the State of São Paulo.* São Paulo: British Chamber of Commerce, 1950.

    Contains statistical data on the industrial, financial, business, geographical, and social environment to attract visitors and potential investors.

20. São Paulo. Departamento Estadual de Estatística. *São Paulo, 1889-1939: dados gerais do estado.* São Paulo: Imprensa Oficial, 1940.

    A useful compendium of statistics on finance, population, transportation, shipping, education, and mortality for the State of São Paulo from 1889 to 1939.

21. Secretaria General de la OEA. *América en cifras, 1977.* 3 vols. Washington, D.C.: Organization of American States 1978-79.

    Contains comparative data for the American Republics on economics, demography and social change. Most of the series span the years from 1950 through 1977.

22. *78 anos de receita federal, 1890/1967.* Rio de Janeiro: Ministério da Fazenda. Assessoria de Estudos, Programaçao e Avaliação, 1968.

    Contains detailed tables on the budgetary breakdown of state revenues for each year between 1890 and 1967.

23. United States-Brazil Fulbright Commission. *Welcome to Brazil.* Rio de Janeiro: Fulbright Commission, 1968.

    Offers a wealth of statistical information about Brazilian life for arriving Fulbright fellows. Includes a detailed description of the educational system.

24. Weil, Thomas E. *Area Handbook for Brazil.* Washington, D.C.: Superintendent of Documents, United States Government Printing Office, 1971.

    A compendium of statistics on population, agriculture, natural resources, social sciences and geography. Also includes summaries of political events.

2. Biographical Dictionaries

25. *Autoridades brasileiras.* Rio de Janeiro: Departamento Administrativo do Serviço Público, 1962.

    Lists all major office holders, governors, and mayors of state capital cities during the Quadros and Goulart administrations.

26. Behor, Ely. *Vultos do Brasil.* São Paulo: Livraria Exposição do Livro, 1968.

    A biographical dictionary of important persons from Brazilian history, mostly from political life.

27. Beloch, Israel. "Dicionário histórico-biográfico brasileiro." *Revista de Ciência Política*, 21 (July-September 1978), 29-52.

    Contains excerpts and examples from the yet-uncompleted historical-biographical dictionary for modern Brazil being compiled by Rio de Janeiro's research documentation center, CPDOC.

28. Bittencourt, Adalzira. *Dicionário biográfico de mulheres ilustres, notaveis e intelectuais do Brasil.* 2 vols. Rio de Janeiro: Editôra Pongetti, 1969-70.

    Provides biographical sketches of notable Brazilian women from colonial times to the present.

29. Brasil. Congresso. Câmara dos Deputados. Biblioteca. *Deputados brasileiros (1967-1971).* Brasília: Câmara dos Deputados, 1968.

    A lengthy (761 pp.) sourcebook containing biographical information on all federal congressmen during the period 1967-1968.

30. Brasil. Ministério das Relações Exteriores. *Quem é quem nas artes e nas letras do Brasil.* Rio de Janeiro: Ministério das Relações Exteriores, 1965.

    A Who's Who of contemporary arts and letters, including persons whose deaths occurred after 1945.

31. Brinches, Victor M.F. *Dicionário bio-bibliográfico luso-brasileiro.* Rio de Janeiro: Fundo da Cultura, 1965.

    A bio-bibliographical dictionary emphasizing cultural and historical ties between Portugal and Brazil.

32. British Chamber of Commerce. São Paulo. *Personalidades do Brasil.* São Paulo: British Chamber of Commerce, 1934.

    Contains biographical sketches of Brazilian officials, commercial leaders, and foreign (mostly British) businessmen.

33. Coutinho, Afrânio. *Brasil e brasileiros de hoje: enciclopêdia de biografias.* 2 vols. Rio de Janeiro: Sul Americana, 1961.

    A Who's Who of political, commercial, and cultural leaders.

34. Coutinho, Afrânio. *Introdução à literatura no Brasil.* Rio de Janeiro: Civilização Brasileira, 1964.

    A reference guide to Brazilian literature and cultural life, spanning the entire period since early colonization.

35. Guimaraẽs, Argeu de Segadas Machado. *Diccionário bio-bibliográphico brasileiro de diplomacia, política exterior e direito internacional.* Rio de Janeiro: Ministério das Relações Estrangeiras, 1938.

    Contains biographies for all Brazilian diplomats and specialists in international affairs through the beginning of the Estado Nôvo.

36. Hilton, Ronald, ed. *Who's Who in Latin America. Part VI: Brazil.* 3rd ed. Stanford: Stanford University Press, 1948.

    Contains capsule biographies of nearly 2,000 notable Brazilians from government, science, letters, and commerce. Emphasis falls on persons connected to international affairs.

37. Maciel, Paulo. *Quem é quem em Brasilia.* Brasília: Ed. Alvorada, 1968.

    A 135-page Who's Who for Brasília, listing mostly government officials and diplomats.

38. Martin, Percy Alvin, ed. *Who's Who in Latin America.* Stanford: Stanford University Press, 1935.

    Includes Brazilian figures from government, the arts, and business.

39. Nóbrega, Apolônio Carneiro da Cunha. "Disceses e bispos do Brasil." *Revista do Instituto Histórico, Geográfico Brasileiro*, 222 (1954), 3-328.

    Enumerates all of the bishops and new ecclesiastical divisions created since the colonial period.

40. Ribeiro, João de Souza. *Dicionário biobibliográfico de escritores cariocas (1565-1965)*. Rio de Janeiro: Ed. Brasiliana, 1965.

    Lists hundreds of writers and intellectuals born in or identified with the city of Rio de Janeiro.

41. *Sociedade Brasileira*. Rio de Janeiro: Livraria Francisco Alves, 1979.

    A biographical directory of personalities and institutions comprising "Brazilian Society." Limited mostly to the city of Rio de Janeiro.

42. Vaitsman, Maurício. *Sangue nôvo no Congresso; Deputados de 1959-1962*. Rio de Janeiro: J. Ozon, 1960.

    Contains the biographies of members of Congress elected in the last year of the Kubitschek administration.

43. *Who's Who in the United Nations and Related Agencies*. New York: Arno Press, 1975.

    Offers *curriculum vitae* for 27 Brazilian diplomats accredited to United Nations agencies.

3. Encyclopedias and Handbooks

44. Brasil. Instituto Brasileiro de Geografia e Estatística. *Enciclopédia dos municípios brasileiros*. 36 vols. Rio de Janeiro: Instituto Brasileiro de Geografia e Estatística, 1957-58.

    A multi-volume encyclopedia containing demographic, economic, and social data on each of the more than 3,000 *municípios*, the Brazilian unit of administration roughly equivalent to the United States county.

45. Delpar, Helen, ed. *Encyclopedia of Latin America*. New York: McGraw-Hill, 1974.

    Provides dozens of articles dealing with Brazilian subjects for the modern period. Includes maps, photographs and statistical tables.

46. Florenzano, Éverton. *Moderno dicionário de bôlso de história do Brasil*. Rio de Janeiro: Edições de Ouro, 1964.

Contains several hundred entries, mostly biographical. Notably right-wing in outlook and interpretation.

47. Hispanic Foundation. Library of Congress. *Handbook of Latin American Studies*. Cambridge, Mass.: Harvard University Press, 1936-47; Gainesville: University of Florida Press, 1948-

    An indispensable tool. Includes selective bibliographies, commentary, and information on source materials for research in all fields. After Vol. 26, coverage of social sciences and humanities disciplines alternates annually.

48. Levine, Robert M. *Historical Dictionary of Brazil*. Metuchen, N.J.: Scarecrow Press, 1978.

    Provides more than 2,000 entries dealing with political and historical personages, events, social processes, and Brazilian habits.

49. Martin, Michael Rheta and Gabriel H. Lovett, eds. *Encyclopedia of Latin American History*. rev. ed. Indianapolis: Bobbs-Merrill, 1968.

    Provides brief articles on all aspects of Latin American history, including major Brazilian events, personages, and dates.

50. *Nôvo dicionário de historia do Brasil. Redação dos temas e biografias*. Ed. Brasil Bandecchi *et al*. Saõ Paulo: Ed. Melhoramentos, 1970.

    An illustrated dictionary of Brazilian history emphasizing the colonial and imperial periods, but including political figures from the twentieth century.

51. Sable, Martin H. *A Guide to Latin American Studies*. 2 vols. Los Angeles: Latin American Center, UCLA, 1967.

    Contains a series of essays by topic, statistics, and hundreds of annotated citations of materials in English, Spanish, and Portuguese.

52. Sable, Martin H. *Master Directory for Latin America*. Los Angeles: Latin American Center, UCLA, 1965.

    Lists official United States government agencies, public and private development organizations, and research and educational centers in Brazil as well as outside Brazil with interest in Brazilian studies.

53. *Staden Jahrbuch; beiträge zur Brasilkunde*. Vol. 1- São Paulo: Instituto Hans Staden, 1953-

An annual, illustrated, German-language handbook written for European-based specialists and researchers.

54. Teixeira de Oliveira, José. *Dicionário brasileiro de datas históricas*. Rio de Janeiro: Irmaõs Pongetti, 1950.

A long (423 pp.) historical dictionary stretching back to the colonial period, emphasizing political events.

B. RESEARCH AND LIBRARY GUIDES

55. Andrade, Margaretta de. *The Expansion of Brazilian Studies and Portuguese Language Instruction in the United States*. Washington, D.C.: Brazilian-American Cultural Institute, 1969.

Surveys university programs and library holdings on Brazil in the late 1960's. Partially complete.

56. Bartley, Russell H. and Stuart L. Wagner. *Latin America in Basic Historical Collections: A Working Guide*. Stanford: Hoover Institute Press, 1972.

Describes the major archival and basic collections in the United States.

57. *Bibliographic Guide to Latin American Studies: 1978*. 3 vols. Boston: G.K. Hall, 1979.

Serves as an annual supplement to the *Catalog of the Latin American Collection of the University of Texas Library*.

Strong on Brazil.

58. Cardozo, Manuel S. *A Guide to the Manuscripts in the Lima Library*. Washington, D.C.: Catholic University of America, 1941.

Describes the holdings of the library of Brazilians donated by historian and diplomat Manoel de Oliveira Lima to the Catholic University.

59. Carvalho, Alfredo Ferreira de. *Bibliotheca exótico-brasileira. Publicada em virtude de autorização Legislativa do Governo do Exmo. Sr. Dr. Estácio de Albuquerque Coimbra, Governador do Estado de Pernambuco.* 3 vols. Rio de Janeiro: Empreza Graphica Editôra, 1929-1930.

    An extensive bibliography on "exotic Brasiliana," mostly works by foreign authors on Brazil, translations, and articles in foreign publications.

60. Catholic University of America Library. *Bibliographical and Historical Description of the Rarest Books in the Oliveira Lima Collection at the Catholic University of America.* Washington, D.C.: Catholic University Press, 1926.

    Guide to the Oliveira Lima collection, donated to Catholic University by the Pernambucano historian as a gesture of appreciation to the country in which he served for many years as ambassador.

61. Committee on Latin America, The. *Latin American Economic and Social Serials.* London: Clive Bingeley, Ltd., 1969.

    Lists about 200 serials for Brazil.

62. Cortés Conde, Roberto and Stanley J. Stein, eds. *Latin America: A Guide to Economic History, 1830-1930.* Berkeley: University of California Press, 1977.

    Contains 4,552 entries, annotated in detail, divided into country sections. Part 4, on Brazil (pp. 182-273), is by Nícea Vilela Luz.

63. De Noia, John, comp. *A Guide to the Official Publications of the Other American Republics. Vol. III: Brazil.* Washington, D.C.: Library of Congress, 1948.

    Classifies the Library of Congress's holdings by cabinet ministries, with brief additional sections devoted to the judicial and legislative branches.

64. Dias, Cícero. *Catálogo dos documentos referentes ao Brasil.* Rio de Janeiro: Ministério das Relações Exteriores, 1975.

    Lists collections of archival material and state papers in French depositories on subjects dealing with Brazil.

65. Gillett, Theresa. *Catalog of Luso-Brazilian Material in the University of New Mexico Libraries.* Albuquerque: University of New Mexico Press, 1970.

66. Gorham, Rex. *The Folkways of Brazil.* New York: New York Public Library, 1944.

    A library guide to sources on Brazilian studies, first published serially in the *Bulletin of the New York Public Library* in 1941 and 1942.

67. Harrison, John P. "The Archives of the United States Diplomatic and Consular Posts in Latin America." *Hispanic American Historical Review*, 33 (February 1953), 168-183.

    Uses consular reports for Salvador, Bahia as a case study of the type and quality of materials available for researchers working in the archives of the Department of State.

68. Hilton, Ronald, ed. *Handbook of Hispanic Source Materials and Research Organizations in the United States.* 2nd ed. Stanford: Stanford University Press, 1956.

    Includes coverage of Brazilian sources and library collections.

69. Hispanic Society of America. Library. *Catalog.* 3 vol. Boston: G.K. Hall, 1962.

    Volume III (pp. 1460-1494) covers entries listed under the title "Brazil."

70. Hutchinson, H.W. *Field Guide to Brazil.* Washington, D.C.: National Academy of Sciences / National Research Council, 1960.

    A somewhat dated but otherwise useful guide for researchers, offering basic information about research opportunities, preparations for the field, professional relationships, and physical adjustment.

71. Institute of Latin American Studies. University of London. *Guide to Latin American Collections in London Libraries.* London: Institute of Latin American Studies, 1967.

    Includes official and non-official sources.

72. Jackson, William Vernon, comp. *Catalog of Brazilian Acquisitions of the Library of Congress, 1964-1974.* Boston: G.K. Hall, 1977.

    Divides the massive listing of photo-reproduced cards into 31 subjects ranging from general works to naval science.

73. Jackson, William V. *Library Guide for Brazilian Studies*. Pittsburgh: University of Pittsburgh Press, 1964.

Discusses general and special collections, manuscript sources, government publications, periodicals, and materials in the humanities. An updated guide is being compiled.

74. *Latin American and Caribbean Official Statistical Serials on Microfiche*. Cambridge, England: Chadwyck-Healy Ltd., 1978.

Catalogs data available for researchers. The Brazilian holdings include the *Anuário estatístico* for 1908-1913 and 1935-1969.

75. Levine, Robert M., ed. *Brazil: Field Research Guide in the Social Sciences*. New York: Institute of Latin American Studies, Columbia University, 1966.

Intended as a practical interdisciplinary guide to archival and field research. Illustrates the burgeoning interest in Brazilian studies in the United States in the early and mid-1960's.

76. MacCarthy, Cavan. *Developing Libraries in Brazil with a Chapter on Paraguay*. Metuchen, N.J.: Scarecrow Press, 1975.

Criticizes what the author, an English librarian, considers to be the attitude in Latin America that libraries are to protect books from the people.

77. Manchester, Alan K., ed. "Descriptive Bibliography of the Brazilian Section of the Duke University Library." *Hispanic American Historical Review*, 13 (1933), 238-266; 495-523.

Covers the whole of Brazilian history, citing articles as well as books.

78. Menezes, Jõao Barreto de. *Nôvo catálogo geral systemático da bibliotheca da Faculdade de Direito de Recife*. Recife: Typographia Central, 1932.

Summarizes the holdings of the Recife Law School Library, one of Brazil's best.

79. "Microfilmagem no Arquivo Municipal de São Paulo." *Mensário do Arquivo Nacional* (Rio de Janeiro), 11 (November 1978), 31.

Describes the São Paulo Municipal Archive's project of microfilming more than 900 volumes of documents, numbering more than 100,000 letters, reports, registers, and legislative acts.

80. Morgan, Dale L. and George P. Hammond, comps. *A Guide to the Manuscript Collections of the Bancroft Library*. Berkeley: Bancroft Library, 1963.

    Includes listings of documents from British firms operating in Brazil during the twentieth century.

81. Nagel, Rolf. "Observações sobre as fontes da história do século xx." *Mensário do Arquivo Nacional* (Rio de Janeiro), 9 (August 1978), 14-16.

    A German historian describes documentary sources on Brazil in the Dusseldorf state archive.

82. New York Public Library. Reference Department. *Dictionary Catalog of the History of the Americas*. 28 vols. Boston: G.K. Hall, 1961. *First Supplement*. 9 vols. 1973.

83. Norman, James. "Researcher's Paradise." *Americas*, 25 (January 1963), 19-21.

    Describes the extensive Latin American (and Brazilian) collection at the University of Texas library.

84. Pásztor, Lajos. *Guída della fonti per la storia dell' America Latina negli archivi della Santa Sede e negli archivi ecclesiastici d'Italia*. Vatican City: n.p., 1970.

    A catalog of materials in Vatican and other Italian ecclesiastical libraries dealing with Latin America.

85. "Perfís institucionais de instituições brasileiras em ciências sociais: Centro de Pesquisa e Documentação de História Contemporânea do Brasil (CPDOC)." *Dados*, 16 (1977), 5-10.

    Describes the efforts to create a depository for archival, library, and statistical materials for the study of contemporary Brazilian social history. Lists collections open to researchers.

86. Rio de Janeiro. Bibliotheca Nacional. *Publicações da Bibliotheca Nacional catálogo, 1873-1974*. 2nd ed. Rio de Janeiro: Bibliotheca Nacional, 1978.

    A 120-page catalog of publications issued by the National Library, many of them bibliographical.

87. Rodrigues, José Honório. *A pesquisa histórica no Brasil.* 3rd ed. São Paulo: Companhia Editôra Nacional, 1978.

    Reviews in comprehensive detail the sources for historical research on Brazil, emphasizing bibliography, journals and periodicals, and archival and official collections, foreign as well as domestic.

88. Rodrigues, José Honório. *A situação do Arquivo Nacional.* Rio de Janeiro: n.p., 1959.

    Laments the decline in the quality of collected documents for the period after the fall of the Empire. Only the presidential series is noteworthy for the post-1930 period.

89. Sable, Martin H. *Guide to Nonprint Materials for Latin American Studies.* Detroit: Blaine Ethridge Books, 1979.

    An annotated bibliography-directory listing such nonprint materials as films, slides, photos, videotapes, records, paintings, maps, microforms, and musuem collections.

90. Souza, Alvaro Paulino Soares de. *Catálogo systematico da bibliotheca da Faculdade de Medicina do Rio de Janeiro. Publicações entradas de 1930 a 1934.* Rio de Janeiro: Imprensa Nacional, 1936.

    A short listing of the holdings added to the Rio de Janeiro Medical School between 1930 and 1934. Includes materials of interest to historians of the social history of Brazilian medicine.

91. Taeuber, Irene B., comp. *General Censuses and Vital Statistics in the Americas.* Washington, D.C.: Government Printing Office, 1943; rpt. Detroit: Blaine Ethridge Books, 1974.

    Lists in detail all national, state, and city censuses available to researchers. Brazil's coverage (pp. 13-22) spans the years between 1872 and 1940.

92. United States Department of State. Office of Intelligence Research and Analysis. *Some Brazilian Maps and Map Sources. Preliminary Lists of Publishing Agencies, Maps and Atlases of Brazil.* Washington: Department of State, 1946.

93. University of Texas Library, Austin. *Catalog of the Latin American Collection.* 31 vols. Boston: G.K. Hall, 1969.

One of the world's major collections: strong on Brazil.

94. Welsh, Doris Varner. *A Catalog of the William B. Greenlee Collection of Portuguese History and Literature and the Portuguese Materials in the Newberry Library.* Chicago: Newberry Library, 1953.

Although most of the holdings deal with the colonial period the library collection is invaluable for general background.

C. PERIODICAL INDEXES

94a. Brasil. Departamento Nacional de Estatística. *Estatística da imprensa periodica no Brasil (1929-1930).* Rio de Janeiro: Departamento Nacional de Estatística, 1931.

Lists all daily, weekly, and monthly serial periodicals published across the country in 1929-30 as well as data on claimed circulation.

95. Charno, Steven M. *Latin American Newspapers in the United States: A Union List Compiled in the Serial Division, Library of Congress.* Austin, Texas: University of Texas Press, 1969.

Published for the Conference of Latin American History. Does not include several microfilmed newspaper runs made available after the guide's publication, including *O Estado de São Paulo.*

96. Fernandez, Oscar. *A Preliminary Listing of Foreign Periodical Holdings in the United States and Canada which give coverage to Portuguese and Brazilian Language and Literature.* Iowa City: University of Iowa, 1968.

97. Gardner, Mary A. *The Press of Latin America: A Tentative and Selected Bibliography in Spanish and Portuguese.* Austin: Institute of Latin American Studies, 1973.

A short (34 pp.) guide published by the Institute of Latin American Studies of the University of Texas.

98. Grossmann, Jorge, ed. *Index to Latin American Periodicals: Humanities and Social Sciences.* Vols. I & II.

Boston: G.K. Hall, 1961-62; Vols. III-X. Metuchen, N.J.: Scarecrow Press, 1963-1970.

99. Lombardi, Mary. *Brazilian Serial Documents: A Selective and Annotated Guide.* Bloomington: Indiana University Press, 1974.

Lists 1370 serials published by autonomous Brazilian federal agencies and by the executive, judicial, and legislative branches, through 1971. Includes a useful index.

100. Pan American Union. Columbus Memorial Library. *Index to Latin American Periodical Literature, 1929-1960.* 8 vols. Boston: G.K. Hall, 1962. *First Supplement.* 2 vols. 1968.

Extends the listing of periodicals formerly published under the title *List of Books Accessioned and Periodical Articles Indexed in the Columbus Memorial Library of the Pan American Union* (1952-1960).

101. Paula, Eurípides Simões de. "Revistas de história existentes em algumas bibliotecas em São Paulo." *Revista de História* (São Paulo), 6:14 (April-June 1953), 483-485.

Lists the extensive collection of history journals in São Paulo libraries.

102. Research Publications, Inc. *Bibliography and Reel Index: A Guide to the Microform Edition of International Census Publications, 1945-1967.* Woodbridge, Conn.: Research Publications, Inc., 1976.

103. Rodrigues, José Honório. *Índice anotado da Revista do Instituto Arqueológico, Histórico e Geográfico Pernambucano.* Recife: RIAHG, 1961.

An annotated index to the journal of Recife's principal research center, the Institute of Archaeology, History, and Geography.

104. Rodrigues, José Honório. *Índice anotado da Revista do Instituto do Ceará.* Fortaleza: Instituto do Ceará, 1959.

An annotated index to the journal of the Ceará Institute.

105. Vieira da Cunha, Mário Wagner. "As publicações de administração pública no Brasil (1938-1945)." *Sociologia*, 16 (1954), 21-45.

Indexes the articles published in the *Revista do Serviço Público* on public administration in Brazil since the creation of the DASP (Administrative Department of the Public Service) in 1938.

106. Zimmerman, Irene. *A Guide to Current Latin American Periodicals: Humanities and Social Sciences.* Gainesville, Fla.: Kallman Publishing Co., 1961.

Lists 89 periodicals pertinent to Brazilian studies.

107. Zubatsky, David. "A Bibliography of Cumulative Indexes to Luso-Brazilian Journals of the 19th and 20th Centuries." *Luso-Brazilian Review*, 8 (December 1971), 71-81.

D. GENERAL BIBLIOGRAPHIES

108. "Algumas fontes bibliograficas sôbre Oliveira Viana." *Autores e Livros* (Rio de Janeiro) 4 (1943), 174.

A bibliography of writing by and about conservative historian Oliveira Vianna.

109. Basseches, Bruno. *A Bibliography of Brazilian Bibliographies / Uma bibliografia das bibliografias brasileiras.* Detroit: Blaine Ethridge Books, 1978.

Contains 2,488 entries, an index, and an introduction by historian José Honório Rodrigues. Extensive but uncritical.

110. Bayitch, S.A. *Latin America and the Caribbean; a Bibliographical Guide to Works in English.* Coral Gables, Fla.: University of Miami Press, 1967.

A guide to works on law, history, politics, and economic development.

111. Behrendt, F. *Modern Latin America in Social Science Literature: A Selected, Annotated Bibliography of Books, Pamphlets, and Periodicals.* Albuquerque: University of New Mexico Press, 1949.

112. Bernstein, Harry. *A Bookshelf on Brazil.* Albany: State Education Department, Office of Foreign Area Studies, 1964.

Lists 104 English-language sources on Brazil subdivided into 16 topical categories. Entries are also coded according to relative usefulness.

113. *Bibliografia brasileira de ciências sociais.* Rio de Janeiro: Instituto Brasileiro de Bibliografia e Documentação, 1964.

A basic bibliography of articles and books in the social sciences.

114. *Bibliografia do Centro Latino-Americano de Ciências Sociais.* Rio de Janeiro: CLAPCS, 1962.

A comprehensive, working bibliography on Brazilian and Latin American studies compiled by the librarians of the UNESCO-sponsored research center in Rio de Janeiro.

115. "Bibliografia estrangeira sôbre o Brasil." *Boletim Geográfico* (Rio de Janeiro), 1 (1943-1944), 1-15.

A bibliography of foreign studies of Brazil's geography, climate, and population.

116. "Bibliografia preliminar de teses brasileiras." *IV Congresso Brasileiro de Biblioteconomia e Documentação.* Fortaleza: n.p., 1963.

Offers one of the first nationally-coordinated lists of university dissertations on Brazilian subjects.

117. "Bibliografia sôbre o Amapá." *Boletim da Biblioteca da Sudene* (Recife), 5 (February 1966), 30-44.

Lists studies dealing with the Amazonian federal territory of Amapá, adjacent to Pará.

118. "Bibliografia sôbre a meterologia do Brasil." *Noticias Bibliográficas* (Rio de Janeiro), 45 (1963-64), 132-162.

A bibliography of works on Brazil's climate and rainfall.

119. Brasil. Conselho Nacional de Estatística. *Bibliografia geográfica-estatística brasileiro.* Rio de Janeiro: Conselho Nacional de Estatística, 1956.

A bibliography of publications offering census and demographic data for the period 1936-1950.

120. Brasil. Instituto Brasileiro de Bibliografia e Documentação. *Amazônia: bibliografia.* Rio de Janeiro: Instituto Brasileiro de Bibliografia e Documentação, 1963.

A lengthy bibliography of works dealing with the Amazon region, from the first exploratory incursion in 1614 to 1962.

121. Brasil. Ministério das Relações Exteriores. Biblioteca. *Traduções de autores brasileiros e livros sobre o Brasil escritos em idioma estrangeiro.* Rio de Janeiro: Ministerio das Relações Exteriores, 1960.

A bibliography of works by Brazilian authors or about Brazil published abroad in translation.

122. *The Brazilian Model: Political Repression and Economic Expansion.* Washington, D.C.: CoDoC, June 1974.

A bibliography of left-oriented sources not usually known to researchers, covering Brazil since 1964.

123. Burns, E. Bradford. "A Working Bibliography for the Study of Brazilian History." *The Americas*, 22 (July 1965), 54-88.

Subdivides entries by topic and chronology.

124. Chaffee, Wilber A. and Honor M. Griffin. *Dissertations on Latin America by U.S. Historians, 1960-1970.* Austin: University of Texas Press, 1971.

Lists dissertations produced during the "takeoff" decade for Latin American studies.

125. Coordenação de Aperfeicoamento de Pessoal de Nível Superior (CAPES). *Pos-graduação no Brasil: relação das dissertações e teses defendidas jan. 1974 a jun. 1975.* Brasília: Ministério da Educação e Cultura, 1975.

Lists theses and dissertations successfully defended at Brazilian universities.

126. Deal, Carl W., ed. *Latin America and the Caribbean: A Dissertation Bibliography.* Ann Arbor, Michigan: University Microfilms International, 1978.

Cites 7,200 dissertations from United States and Canadian universities, superseding *Latin America: A Catalog of Dissertations* (1974). Entries are arranged by academic discipline and by country.

127. Dorn, Georgette M. *Latin America, Spain and Portugal: An Annotated Bibliography of Paperback Books*. Washington, D.C.: Hispanic Foundation, 1976.

Offers capsule annotations on books, some of which have since gone out of print.

128. Griffin, Charles C., ed. *Latin America: A Guide to the Historical Literature*. Austin: University of Texas Press, 1971.

A detailed, annotated 700-page bibliography covering Latin American history. Includes sections on Inter-American and foreign relations. Republican Brazil is treated by John D. Wirth (pp. 607-618).

129. Gropp, Arthur E., comp. *A Bibliography of Latin American Bibliographies*. Metuchen, N.J.: Scarecrow Press, 1968. *Supplement*, 1971.

Updates the 1942 edition by C.K. Jones (Hispanic Foundation). Lists entries by subject area.

130. Hanson, Carl A. "Dissertations on Luso-Brazilian Topics, 1892-1970." *The Americas*, 30 (January 1974), 374-403.

Lists 683 dissertations by topic, from all disciplines, ranging from anthropology to zoology.

131. Harmon, Ronald M. and Bobby J. Chamberlain, comps. *Brazil: A Working Bibliography in Literature, Humanities, and the Social Sciences*. Tempe, Ariz.: Center for Latin American Studies, Arizona State University, 1975. Special Study No. 14.

Contains 854 entries by topic. Strong coverage of the arts and humanities as well as history.

132. Harvard University. Bureau of Economic Research in Latin America. *The Economic Literature of Latin America: A Tentative Bibliography*. Vol. I. Cambridge, Mass.: Harvard University Press, 1935-36.

Divided into national bibliographies and further subdivided into four topics, the last of which deals with the period since Independence. Contains 6,244 entries for South American nations.

133. Humphreys, Robin. *Latin American History: A Guide to the Literature in English*. 2nd ed. New York: Oxford University Press, 1958.

Brazil is treated on pp. 65-69; 90-91; 119-128. Entries are annotated in review article style.

134. Institut für Iberoamerika-Kunde. *Ausgewählte neuere Literatur* (Hamburg), 3 (1977).

A well-indexed bibliographic guide listing Latin American and West German articles and books on Latin American themes.

135. Institute of Latin American Studies, University of London. "Theses in Latin American Studies at British Universities in Progress and Completed." London: Institute of Latin American Studies, 1977.

Lists Master's and Doctoral theses and dissertations in the humanities, social sciences, and sciences.

136. Instituto Brasileiro de Geografia e Estatística. *Estudos sobre as línguas extrangeiras e aborigenes faladas no Brasil.* Rio de Janeiro: Instituto Brasileiro de Geografia e Estatística, 1950.

Catalogs studies of foreign and indigenous languages spoken in Brazil.

137. Instituto Nacional do Livro. *Bibliografia brasileira.* 11 vols. Rio de Janeiro: Instituto Nacional do Livro, 1941-

An annual bibliography of newly published works produced by the National Publishing Institute. In November 1967 it adopted a monthly format (*Bibliografia brasileira mensal*).

138. Lauerhass, Ludwig, Jr. *Communism in Latin America: A Bibliography. The Post-War Years (1945-1960).* Los Angeles: Center for Latin American Studies, UCLA, 1962.

Contains listings on communism in the hemisphere, in South America, and in specific countries. Most of the citations are Cold War pieces.

139. McGreevey, William Paul. *A Bibliography of Latin American Economic History, 1760-1960.* Berkeley: Center for Latin American Studies Working Papers, 1968.

A 60-page unannotated bibliography, organized by country and general themes.

140. Maia, Jorge de Andrade. *Catâlogo das tesas inaugurais defendidas perante a Faculdade de Medicina da Univer-*

sidade de São Paulo, 1919-1935. São Paulo: Faculdade da Medicina, 1935.

Lists all of the theses for advanced degrees accepted by the São Paulo Medical School between 1919 and 1935.

141. *Manual bibliográfico de estudos brasileiros*. Rio de Janeiro: Gráfica Editôra Souza, 1949.

A bibliography on Brazilian studies strongest on art, history, literature, and ethnology.

142. Martins, Ari Peixoto. "Bibliografia gaúcha." *Revista das Academias de Letras* (Rio de Janeiro), 32 (1941), 151-161.

A bibliography of materials related to the life and culture of the State of Rio Grande do Sul.

143. Martins, Maria Thereza Coelho. *Publicações do Ministério do Trabalho, Indústria e Comércio*. Rio de Janeiro: Serviço de Documentação, 1954.

Catalogs publications issued by the federal Ministry of Labor, Industry, and Commerce through the final year of Vargas's presidency.

144. Montgomery, Emma G. and Sandra F. Brenner. *Acquisition of Brazilian Official Publications: Monograph*. Eighth Seminar on the Acquisition of Latin American Library Materials. Madison, Wisconsin: University of Wisconsin, 1963.

A short but detailed list of official government publications.

145. Morais, Ruben Borba de. *Manual bibliográfico de estudos brasileiros*. Rio de Janeiro: Ed. Sousa, 1949.

Includes sections on music, art, and culture in a survey of Brazilian studies.

146. Okinshevich, Leo, comp. *Latin America in Soviet Writings: A Bibliography*. 2 vols. Baltimore: Johns Hopkins University Press, 1965.

Vol. I covers 1917 to 1958; Vol. II, 1959 to 1964. Divides entries into 25 subject areas. Partially annotated.

147. Pedrosa, Carlos. "Bibliografia estrangeira sôbre o Brasil, 1937-1941." *Cultura Política* (Rio de Janeiro),

1 (1937), 262-268; 301-311; 1 (1938), 302-316, 330-348; 2 (1941), 268-277, 232-236.

Surveys foreign writing on Brazilian subjects, mostly in the area of trade and economics.

148. Reis, Antônio Simões dos. *Bibliografia das bibliografias brasileiras.* Rio de Janeiro: Imprensa Nacional, 1942.

The major bibliography of Brazilian bibliographies written before the Second World War.

149. Rio de Janeiro. Centro de Estudos Sociais. *Bibliografia sôbre o Estado da Bahia.* Rio de Janeiro: Fundação Getúlio Vargas, 1953.

A 50-page bibliography dealing with the State of Bahia, concentrating on topics related to health care, education, and economic conditions.

150. Rio de Janeiro. Universidade. Faculdade de Filosofia. Centro de pesquisas de Geografia do Brasil. *Bibliografia Geográfica do Brasil. 1951-1955.* 5 vols. Rio de Janeiro: Universidade de Rio de Janeiro, 1954-1957.

An exhaustive bibliography covering geography, geology and land use.

151. Rogers, Francis M. and David T. Haberley. *Brazil, Portugal and Other Portuguese Speaking Lands; A List of Books primarily in English.* Cambridge, Mass.: Department of Romance Languages and Literature, Harvard University, 1968.

A 73-page checklist ranging broadly from history through literature and philosophy.

152. Sable, Martin H., ed. *Communism in Latin America: an International Bibliography, 1900-1945, 1960-1967.* Los Angeles: Latin American Center, University of California, 1968.

153. Sable, Martin H. *Latin American Studies in the Non-Western World and Eastern Europe: a Bibliography on Latin America in the Languages of China, Asia, the Middle East, and Eastern Europe.* Metuchen, N.J.: Scarecrow Press, 1970.

An interesting compendium of articles and studies in non-Western languages. Most entries on Brazil deal with race, economic development, and military rule.

154. Shaw, Bradley A., comp. *Latin American Literature in English Translation: An Annotated Bibliography.* New York: New York University Press, 1976.

Lists translations of novels, plays and selected literary essays which have appeared in book form up to 1975. Indexed by title, author, and countries of origin.

155. Souza, José Galante de. *Índice de bibliografia brasileira.* Rio de Janeiro: Instituto Nacional de Livro, 1963.

A long (440 pp.) index to Brazilian bibliography.

156. Superintendência do Desenvolvimento do Nordeste. *Bibliografia sôbre a SUDENE e o nordeste.* Recife: SUDENE, 1969.

An extensive (385 pp.) listing of articles, studies, and documentary sources dealing with the Northeast's regional development agency.

157. Swigart, Joseph E. and John D. Wirth, comps. "Historical Research in Brazil: Recent Contributions." Rio de Janeiro: n.p. [November 1976].

Contains nearly three hundred titles of historical work recently published in Brazil, including theses and dissertations completed from 1974 to 1976.

158. Topete, José Manuel. *A Working Bibliography of Brazilian Literature.* Gainesville: University of Florida Press, 1957.

A thorough, partially-annotated bibliography stressing general reference works, criticism, novelists, poetry, and theater.

159. United States Department of State. External Research Staff. *Brazil--A Selected Bibliography.* Washington, D.C.: Department of State, 1964.

A partially-annotated 40-page list of writing on Brazil, including European and Russian sources.

160. Villas-Boas, Pedro Leite. *Bibliografia do regionalismo gaúcho.* Pôrto Alegre: Imprensa Moliterni, 1967.

A 58-page bibliography of Rio Grande do Sul folklore, history, and regional culture.

161. Weaver, Jerry L., ed. *Latin American Development: A Selected Bibliography (1950-1967).* Santa Barbara, Calif.: American Bibliographic Center, 1969.

Defines "development" so broadly as to encompass all of the social science literature. Brazil is treated on pp. 25-32.

162. Zimmerman, Irene. *Current National Bibliographies of Latin America*. Gainesville: University of Florida Press, 1971.

Discusses the "state of the art" of national bibliography, defined as works published in Latin America about Latin American subjects. Considers Brazilian bibliographies to be relatively well-developed.

II.
General Histories and Historiography

A. GENERAL HISTORIES

163. Bishop, Elizabeth. *Brazil*. New York: Time Incorporated, 1962.

A narrative general history and interpretation of Brazilian culture written for general readers. Lavishly illustrated.

164. Bruno, Ernani Silva. *História do Brasil, geral e regional*. 7 vols. São Paulo: Cultrix, 1966-1967.

Regional studies written for the general reader offering geographic, economic, and some historical background.

165. Dos Passos, John. *Brazil on the Move*. Garden City, N.Y.: Doubleday, 1963.

A popularly-written book-length essay emphasizing Brazil's Lusitanian heritage and future promise.

166. Fausto, Bóris, ed. *História geral da civilização brasileira. Tomo III. O Brasil republicano. 1° vol. Estrutura do poder e economia (1889-1930)*. São Paulo: DIFEL, 1975.

One of the first published studies to bring together analysis by scholars from Brazil and outside. Stresses economic history and the political organization of society. Contains item 479.

167. Fausto, Bóris, ed. *História geral da civilização brasileira. Tomo III. O Brasil republicano. 2° vol*. 2nd ed. São Paulo: DIFEL, 1978.

Emphasizes society and political culture.

168. Hill, Lawrence F., ed. *Brazil*. Berkeley: University of California Press, 1947.

A collection of essays by Brazilian and foreign scholars

looking at Brazilian history broadly, through a cultural as well as a socio-political prism.

169. Hilton, Ronald. *The Latin Americans: Their Heritage and Their Destiny*. New York: J.B. Lippincott, 1973.

Emphasizes the European origin of the population of southern Brazil as the key to the more rapid development of that region. A general historical overview.

170. James, Preston. *Brazil*. New York: Odyssey Press, 1946.

The major single-volume study of the Brazilian subcontinent.

171. Mauro, Frédéric, ed. *L'Histoire quantitative de Brésil de 1800 à 1930*. Paris: Centre National de la Recherche Scientifique, 1973.

Frames Brazil's historical evolution through the use of quantitative methodology and application of the so-called French *Annales* school of social history.

172. Momsen, Richard. *A Giant Stirs*. Princeton, N.J.: Van Nostrand, 1968.

The "giant" is Brazil.

173. Monbeig, Pierre. *Le Brésil*. Paris: Presses Universitaires de France, 1954.

Follows the French tradition of interpreting Brazil as a society divided into conflicting parts, the modern and the traditional. Emphasizes Brazil's economic growth and its future potential as a world power.

174. Niedergang, Marcel. *Les vingt Amériques Latines*. rev. ed. Paris: Editions du Seuil, 1969.

A general overview pointing out the confident attitude of Brazilians and their feeling that throughout their history, God has favored them.

175. Poppino, Rollie E. *Brazil: the Land and People*. New York: Oxford University Press, 1968.

Emphasizes Brazil's physical diversity and its economic development. Argues that regardless of their political views, Brazilians share a common vision of a prosperous future. Includes an excellent bibliographic essay.

176. Prado, Caio, Júnior. *História econômica do Brasil*. São Paulo: Ed. Brasiliense, 1963.

Provides a Marxist analysis of the entire sweep of Brazilian history.

177. Rivera, Jules. *Latin America: A Sociocultural Interpretation*. New York: Halstead Press, 1978.

Looks at Latin America (and Brazil) through a sociological framework rather than through traditional political analysis. Stresses Brazil's failures.

178. Rodman, Selden. *The Brazil Traveler*. New York: Devin Publishers, 1975.

Accentuates the positive and magical side of Brazilian life and its historical evolution.

179. Salles, Pedro. *Históría da medicina no Brasil*. Belo Horizonte: Ed. G. Holman, Ltda., 1971.

A general history of Brazil emphasizing medicine and efforts to improve the state of public health.

180. Sayers, Raymond S., ed. *Portugal and Brazil in Transition*. Minneapolis: University of Minnesota Press, 1968.

Contains twenty-six papers on aspects of Brazilian history and culture, from the Sixth International Colloquium on Luso-Brazilian Studies. Includes items 1261, 1519.

181. Schurz, William Lytle. *Brazil, the Infinite Country*. New York: Dutton, 1961.

A well-organized general overview.

182. Stepan, Nancy. *Beginnings of Brazilian Science*. New York: Science History Publications, 1975.

A history of Brazil since the late nineteenth century, emphasizing the evolution of its scientific tradition and efforts of Oswaldo Cruz and others to develop research capabilities.

183. Tannenbaum, Frank. *Ten Keys to Brazil*. New York: Random House, 1963.

Provides a general overview of Latin American history. Brazil is considered different owing to its relatively calmer evolution and its tradition of toleration.

184. Wagley, Charles. *An Introduction to Brazil*. rev. ed. New York: Columbia University Press, 1971.

Puzzles the riddle of the proverb "Brazil is rich but the Brazilians are poor." Provides a sensitive portrait of the nation and its historical evolution.

B. HISTORIOGRAPHY

185. Boehrer, George C. "Brazilian Historical Bibliography: Some Lacunae and Suggestions." *Revista Interamericana de Bibliografia*, 11 (1961), 137-144.

Discusses areas in need of further study--mostly in intellectual and political history--and the state of research materials in the field.

186. Burns, E. Bradford, ed. *Perspectives on Brazilian History*. New York: Columbia University Press, 1967.

Provides selections from Capistrano de Abreu, Jose Honório Rodrigues, Sérgio Buarque de Holanda and other major historians. A brief essay precedes each excerpt.

187. Byars, Robert S. and Joseph L. Love, eds. *Quantitative Social Science Research on Latin America*. Urbana: University of Illinois Press, 1973.

Contains seven articles dealing with current quantitative research in disciplines from history to archaeology. The appendix lists data banks containing Latin American materials, including those at the Center of Social and Political Data of the Federal University of Minas Gerais.

188. Carone, Edgard. "Oligarchias: definição e bibliografia." *Revista da Administração de Empresas* (Rio de Janeiro), 12 (January-March 1972), 81-92.

Provides detailed commentary on several dozen Brazilian studies of political elites and oligarchies. Concentrates on the republican period.

189. Cavalcanti, Themistocles Brandão. "Tópicos de uma história política." *Revista de Ciência Política*, 21 (July-September 1978), 5-26.

Suggests revisionist interpretations for five themes in Brazilian historiography, including the meaning of Vargas-era *tenentismo*.

190. Céspedes, Guillermo. "Brazil: the View from Spanish American History." *The History Teacher* (March 1969), 44-49.

Contends that more similarities than differences characterize Brazil's relationship to its Spanish-speaking neighbors.

191. Chagas Cruz, Carlos Henrique Davidoff. "História e ideologia na década de 30." Master's Thesis. Departamento de Ciências Sociais, Universidade Estadual de Campinas, 1976.

Contrasts the dual strains of "conciliation" and "authoritarianism" which have survived from the experience of the 1930s, through a study of the writings of Gilberto Freyre, Buarque de Holanda, Oliveira Vianna, and Azevedo Amaral.

192. Dulles, John W.F. "The Contribution of Getúlio Vargas." *Man, State, and Society in Latin American History.* Ed. Sheldon B. Liss and Peggy K. Liss. New York: Praeger, 1972, pp. 384-393.

Describes Vargas as a level-headed but not emotionless leader, one who subordinated special-interest loyalties to the needs of the people.

193. Esquenazi-Mayo, Roberto and Michael C. Meyer, eds. *Latin American Scholarship since World War II: Trends in History, Political Science, Literature, Geography, and Economics.* Lincoln: University of Nebraska Press, 1971.

194. Fausto, Bória. *A revolução de 1930: historiografia e história.* São Paulo: Ed. Brasiliense, 1970.

Argues that the urban middle class, formally recognized politically for the first time after Vargas's victorious coup in 1930, was basically hostile to industrialization, since it feared the possible mobilizing impact industrial growth would have on the working class.

195. Fernandes, Florestan. "The Social Sciences in Latin America." *Social Science in Latin America.* Ed. Manuel Diégues Júnior and Bryce Wood. New York: Columbia University Press, 1967, pp. 19-54.

Urges scholars, especially in the United States, to "revolutionize" their approach to observation and analysis and to cooperate with Brazilians seeking social change.

196. Flynn, Peter. "Brazil: Authoritarianism and Class Control," *Journal of Latin American Studies*, 6 (November 1974), 315-333.

Discusses the contributions of Erikson, Rosenbaum and Tyler, Quartim, Roett, Schneider, Stepan, Schmitter and others.

197. Holanda, Sérgio Buarque de. "Historical Thought in Twentieth Century Brazil." *Perspectives on Brazilian History*. Ed. E. Bradford Burns. New York: Columbia University Press, 1967, pp. 181-196.

Examines the impact of positivism, modernism, and nationalism on modern Brazilian political life.

198. "Independence or Death: A história do Brazil." *Veja* (São Paulo), 168 (Nov. 24, 1971), 32-38.

One of the opening shots in the press attack on foreign "Brazilianists" who are accused of rewriting Brazilian history from basic ignorance.

199. Leão, A. Carneiro *et al*. *A margem da história da República (ideais, crenças e afirmações). Inquerito por escriptores da geração nascida com a República*. Rio de Janeiro: José Olympio, 1924.

A major historiographical contribution by writers self-described as of the "Republican Generation," and collectively lamenting Brazil's lack of "national consciousness."

200. Levi, Darrell E. "Brazilian Nationalism: An Introduction." *Canadian Review of Studies in Nationalism*, 3 (1976), 114-122.

A review article on the post-1930 rise of nationalistic consciousness. Faults the nationalism of the Vargas years and after for failing to embrace the interests of the entire nation.

201. Levine, Robert M. "Letter from Recife." *Luso-Brazilian Review*, 7 (December 1970), 114-121.

Discusses the research climate in the Northeast's major city and problems caused by inadequate facilities for the storage of historical materials.

202. Levine, Robert M. "The Vargas Era Revisited." Paper presented to the Seminar on Brazilian Studies, State University of New York at Stony Brook, April 1979.

Uses previously uncited diplomatic records from British and United States sources to analyze the evolving historiography of the Vargas pre-Estado Nôvo period. Finds a growing attempt to redefine the role of the Brazilian State and a corresponding shift away from dismissing Vargas as an inscrutable personality.

203. Love, Joseph L. "An Approach to Regionalism." *New Approaches to Latin American History* (item 408), pp. 137-155.

Appraises opportunities for research at the regional level, citing examples of new methodological approaches drawn from the social science literature.

204. Luz, Nícea Vilela. "Ensaio de interpretação: historiografia brasileira." *Latin America: A Guide to Economic History*. Ed. Roberto Cortés Conde and Stanley J. Stein. Berkeley: University of California Press, 1977, pp. 165-181.

Reviews the historiography of Brazil's economic development for the hundred years culminating in the 1930 Revolution. Credits the nationalistic movements of the 1920's with awakening the interest of Brazilian intellectuals in their nation's economic state, preparing them to wrestle later with the reality of national underdevelopment.

205. Mota, Carlos Guilherme, ed. *Brasil em perspectiva*. São Paulo: DIFEL, 1969.

A collection of historiographically-minded essays spanning modern Brazilian social and political history, especially the Vargas period (1930-1954). Contains items 440, 516, 683, 687, 888.

206. Mota, Carlos Guilherme. "A historiografia brasileira nos últimos quarenta anos: tentativa de avaliação crítica." *Debate e Crítica*, 5 (1975), 1-26.

Comments on the major themes in Brazilian historical scholarship since 1935, including the role of the state, liberalism, and authoritarianism.

207. Pessôa Ramos, Dulce Helena Alvares. "As teses americanas sôbre o Brasil (1960/1970)." Master's Thesis. University of São Paulo, 1977.

Criticizes angrily the failings of a decade of writing on Brazil by American "Brazilianists." The author's selections seem to have been taken at random although several dozen dissertations are analyzed.

208. Pinheiro, Paulo Sérgio. "Mr. Dulles Rides Again (dessa vez na história social)." *Estudos CEBRAP* (São Paulo), 9 (July-September 1974), 155-166.

Provides a sarcastic critique of two of John W.F. Dulles's recent works, attacking, by extension, some of the work of foreign "Brazilianists."

209. Rodrigues, José Honório. "Brazilian Historiography: Present Trends and Research Requirements." *Social Science in Latin America*. Ed. Manuel Diégues Júnior and Bryce Wood. New York: Columbia University Press, 1967, pp. 217-240.

Suggests that scholars give priority to economic and political history as well as to studies of vested interests and economic groups.

210. Rodrigues, José Honório. *Conciliação e reforma no Brasil: um desafio histórico-político*. Rio de Janeiro: Civilização Brasileira, 1965.

Argues that the Brazilian political elite has traditionally avoided conflict in favor of conciliation in order to maintain power and resist social change.

211. Rodrigues, José Honório. "O ensino da história e a reforma universitária." *Revista Civilização Brasileira*, 4 (September-December 1968), 3-39.

Advocates new ways of teaching and studying Brazilian history at the university level.

212. Rodrigues, José Honório. *História, corpo do tempo*. São Paulo: Ed. Perspectiva, 1976.

Contains a series of historiographical essays on various themes frequently discussed by historians of Brazil, including political behavior, foreign influence, and the alleged national tendency toward conciliation rather than belligerency.

213. Rodrigues, José Honório. *História e historiadores do Brasil*. São Paulo: Companhia Editôra Nacional, 1965.

Speculates on the strengths and weaknesses of the existing historiography and calls for more far-reaching studies on such topics as nationalism and political ideology.

214. Rodrigues, José Honório. "O sentido da história do Brasil." *Revista de História*, 100 (1974), 515-528.

Finds a gulf separating historical thinking and historical events, and advocates further study of nationalism and Brazilian national society.

215. Rodrigues, José Honório. *Vida e história*. Rio de Janeiro: Civilização Brasileira, 1966.

A collection of historiographical essays ranging from a criticism of revisionism and historical judgment to analyses of foreign view of Brazilian history. History, the author avers, is a "question of conscience."

216. Skidmore, Thomas E. "The Historiography of Brazil, 1889-1964." *Hispanic American Historical Review*. Part I: 55 (November, 1975), 716-749; Part II, 56 (February, 1976), 81-109.

Focuses on work appearing, in Brazil and outside, between 1960 and 1972. Part I treats political history; Part II, economic history and state and local politics as well as foreign relations.

217. Skidmore, Thomas E. "Letter from Brazil: Recent Publications in History and the Social Sciences." *Luso-Brasilian Review*, 4 (December 1967), 111-119.

Shows that most new studies fall into the category of political history, although economics and geography also have received attention.

218. Souza, Amaury de. "The Cangaço and the Politics of Violence in Northeast Brazil." *Protest and Resistance in Angola and Brazil: Comparative Studies*, pp. 109-131.

Reviews the literature on the *cangaceiro*, the bandit-folk hero of the early twentieth century northeast who often acted as the enforcing arm of coastal political machines and their *coronel* clients.

219. Stein, Stanley J. "Latin American Historiography: Status and Research Opportunities," *Social Science Research on Latin America*. Ed. Charles Wagley. New York: Columbia University Press, 1964, pp. 86-124.

Argues that historians must redefine and reinterpret the interpretations, questions, and assumptions made by earlier scholars in order to remain dynamic. Urges studies of the "tenacity of conservatism" and the persistence of traditionalism.

220. Sodré, Nelson Werneck. *O que se deve ler para conhecer o Brasil.* 4th ed. Rio de Janeiro: Civilização Brasileira, 1973.

Provides commentary and bibliographic references for 46 topics on Brazilian studies. Limited for the most part to material published in Brazil.

221. Turner, J. Michael. "Brazilian and African Sources for the Study of Cultural Transferences from Brazil to Africa." Paper presented to the Latin American Studies Association, Houston, November 1977.

Examines current writing on Afro-Brazilian themes with suggestions for projects which need to be done.

222. Vianna, Hélio. "Atuais tendências da historiográfia brasileira." *Revista Interamericana de Bibliografia* (Washington, D.C.), 13 (January-March 1963), 30-59.

Emphasizes the importance of biographies and memoir literature in current Brazilian historical scholarship.

223. Warren, Doanld Jr. "The 'Atlantic Vocation' and Teaching Brazilian History." *Luso-Brazilian Review*, 5 (Summer 1968), 75-85.

Asks instructors and textbook writers not to consider Brazil "about the same as Spanish-speaking lands but just less so."

224. Williams, Margaret Todaro. "Social Psychology and Latin American Studies." *Latin American Research Review*, 9 (Spring 1974), 141-153.

Uses various themes from contemporary Brazilian society--*machismo*, *macumba* and *candomblé*, the role of women, right-wing Catholicism--to discuss future opportunities for researchers.

III.
State and Polity

A. THEORETICAL ANALYSES

1. General Analyses

225. Almeida, Martins de. *O Brasil errado.* Rio de Janeiro: Schmidt Editôra, 1932.

Attacks Brazil's republican institutions for avoiding the inherent conflict between economic growth and the social needs of the population.

226. Azambuja, Darcy. *Teoria geral do Estado.* Pôrto Alegre: Ed. Glôbo, 1962.

Offers a history of the theoretical basis of Brazilian thought from a juridical perspective.

227. Benavides, Paulo. *A crise política brasileira.* Rio de Janeiro: Ed. Forense, 1969.

Demonstrates that although in theory Brazil's political system has been bipartite, in fact it remains, in sociological terms, a one-party system.

228. Busey, James L. "Brazil's Reputation for Political Stability." *Western Political Quarterly*, 18 (December 1965), 866-880.

Calls the events of 1964 "passing portents in a gathering storm," since for more than half a century Brazil has postponed solutions for social and economic reform while maintaining "stability" at almost any cost.

229. Calmón, Pedro. *História das ideias políticas.* Rio de Janeiro: Freitas Bastos, 1952.

A straightforward history of Brazilian political thought filled with copious quotes and references.

230. Calavcanti, Themistocles Brandão. *Teoria do Estado.* Rio de Janeiro: Ed. Borsoi, 1958.

Provides a long (532 pp.) treatise on the history of Brazilian political theory.

231. Chacon, Vamireh. *Historia das ideias socialistas no Brasil.* São Paulo: Editorial Grijalbo, 1977.

A rapid view of the major currents in Brazilian sociological thought, stressing philosophical theory.

232. Chacon, Vamireh. "State Capitalism and Bureaucracy in Brazil." Paper presented to the Latin American Studies Association, Houston, November 1977.

Discusses the prospects for a return to democracy in a society where executives are ill-trained; illiteracy runs rampant; agriculture is neglected; church militancy is considered subversive; and where two-thirds of the population barely earn subsistence wages.

233. Cintra, Antônio Octávio. "A política tradicional brasileira." *Cadernos do Departamento de Ciência Política* (Belo Horizonte) 1 (1974), 59-112.

Examines the Brazilian political system from the perspective of the center-periphery model utilized by many Latin American social scientists.

234. Donald, Carr Lowe. "The Brazilian *Município*: The Myth of Local Self-Government." Diss. University of Texas, 1959.

Points to the detrimental effect of centralism on popular attitudes towards government and upon local administration.

235. Duarte, Pereira Osny. *Quem faz as leis no Brasil?* 3rd ed. Rio de Janeiro: Civilizaçao Brasileira, 1963.

Calls João Goulart an agent of the national bourgeoisie, too weak to resist foreign economic aggression.

236. Faoro, Raymundo. *Os donos do poder: formação do patronato politíco brasileiro.* 3rd ed. 2 vols. Pôrto Alegre: Ed. Glôbo, 1976.

Examines the internal antagonisms which preserve disunity and fuel conflict among interest groups to the detriment of the Brazilian people. A major analysis of Brazilian political society, first published in 1958.

237. Figueiredo, Marcus. "*Cultura Política*: revista teórica do Estado Nôvo." *Dados*, 4 (1968), 221-246.

A much-needed annotated bibliography of 232 articles from the Estado Nôvo journal *Cultura Política*, published between 1941 and 1945.

238. Fontes, Lourival. "Democracia, eleição, representação." *Cultura Política*, 1 (August 1941), 5-9.

Vargas's propaganda chief and intellectual protegé explains the regime's stance against representative democracy.

239. Freels, John W., Jr. "The Many Shades of Revolutions in Brazilian Political Literature." Riverside, Calif.: Latin American Research Program, University of California, Riverside, 1966.

Considers the "Brazilian Revolution" to be an ambiguous term used by reformists and opponents of change alike. Argues that the military regime uses the term in a counter-revolutionary sense.

240. Furtado, Celso. *A pre-revolução brasileira*. Rio de Janeiro: Fundo da Cultura, 1962.

Presents an analytical framework for "pre-revolutionary" conditions for Brazilian society.

241. Holanda, Sérgio Buarque de. *Raizes do Brasil*. 5th ed. Rio de Janeiro: José Olympio, 1969.

One of the seminal works of Brazilian historical thought, first published in 1936. Seeks to understand Brazil's roots through its rural heritage, patterns of settlement, and national style.

242. Jaguaribe, Hélio. "Brazilian Nationalism and the Dynamics of Political Development." *Studies in Comparative International Development*, 2 (1966). St. Louis: Washington University, 1966.

Argues that only the removal of the causes of tension within Brazilian society can resolve the post-1964 impasse. The proletariat must receive its share of the nation's wealth before stability is possible.

243. Jaguaribe, Hélio. *The Brazilian Structural Crisis*. Riverside, Calif.: Latin American Research Program, University of California, Riverside, 1966.

Calls the Brazilian political system "colonial fascist," subservient to the United States, and frozen at an incipient level of development.

244. Jaguaribe, Hélio. "The Dynamics of Brazilian Nationalism." *Obstacles to Change in Latin America*. Ed. Claude Veliz. London: Oxford University Press, 1965, pp. 162-187.

Calls for a reconstituted national front comprised of the national bourgeoisie, the new technocratic middle class, and urban workers.

245. Jaguaribe, Hélio. *Political Development: A General Theory and a Latin American Case Study*. New York: Harper &,Row, 1973.

Pleads for reformers and moderates to seize hold of the powerful state apparatuses built by military regimes in Brazil, Argentina and elsewhere and reorient them to social and national developmental goals mobilized by popular participation.

246. Johnson, John J. *Political Change in Latin America: the Emergence of the Middle Sectors*. 2nd ed. Stanford: Stanford University Press, 1961.

Argues that the "middle sectors" act to acquire political power, and are the key to understanding the dynamics of political change.

247. Keith, Henry H. and S.F. Edwards, eds. *Conflict and Conformity in Brazilian Society*. Columbia, S.C.: University of South Carolina Press, 1969.

Collected papers speculating on Brazil's purported capacity to absorb conflict and achieve conciliation through moderation and compromise.

248. Luz, Nícea Vilela. "A década de 20 e suas crises." *Revista do Instituto de Estudos Brasileiras*. (São Paulo), 6 (1969), 67-75.

Considers the socio-economic tensions of the 1920's responsible for awakening national consciousness, setting the stage, in turn, for the more radical programs of the 1930's.

249. Machado Neto, A.L. *Os valores políticos de uma élite provinciana*. Salvador: Ed. Progresso, 1958.

Examines the political values of the middle and upper class electorate in urban Bahia, finding large doses of moralism and residues of traditional attitudes. In spite of observable penetration of progressive ideology, old values persist.

250. Magalhães, Agamemnon. *O Estado e a realidade contemporânea*. Rio de Janeiro: n.p., 1933.

Blames socio-economic polarization and rural poverty for Brazil's ills. The author, Vargas's Labor Minister, publicly championed national solutions for regional problems, and a strong executive branch of the government.

251. Marcadante, Paulo. *A consciência conservadora no Brasil*. Rio de Janeiro: Ed. Saga, 1965.

Finds conservative ideology, the basis of Brazilian political thought, to be the direct legacy of economic liberalism and neo-feudal forms of land tenure.

252. Martins, Paulo. *Problemas nacionaes*. São Paulo: Revista dos Tribunaes, 1935.

Outlines a political plan of action for the newly elected National Congress to which the author was elected in 1934. Calls for increased international trade with accompanying safeguards against exploitation by foreign interests.

253. Mello Franco, Afonso Arinos de. *Evolução da crise brasileira*. São Paulo: Companhia Editôra Nacional, 1965.

The "Brazilian crisis," as he sees it, is total: social, military, political, administrative, moral, monetary, educational, fiscal, national. It has persisted since 1930, and threatens to paralyze the entire present generation.

254. Mello Franco, Afonso Arinos de. *Preparação ao nacionalismo*. Rio de Janeiro: José Olympio, 1934.

Attacks the enemies of Brazilian nationhood, including liberal-democratic Jews, and advocates government by the "clean blooded and well-born."

255. Menezes, Aderson de. *Teoria geral do Estado*. Rio de Janeiro: Ed. Forense, 1960.

Offers a lengthy history of Brazilian political thought, mostly in its abstract juridical dimension.

256. Moore, R. Barrington. *Injustice: The Social Bases of Obedience and Revolt.* New York: M.E. Sharpe, 1978.

Attributes the inability of citizens under authoritarian rule to react other than with docility to the limitations imposed on their "social and cultural space."

257. Oliveira, Franklin de. *Quê é a revolução brasileira?* Rio de Janeiro: Editôra Civilização Brasileiro, 1962.

Discusses the problems posed by Brazil's pre-revolutionary, semi-feudal peasantry and its working class, which he considers "more reformist than revolutionary."

258. Oliveira, Franklin de. *Revolução e contra-revolução no Brasil.* Rio de Janeiro: Civilização Brasileira, 1962.

Calls for a nationalist, innovative, and humane expression of revolutionary spirit to overcome Brazilian suffering.

259. Oliveira Torres, João Camillo de. *A formação do federalismo no Brasil.* São Paulo: Companhia Editôra Nacional, 1961.

Emphasizes the historical tension between centralization and federalism.

260. Oliveira, Vianna. *A evolução do povo brasileiro.* São Paulo: Companhia Editôra Nacional, 1932.

Argues that centralization holds the key to the Brazilian future, "a definitive triumph over the centrifugal forces of provincialiam and localism." This view became the basis for the nationalistic ideology of Vargas's Estado Nôvo.

261. Packenham, Robert A. "Yankee Impressions and Brazilian Realities." *The Wilson Quarterly*, 1 (August 1976), 63-72.

Contends that Brazil's regime is neither totalitarian nor democratic; the military is not monolithic; the fading economic boom nonetheless helped to keep radical opponents from gaining middle-class support.

262. Pompermayer, Malori José. "Autoritarismo no Brasil." Masters Thesis. Universidade Federal de Minas Gerais, 1970.

Constructs a theoretical model of the Brazilian authoritarian structure as a vehicle for understanding possibilities for political relaxation.

263. Rachum, Ilan. "Nationalism and Revolution in Brazil, 1922-1930." Diss. Columbia University, 1970.

Reviews the rise of nationalism in culture as well as within the political-military sphere in the 1920s, setting the stage for the Liberal Alliance and the 1930 Revolution.

264. Ramos, Alberto Guerreiro. *Mito e verdade da revolução brasileira*. Rio de Janeiro: Zahar, 1963.

Calls Brazil excessively internationalized, warning that the State must reorganize itself to encompass the needs of newly emerging social classes.

265. Ramos, Alberto Guerreiro. "Typology of Nationalism in Brazil: A Case of Political Breakdown." Paper presented to the University of California Project, "Brazil-Portuguese Africa," UCLA-University of California, Riverside, March 1968.

Examines the myths of Brazilian nationalist theory that the nation is a closed system; that there is a monolithic dominant class, the national bourgeoisie; and that the proletariat play a messianic role.

266. Roett, Riordan. *Brazil: Politics in a Patrimonial Society*. rev. ed. New York: Praeger, 1978.

Defines Brazil as a patrimonial state with a flexible and paternalistic commitment to the preservation of the nation. Authority is exercised by the elite, which dominates the bureaucratic apparatus.

267. Sampaio, Nelson de Souza. *Prôlogo à teoria do Estado*. Rio de Janeiro: Ed. Forense, 1960.

Discusses the historical and theoretical basis of Brazilian political thinking over time.

268. Santa Rosa, Virgínio. *O sentido do tenentismo*. Rio de Janeiro: Schmidt Editôra, 1933.

Argues that industrialists and land owners dominated Brazil before 1930 and that the Liberal Alliance signified victory for the emerging urban bourgeoisie. Reprinted in 1963 as *Que foi o tenentismo?* in the *Cadernos do Povo* series.

269. Santos, Wanderley Guilherme dos. "A imaginação politico-social brasileira." *Dados*, 4 (1968), 182-193.

Analyzes the "Brazilian political imagination, choosing studies by Fernando de Azevedo, Gurreiro Ramos, Djacir Menezes and Florestan Fernandes as having had substantial influence on what the author calls the "national memory."

270. Schmitter, Philippe C. *Interest Conflict and Political Change in Brazil.* Stanford: Stanford University Press, 1971.

Analyzes the political process from a comparative theoretical standpoint.

271. Schmitter, Philippe C. "Still the Century of Corporatism?" *The New Corporatism: Social-Political Structures in the Iberian World.* Ed. Frederick B. Pike and Thomas Stritch. Notre Dame, Indiana: University of Notre Dame Press, 1974, pp. 85-131.

Explores alterantive usages of the concept of corporatism, which, the author contends, is frequently misused. Defines the Brazilian variety as "state corporatism," in contrast to the pluralist variety found elsewhere.

272. Schmitter, Philippe C. "The Portugalization of Brazil?" *Authoritarian Brazil* (item 431), pp. 179-232.

Examines Brazil's post-1964 rule as a developmental model of authoritarian political domination. Claims the price of this non-revolutionary response to the strains of modernization is to be restricted political choice and limited free inquiry.

273. Schneider, Ronald M. *The Political System of Brazil: Emergence of a 'Modernizing' Authoritarian Regime, 1964-1970.* New York: Columbia University Press, 1971.

Analyzes military politics in the first six years of the "Revolution." Notes the existence of deep cleavage within the military ranks and emphasizes maneuverings within the armed forces hierarchy.

274. Skidmore, Thomas E. "Brazil: From Revolution to Miracle." *Latin American Review of Books*, 1 (Spring 1973), 103-109.

Reviews five studies on contemporary Brazil, emphasizing the role of the military, the function of official repression, and economic performance.

275. Soares, Glaúcio Ary Dillon. "As bases ideolôgicas do Lacerdismo." *Revista Civilização Brasileira*, 1 (September 1965), 49-70.

Finds the political ideology of Carlos Lacerda, the flamboyant governor of Guanabara prior to the 1964 coup, to combine upper class values with anti-interventionist biases.

276. Sobrinho, Barbosa Lima. *Desde quando somos nacionalistas?* Rio de Janeiro: Civilização Brasileira, 1963.

Surveys the history of Brazilian nationalism, defending the patriotic variety but warning against blind nativism. Compares English and United States imperialism and finds the former more generous, less ostentatious, more tolerant, and more able.

277. Sodrê, Nelson Werneck. *Histôria da burguesa brasileira*. 2nd ed. Rio de Janeiro: Civilização Brasileira, 1967.

Finds Brazil's national bourgeoisie timid and vacillating, threatened by three historical forces: *latifunda*, imperialism, and proletarian demands.

278. Sodrê, Nelson Werneck. *Introdução a Revolução Brasileira*. Rio de Janeiro: Civilização Brasileira, 1963.

The electorate, he warns, is *not* the "people" and the voting process is a sham, since the masses are disproportionately represented.

279. Torres, Alberto. *O problema nacional brasileiro*. 3rd ed. São Paulo: Companhia Editôra Nacional, 1938.

Published in 1914 but highly influential a generation later. Calls for Brazilian economic independence from colonialism and "Brazilian solutions to Brazilian problems."

280. Unger, Roberto Mangabeira. *Knowledge and Politics*. New York: Free Press, 1975.

Constructs a theoretical post-authoritarian social structure for Brazil in which the society comes to predominate over the state and where technocrats are restricted to auxiliary functions and are subordinated to political choice.

281. Weffort, Francisco C. "State and Mass in Brazil." *Masses in Latin America*. Ed. Irving Louis Horowitz, New York: Oxford University Press, 1970, pp. 385-406.

Argues that nationalism produced a climate of false expectation whereby the actions of both the State and popular political organization became increasingly guided by the belief that the government could control any possible reaction from the right.

2. The Left

282. Alexander, Robert J. *Communism in Latin America.* New Brunswick: Rutgers University Press, 1957.

Discusses Luis Carlos Prestes and the Brazilian Communist Party within a Cold War framework.

283. Alexander, Robert J. *Trotskyism in Latin America.* Stanford: Hoover Institute Press, 1973.

Includes treatment of the dissident Trotskyite faction in the PCB during the late 1920's and early 1930's.

284. Amado, Jorge. *Homens e coisas do Partido Comunista.* Rio de Janeiro: Ed. Horizonte, 1946.

A short (63 pp.) essay describing Brazilian Communist Party leadership and discussing its goals.

285. Amado, Jorge, ("My People are Fighting"). *Molodoi Kolkhoznik* (Moscow), 2 (February 1952) 7ff.

The novelist praises the survival of militancy against imperialism despite government suppression of the P.C.B.

286. Amado, Jorge. *Vida de Luis Carlos Prestes: O Cavaleiro da Esperança.* São Paulo: Ed. Martins, 1945.

Portrays the life of Prestes, the "Knight of Hope," in glowing praise. After the P.C.B. was stripped of its legality in 1947 the biography was suppressed; it is usually not listed in Amado's bibliography.

287. Amazonas, João, Carlos Marighela and Maurício Grabois. *Em defesa dos mandatos do povo e pela renúncia do ditator.* Rio de Janeiro: Ed. Vitória, 1948.

Three Communist Party theoreticians attack President Dutra and argue that social justice will only be won by popular militancy.

288. Arraes, Miguel. *Brazil: The People and the Power.* Tr. Lancelot Sheppard. Baltimore: Penguin Books, 1972.

Analyzes Brazilian conditions from the prespectives of the left.

289. *A bancada comunista na constituinte de 1946.* Rio de Janeiro: Ed. Horizonte, 1947.

Explains the platform of the Communist Party at the 1946 national Constituent Assembly.

290. Barata, Agildo. *Vida de um revolucionário.* Rio de Janeiro: Ed. Melso, 1963.

The author outlines his stormy revolutionary career as a *tenente* member of the Prestes Column and later as a militant leftist.

291. Basbaum, Leôncio. *Uma vida em seis tempos (memórias).* São Paulo: Ed. Alfa-Omega, 1976.

A posthumous autobiographical glimpse of life in the Communist Party and the distance between party leadership and the "masses."

292. Bastos, Abguar. *Prestes e a revolução social.* Rio de Janeiro: Ed. Calvino, 1946.

A detailed, larger-than-life portrayal of the life of Communist Party leader Luis Carlos Prestes.

293. *Carlos Marighela.* Havana: Ed. Tricontinental, 1970.

A Cuban-published collection of the Brazilian guerrilla's writing, prefaced by a biographical sketch.

294. Chernov, L. "Indefatigable Fighters for the Interests of the Brazilian People." *Agitator*, 12 (June 1958), 38-41.

A Soviet writer optimistically views the P.C.B.'s prospects for social progress and raised social awareness among the lower classes.

295. Claudin, Fernando. *La crise du mouvement communiste (du Komintern au Kominform).* Paris: n.p., 1972.

A history of the Communist International, including its role in Brazil in the 1930's.

296. Collitti-Pischel, Enrica and Chiara Robertazzi. *L'Internationale Communiste et les problèmes coloniaux, 1919-1935*. Paris: Mouton, 1968.

Touches on Comintern activity in Brazil through the ill-fated 1935 revolt.

297. Colombo, Pedro. *Quem faz a revolução no Brasil?* São Paulo: Ed. Martins, 1964.

Argues that communists seek to impose Soviet domination over Brazil, and are aided by Catholics and even priests.

298. Dillon, Dorothy. *International Communism and Latin America: Perspective and Prospects*. Gainesville: University of Florida Press, 1962.

Surveys the "rising curve" of Sino-Soviet Bloc interest in Latin America from the mid-1920's, through the Comintern's popular front strategy of the 1930's, through the Cold War. Brazil was second only to Cuba as recipient of Soviet aid to Latin America between 1959 and 1961.

299. Dos Santos, Theotônio. "Brazil." *Latin America: The Struggle for Dependency and Beyond*, Ed. R.H. Chilcote and J.C. Edelstein. New York: Halsted Press, 1974, pp. 409-490.

Contends that socialism, "the only popular solution," and fascism, "the only capitalist alternative," will continue to struggle at the center of Brazil's historical process.

300. Dulles, John W.F. *Anarchists and Communists in Brazil, 1900-1935*. Austin: University of Texas Press, 1973.

Describes the rise of anarcho-syndicalism in the first decade of the century and the rise of the Brazilian Communist Party, most of whose founders and theoreticians came from anarchist ranks. By 1935 the tide had turned, the military held control, and the left was crushed.

301. Gorender, Jacob. "Brazil in the Grip of Contradictions." *World Marxist Review*, 6 (February 1963), 27-32.

An interesting view of Brazil from the left during the heady days at the Goulart administration.

302. Holanda, Nestor de. *Como seria o Brasil socialista?* Rio de Janeiro: Civilização Brasileira, 1963.

Explains that a socialist Brazil would bring a better life to the Brazilian people without sacrificing traditional institutions.

303. Lacerda, Fernando, Luis Carlos Prestes, and "Sinani." *A luta contra o prestismo e a revolução agrária e anti-imperialista.* Rio de Janeiro: Partido Comunista do Brasil, 1934.

Explains the Communist Party's position on land reform, imperialism and "prestismo," defined as a vacillating, petty-bourgeois mentality which lacks sufficient assertiveness to pursue revolutionary goals. Also attacks Trotskyites.

304. Levine, Robert M. "A revolução de 1935." *Cuadernos Brasileiros*, 10 (January-February 1968), 47-59.

Explores the social environment out of which the unsuccessful and short-lived insurrectionary movement of November 1935 erupted.

305. Machado, Augusto [Leôncio Basbaum]. *O caminho da revolução.* Rio de Janeiro: Ed. Vitória, 1934.

A Marxist analysis by a then-ranking member of the Brazilian Communist Party, under a pseudonym.

306. Marighela, Carlos. *For the Liberation of Brazil.* Tr. John Butt and Rosemary Sheed. Middlesex, England: Penguin Books, 1971.

Offers a primer for urban warfare. Marighela was the Marxist guerrilla leader gunned down in an ambush by São Paulo police in 1971.

307. Marighela, Carlos. *Por que resistí à prisão.* Rio de Janeiro: Contemporâneas, 1965.

The author, killed later in a police ambush, explains his reasons for resistance.

308. Patric, Anthony. *Toward the Winning Goal.* Rio de Janeiro: Ed. Vitória, 1940.

Laments the suppression of the Communist Party and Vargas's seemingly fascist leanings.

309. Peralva, Osvaldo. *O Retrato.* Pôrto Alegre: Ed. Globo, 1962.

Memoirs by a former communist in the form of a history of the Brazilian movement through its schism in the mid-1950's. Criticizes party officials for mistrusting their intellectuals and ultimately turning on them.

310. Pereira, Astrojildo. *Formação do PCB*. Rio de Janeiro: Ed. Vitória, 1962.

One of its founders relates the early history of the Brazilian Communist Party. Notes the difficulties of forging ties with the apolitical working classes.

311. Pereira, Astrojildo. *Interpretação*. Rio de Janeiro: Casa do Estudante do Brasil, 1944.

Pleads for the restoration of legal status for the Brazilian Communist Party and for mobilization against fascism.

312. Polícia Civil do Distrito Federal. *Arquivos da Delegacia Especial de Segurança Política e Social*. Vol. 3. Rio de Janeiro: DESPS, 1938.

Reproduces the most important of the documents captured from Communist Party activists after the 1935 insurrection, confirming Comintern interest in fomenting social insurrection.

313. Prestes, Luis Carlos. "The Brazilian Communist Party in its Struggle for Peace, Liberty, and National Independence." *Kommunist* (Moscow), 31 (February 1955), 87-102.

Analyzes Brazilian events and predicts better fortunes for the Party cause as its message spreads among the masses.

314. Prestes, Luis Carlos. "Brazilian Communists in the Fight for Democracy." *Marxism in Latin America*. Ed. and Tr. Luis E. Aguilar. New York: Borzoi Books, 1968, pp. 139-144.

Warns that the Brazilian Communist Party must lead and not be "swept along by the spontaneous movement of the popular masses" or by popular opinion, which is nurtured by the bourgeois press in order to subvert class interests.

315. Prestes, Luis Carlos. *5 cartas da prisão*. Rio de Janeiro: Ed. Horizonte, 1948.

Five letters written from prison by the Communist Party chieftain, on social issues.

316. Prestes, Luis Carlos. *Os communistas na luta pela democracia.* Rio de Janeiro: Partido Comunista Brasileiro, 1945.

 States the objectives and goals of the Brazilian Communist Party on the eve of its legalization following Prestes' release from prison.

317. Prestes, Luis Carlos. *Em marcha para um grande Partido Comunista de massa.* Rio de Janeiro: Ed. Horizonte, 1947.

 Explains the Party's campaign to attract mass support as the first step towards ultimate electoral victory.

318. Prestes, Luis Carlos. *Porque os comunistas apoíam Lott e Jângo.* Rio de Janeiro: Ed. Vitória, 1960.

 The Communist leader explains his party's position backing Janio Quadros in 1960.

319. Prestes, Luis Carlos. *Problemas atuais da democracia.* Rio de Janeiro: Ed. Vitória, 1947.

 A collected edition of the letters, speeches, and articles of the chief of the Brazilian Communist Party, emphasizing the strategy of working within the political system.

320. Prestes, Luis Carlos. *The Struggle for Liberation in Brazil.* New York: n.p., 1936.

 The nominal head of the Brazilian Communist Party and its popular front subsidiary, the National Liberation Alliance, offers a nationalistic and anti-fascist program for social change.

321. Quartim, João. *Dictatorship and Armed Struggle.* Tr. David Fernbach. New York: Monthly Review Press, 1972.

 Analyzes socio-economic conditions in Brazil from a Marxist perspective and foresees a struggle for national liberation.

322. Redmont, Bernard S. "Brazilian Communist Outlines Party Policy in Latin America." *World Report* (Oct. 8, 1946), 18-19.

 Sympathetically recounts the goals of the newly-legalized P.C.B. under Prestes.

323. Ribeiro de Castro, Orlando. *E as ordens vieram de Moscou.* Rio de Janeiro: Ed. *A Noite*, 1946.

Charges that the Prestes and the P.C.B. are tools of the Soviet Union and, as a result, should be dealt with severely.

3. The Right

324. "Algumas fontes bibliograficas sôbre Alceu Amoroso Lima." *Autores e Livros* (Rio de Janeiro), 4 (1943), 269.

A bibliography of the works of Alceu Amoroso Lima (Tristão de Athayde), spokesman for the Catholic Right during the 1930's.

325. "Algumas fontes bibliográficas sôbre Raul Bopp." *Autores e Livros* (Rio de Janeiro), 5 (1943), 61.

A short bibliographic listing of works by and about the modernist poet Raul Bopp, who was a member of the fascist Integralist party in the 1930's.

326. Araujo, Ricardo Benzaquen de. "As classificações de Plínio." *Revista de Ciência Política*, 21 (July-September 1978), 161-180.

Classifies the works of the Integralist chieftain, Plínio Salgado, and discusses his major themes: the evils of liberalism, the "two Brasils," anti-communism, and the conservative tradition.

327. Barroso, Gustavo [João Dodt]. *Brasil: colônia de banqueiros.* Rio de Janeiro: Editôra ABC, 1934.

Claims that Brazil lies helplessly under the sway of foreign bankers, mostly Jewish. The author was a leading member of the Academy of Letters and the intellectual chieftain of the fascist Integralists.

328. Barroso, Gustavo [João Dodt]. *O integralismo de norte a sul.* Rio de Janeiro: Civilização Brasileira, 1934.

Analyzes the fascist movement's political platform and implores Brazilian Christians to support Integralist candidates.

329. Barroso, Gustavo [João Dodt]. *A palavra e o pensamento integralista*. Rio de Janeiro: Civilização Brasileira, 1934.

Exhorts his followers to combat their lethargy and plunge into Integralist life with enthusiasm and faithfulness.

330. Barroso, Gustavo [João Dodt]. *Roosevelt es judío*. Buenos Aires: n.p., 1938.

Attacks Roosevelt as a crypto-Jew and enemy of the Brazilian people.

331. Barroso, Gustavo [João Dodt]. *O que o integralista deve saber*. 3rd ed. Rio de Janeiro: Civilização Brasileira, 1935.

Lists the obligations of the Integralist: to stand vigilant, obey orders without question, combat Jewish communism, and face destiny.

332. Barroso, Gustavo [João Dodt]. *A sinagoga paulista*. Rio de Janeiro: Editôra ABC, 1937.

The Integralist's intellectual chieftain scurrilously alleges that Jews control the city of São Paulo.

333. Broxson, Elmer R. "Plínio Salgado and Brazilian Integralism, 1932-1938." Diss. The Catholic University of America, 1972.

Emphasizes Brazilian fascist ideology and the growth of the Integralist Party.

334. Del Pincchia, Menotti. *Questões nacionals*. Rio de Janeiro: José Olympio, 1935.

A leading poet of right-wing persuasion identifies Brazil's lack of assertiveness as a nation as its major weakness.

335. Eulau, Heinz H.F. "The Ideas Behind Brazilian Integralism." *Inter-American Quarterly*, 3 (October 1941), 36-43.

Shows that, despite its claim of originality, Brazilian Integralist ideology is exceedingly similar to fascist political thought of European vintage. Adds that Integralism represents a threat to the interests of the United States and of Pan American unity.

336. Hilton, Stanley E. "Ação Integralista Brasileira." *Luso-Brazilian Review*, 9 (December 1972), 3-29.

Examines the Integralist party (AIB) in terms of its membership and its inability to win support from the ruling civilian-military elite.

337. Medeiros, Jarbas. *Ideologia authoritária no Brasil, 1930/1945*. Rio de Janeiro: Fundação Getúlio Vargas, 1978.

Examines five "authoritarian" Brazilian thinkers: Francisco Campos, Oliveira Vianna, Azevedo Amaral, Alceu Amoroso Lima, and Plínio Salgado. All stood on the right of the political spectrum and have exerted major influence since 1930 during the periods of authoritarian rule.

338. Mota, Arthur. "Bio-Bibliografia: Plínio Salgado." *Revista da Academia Paulista de Letras* (São Paulo), 2 (1939), 136-138.

A brief biography (with complete bibliography) of the Integralist leader through the year 1939, his first year of Portuguese exile.

339. Prado, Eduardo. *A ilusão americana*. 3rd ed. Rio de Janeiro: Civilização Brasileira, 1935.

A new edition, printed for Integralist readers, of the call for economic independence first raised in the 1890's.

340. Reale, Miguel. *O estado moderno*. Rio de Janeiro: José Olympio, 1933.

A book-length essay attributing weakness to liberal democracy and strength to corporatism.

341. Reale, Miguel. *Perspectivas integralistas*. São Paulo: Ed. Odeon, c. 1935.

One of the Integralist Party's leading intellectuals argues for fascist solutions to Brazil's problems.

342. Salgado, Plínio. *Despertemos a nação*. Rio de Janeiro: José Olympio, 1935.

Explains the fascist Integralist ideology and the need for corporatist hierarchy and national solidarity. Brazil, the "true Christian Western civilization," must liberate the rest of Latin America.

343. Salgado, Plínio. *Discursos na Câmara dos Deputados.* Rio de Janeiro: Livraria Clássica Brasileira, 1961.

Speeches delivered to the Chamber of Deputies in 1959 and 1960 by ARENA deputy Salgado, still an ardent Integralist.

344. Salgado, Plínio. *A doutrina do sigma.* Rio de Janeiro: Schmidt Editôra, 1936.

Another version of Integralist ideology: the "doctrine of the Sigma," the A.I.B.'s organizational symbol, analogous to the swastika.

345. Salgado, Plínio. *A quarta humanidade.* Rio de Janeiro: José Olympio, 1934.

Another Integralist diatribe against liberalism and democracy.

346. Salgado, Plínio. *O que é o integralismo.* Rio de Janeiro: Schmidt Editôra, 1933.

Argues that only under fascism can Brazil overcome liberal weakness and restore its lost Catholic faith.

347. Trindade, Hélgio Henrique C. "A Ação Integralista Brasileira: aspectos históricos e ideológicos." *Dados*, 10 (173), 25-60.

Considers Plínio Salgado's role as a "post-modernist" intellectual to have colored Integralist ideology, and sees the anti-liberal and anti-intellectual climate of the 1930's as a fertile ground for Salgado's fascist movement.

348. Trindade, Hélgio. *Integralismo (O fascismo brasileiro na década de 30).* Porto Alegre: Universidade de Rio Grande do Sul, 1974.

Analyzes in detail the composition of the Integralist movement, which was subsequently suppressed although some of its ideas were absorbed under the corporatist Estado Nôvo (1937-1945).

349. Velloso, Mônica Pimenta. "*A Ordem*: uma revista de doutrina política e cultura católica." *Revista de Ciência Política*, 21 (July-September 1978), 117-160.

Chronicles the right-wing phase of the Catholic journal *A Ordem* during the anti-communist and neo-orthodox campaign of the mid- and late-1930's.

B. LAW AND PUBLIC ADMINISTRATION

350. Almeida, Antônio Figuera de. *A Constituição de dez de novembro explicada ao povo.* Rio de Janeiro: Departamento da Imprensa e Propaganda, 1938.

     Explains the 1937 constitution, article-by-article.

351. Almeida, Fernando Henrique Mendes de. *Constituicões do Brasil.* 6th ed. 2 vols. São Paulo: Ed. Saraiva, 1971.

     Compares and analyzes Brazil's constitutions from 1824 through 1969.

352. Andrade, Almir de. *Contribuição à história administrativa do Brasil, na república, até o ano de 1945.* 2 vols. Rio de Janeiro: José Olympio, 1950.

     Traces the history of expanding national bureaucratic agencies, describing in detail the creation of the D.A.S.P., the federal civil service agency.

353. Andrade, Bonifácio de. *Parlamentarismo e a evolução brasileira.* Rio de Janeiro: Ed. B. Álvares, 1962.

     Discusses the system of presidentialism through its crisis period in the early 1960's.

354. Barreto, Carlos Eduardo. *Carteira do advogado: Direito constitucional.* Rio de Janeiro: M. Limonad, 1954.

     Analyzes the national constitutions of 1824, 1891, 1934, 1937 and 1946.

355. "Bibliografia sôbre planejamento administrativo." *Boletim da Biblioteca da Fundação Getúlio Vargas* (Rio de Janeiro), 6 (January 1964), 118-131.

     A bibliography on public administration and planning.

356. Brasil. Congresso, Câmara dos Deputados. Biblioteca. "Administração municipal, Bibliografia." *Boletim da Biblioteca da Câmara dos Deputados* (Brasilia), 9 (January 1960), 101-155.

     A well researched bibliography on *município*-level administration in Brazil, compiled by the library staff of the federal Chamber of Deputies.

357. Brasil. Ministério da Justiça e Negócios Interiores. *Constituições federal e estaduais*. Rio de Janeiro: Imprensa Nacional, 1957.

Contains the federal constitution (1946) as well as each constitution of the twenty-one states (but not Guanabara).

358. Carvalho, Orlando M. *Ensaios de sociologia electoral*. Belo Horizonte: Universidade de Minas Gerais, 1958.

Five essays on electoral law and politics, including three case studies from Minas Gerais in the mid-1950's.

359. Carvalho, Orlando de. *Política do munícipio: ensaio histórico*. Rio de Janeiro: Agir Editôres, 1946.

Analyzes the juridical role of the *município* (county), tracing its juridical roots back to colonial times.

360. Cavalcanti, Themistocles Brandão. *Manual da constituição*. Rio de Janeiro: Zahar, 1963.

Shows that the 1946 Constitution more closely resembles the 1891 charter than the Constitutions of 1934 and 1937, its immediate predecessors.

361. Conn, Stephen. *The Squatters' Rights of Favelados*. Cuernavaca: CIDOC, 1969.

Surveys the juridical rights of *favela* (shanty-town) inhabitants.

362. Crawford, H.P. "Comments on the Constitution of Brazil." *General Legal Bulletin*. Washington, D.C.: United States Department of Commerce, April 1935.

Offers a detailed analysis of the nationalistic 1934 Constitution.

363. Daland, Robert T. *Brazilian Planning*. Chapel Hill, N.C.: University of North Carolina Press, 1967.

An important study of administrative planning and government organization.

364. Daland, Robert T., ed. *Perspectives of Brazilian Public Administration*. Los Angeles: University of Southern California School of Public Administration, 1963.

Provides twelve articles on various aspects of public administration.

365. Duarte Pereira, Osny. *Quem faz as leis no Brasil.* Rio de Janeiro: Civilização Brasileira, 1962.

Argues that pressure groups of businessmen and industrialists control the legislative process.

366. Espínola, Eduardo. *A família no direito civil brasileiro.* Rio de Janeiro: Gazeta Judiciaria Editôra, 1954.

Offers a study of civil laws affecting the family.

367. Garcia-Zamor, Jean-Claude. *An Ecological Approach to Administrative Reform: The Brazilian Case.* Austin: Institute of Latin American Studies, University of Texas, 1971.

Advocates that administrative reform be accompanied by changes in mentality of civil servants to achieve greater efficiency.

368. Gomes, Angela Maria de Castro. "A representação de classes na constituinte de 1934." *Revista de Ciência Política*, 21 (July-September 1978), 53-116.

Considers the experiment with "class" representation during the 1934 constituent assembly to have been a pragmatic effort on the part of the regime to deal with conflicting pressures from the *tenente* nationalists.

369. Graham, Lawrence S. *Civil Service Reform in Brazil.* Austin: University of Texas Press, 1968.

Shows that government employment provides security and social standing for established middle-class elements; at the same time it has been highly coveted by the upwardly mobile urban working class.

370. Grossmann, Jorge. *Bibliography on Public Administration in Latin America.* 2nd ed. Washington: Columbus Memorial Library, 1958.

Contains substantial material on Brazil.

371. Lambert, Francis. "Trends in Administrative Reform in Brazil." *Journal of Latin American Studies*, 1 (November 1969), 167-188.

Briefly traces government planning from the colonial period to Vargas and the DASP, the federal civil service agency established in 1937, noting that it has never truly functioned according to the merit principle.

372. Lucas, Fábio. *Conteudo social nos constituições brasileiros.* Belo Horizonte: Universidade de Minas Gerais, 1959.

Discusses the social content of Brazil's republican-era constitutions.

373. Malloy, James M. *The Politics of Social Security in Brazil.* Pittsburgh: University of Pittsburgh Press, 1978.

Charges that Brazil's social security system fails to meet the needs of the poor in spite of official lip-service to human welfare.

374. Martin, Percy A. "Federalism in Brazil." *Hispanic American Historical Review*, 18 (May, 1938), 143-163.

Traces the evolution of federalism from the Empire through what the author terms its "enthronement" under the Estado Nôvo.

375. Marx, Fritz Morstein. "The Brazilian Civil Service." *Inter-American Quarterly*, 2 (1940), 42-63.

Praises Brazil for having established its Civil Service (DASP), and rationalizes its weaknesses on the grounds that resistance to change is still strong and that time will be needed for attitudes to mellow.

376. Mello Franco, Afonso Arinos de. *História e teoria do partido político no direito constitucional brasileiro.* Rio de Janeiro: Ed. Forense, 1948.

Examines the history of Brazilian political parties, concentrating on their interaction to produce laws or other specific results.

377. Mello Franco, Afonso Arinos de. *Formação constitucional brasileira.* 2 vols. Rio de Janeiro: Ed. Forense, 1960.

A textbook on constitutional history, emphasizing constitutional theory rather than political developments.

378. Miralles, Teresa. *O sistema penal na cidade do Rio de Janeiro.* Rio de Janeiro: Editôra Liber Juris, 1977.

Argues that penal laws and bureaucracy serve to obscure the realities of oppressive conditions in Rio de Janeiro prisons, and that only the poor are incarcerated.

379. Oliveira Torres, João Camillo de. *O presidencialismo no Brasil*. Rio de Janeiro: Ed. *O Cruzeiro*, 1962.

Analyzes the impact of technology, urbanization, and Vargas-era social change on the presidential system.

380. Richardson, Ivan L. *Political Science in Brazil: A Selected Bibliography*. Los Angeles: School of Public Administration, University of Southern California, 1964.

A 40-page annotated bibliography covering law, public administration, government organization and political theory, completed shortly after the 1964 coup.

381. Rodrigues, Leda Beochat. *Direito e polîtica: os direitos humanas no Brasil e nos EUA*. Ed. Ajuris, 1978.

Compares human rights before the law in Brazil and the United States in studies of the courts, individual justices, and the role of habeas-corpus. Illuminates the rather profound distance between the two societies despite structural similarities in their systems of justice.

382. Siegel, Gilbert. "The DASP of Brazil: A History and Analysis." Diss. University of Pittsburgh, 1964.

Outlines the history of Brazil's merit-based Civil Service, established by Vargas in 1938.

383. Wahrlich, Beatriz. *An Analysis of the DASP*. Chicago: Public Administration Clearing House, 1955.

An early evaluation of the civil service system.

C. POLITICAL HISTORY

1. General Studies

384. Álvaro Moises, Josê, Liisa North and David Raby. *Conflicts Within Populist Regimes: Brazil and Mexico*. Toronto: LARU, 1977.

Analyzes unrest in Brazil and Mexico and discusses prospects for further mobilization against the established regimes.

385. Baklanoff, Eric N., ed. *New Perspectives of Brazil.* Nashville: Vanderbilt University Press, 1966.

A collection of essays by ten specialists in history, the behavioral sciences, and the humanities. Contains item 985.

386. Basbaum, Leôncio. *História sincera da República.* Vol. III. 2nd ed. São Paulo: Ed. Edgalit, 1962.

Reviews Brazilian events since 1930's Liberal Alliance coup. The author was a Marxist who loyally adhered to the Brazilian Communist Party until his expulsion for "sectarianism."

387. Bello, José Maria. *A History of Modern Brazil, 1889-1964.* Tr. James L. Taylor. Stanford: Stanford University Press, 1968.

Chronicles the political history of Brazil since the fall of the Empire in detail, passing over social issues. The author, a well-educated member of the landholding elite, was elected governor of Pernambuco but was prevented from taking office by the 1930 Revolution.

388. Bernstein, Harry. *Modern Brazil: An Emerging Nation.* New York: Holt, Rinehart and Winston, 1964.

A somewhat dated but comprehensive general political history. Provides conventional interpretations.

389. Blondel, Jean. *As condições da vida política no Estado da Paraíba.* Rio de Janeiro: Fundação Getúlio Vargas, 1957.

Identifies new forms of behavior replacing waning rural *coronelismo*, such as increased political roles for professionals (physicians, lawyers, notaries) in interior urban centers.

390. Brasil. Congresso, Câmara dos Deputados. Biblioteca. "Eleições e partidos políticos, Bibliografia. *Boletim da Câmara dos Deputados* (Brasília), 13 (January-June 1964), 141-193.

A compilation of articles and studies on elections and political parties in Brazil.

391. Buarque de Holanda, Sérgio. *Raizes do Brasil.* Rio de Janeiro: José Olympio, 1936.

A landmark study of the Brazilian historical tradition

by a São Paulo scholar seeking to understand the failure of democratic institutions to take hold.

392. Burns, E. Bradford, ed. *A Documentary History of Brazil*. New York: Alfred A. Knopf, 1966.

Offers translations of basic documents in Brazilian history from the colonial period to the 1964 *golpe*.

393. Burns, E. Bradford. *A History of Brazil*. New York: Columbia University Press, 1970.

A comprehensive history of Brazil integrating cultural themes and based on the secondary literature in English as well as Portuguese.

394. Burns, E. Bradford. *Latin America: A Concise Interpretive History*. 2nd ed. Englewood Cliffs, N.J.: Prentice-Hall, 1977.

Treats contemporary Brazil as a "military model for change" and as an example of a pragmatic alliance between the elite and the middle class.

395. Burns, E. Bradford. *Nationalism in Brazil: A Historical Survey*. New York: Columbia University Press, 1968.

Regards nationalism as the central theme in Brazil's political evolution, too strong a force to be suppressed by political exigency.

396. Calmõn, Pedro. *Histõria do Brasil*. 7 vols. Rio de Janeiro: Josẽ Olympio, 1959.

A conservative, traditional political history of Brazil.

397. Calogeras, João Pandia. *A History of Brazil*. Tr. Percy A. Martin. Chapel Hill: University of North Carolina Press, 1939.

A comprehensive narrative history by a conservative Brazilian diplomat and historian.

398. Calvert, Peter. *Latin America: Internal Conflict and International Peace*. New York: St. Martin's Press, 1969.

Places Brazilian events in a hemispheric context and ponders the country's unresolved potential.

399. Chevalier, François. *L'Amérique Latine: De l'indépendance à nos jours*. Paris: Presses Universitaires de France, 1977.

Offers an overall treatment of Latin American history based to some extent on French sources which are not widely known.

400. Chilcote, Ronald H. *The Brazilian Communist Party: Conflict and Integration, 1922-1972*. New York: Oxford University Press, 1974.

Chides the Brazilian Communist Party for its "timidity and caution" during the critical years--1945 to 1947--of its legal status under the Dutra presidency.

401. Chilcote, Ronald H., ed. *Protest and Resistance in Angola and Brazil*. Berkeley: University of California Press, 1972.

Emphasizes efforts by local populations to resist colonial and neo-colonial domination despite entrenched hegemony from landowning elites. Contains item 218.

402. De Dubnic, Vladimir Reisky. *Political Trends in Brazil*. Washington, D.C.: Public Affairs Press, 1968.

Assesses Brazilian politics in broad strokes up to and beyond the 1964 coup.

403. Fitzgibbon, Russell H., comp. *Brazil: A Chronology and Fact Book, 1488-1973*. Dobbs Ferry, N.Y.: Oceana Publications, 1974.

Contains translations of documents relating to such post-1930 events as the Estado Nôvo; Brazil's role in the Second World War; Vargas's departure in 1954; Quadros's resignation in 1954; and the post-1964 military government.

404. Fleischer, David V. "A bancada federal mineira: trinta anos de recrutaménto polîtico, 1945/1975." *Revista Brasileira de Estudos Polîticos*, 45 (July 1977), 7-58.

Analyzes political recruitment over a thirty-year period to the federal congressional delegation of Minas Gerais. The new generation comprises younger men trained at the municipal level.

405. Flynn, Peter. *Brazil: A Political Analysis*. London: Ernest Benn, 1978.

Paints a sympathetic case in favor of President Goulart, and is critical of the military regime. The study is long, detailed, and invaluable.

406. Furtado, Celso, et al. *Brasil: tempos modernos*. Rio de Janeiro: Paz e Terra, 1968.

Collected essays on contemporary Brazil by Antônio Callado, Otto Maria Carpeaux, Fernando Henrique Cardoso, Florestan Fernandes and others.

407. Graham, Richard, ed. *A Century of Brazilian History Since 1865*. New York: Alfred A. Knopf, 1969.

Emphasizes aspects of Brazil's economic, historical, and social development which led to the instability which precipitated military intervention in 1964.

408. Graham, Richard and Peter H. Smith, eds. *New Approaches to Latin American History*. Austin: University of Texas Press, 1976.

Offers nine essays as a festschrift honoring Lewis Hanke. Contains item 203.

409. Gunther, John. *Inside Latin America*. New York: Harper and Row, 1941.

Provides for general readers a glimpse of a continent otherwise unknown to them. Stresses Brazil's strategic importance for the United States.

410. Humphreys, Robin A. *The Evolution of Modern Latin America*. London: Oxford University Press, 1946.

Provides a comparative framework within which to view Brazil's general historical evolution.

411. Kingsbury, Robert C. and Ronald M. Schneider. *An Atlas of Latin American Affairs*. New York: Praeger, 1965.

Includes a section on Brazil (pp. 106-123).

412. Lacerda, Carlos. *O poder das ideais*. 4th ed. Rio de Janeiro: Distribuidora Record, 1964.

Collected speeches and articles by Lacerda, the ex-Young Communist League leader who turned to the right in the 1950's and played a leading role as governor of Guanabara in the 1964 coup.

413. Lacombe, Américo Jacobina. *Brazil: A Brief History.* Tr. W.A.R. Richardson, Rio de Janeiro: Ministry of Foreign Relations, 1954.

A brief outline of Brazilian history written specifically for British readers.

414. Love, Joseph L. "Political Participation in Brazil, 1881-1969." *Luso-Brazilian Review*, 7 (December 1970), 3-24.

Shows that political mobilization after the fall of the Empire strengthened the traditional elite through legitimization of rural domination. Eventually, control was shifted to new groups, threatening patriarchal hegemony. A major contribution.

415. Marshall, Andrew. *Brazil.* New York: Walker and Company, 1966.

Blames Brazil's leaders for failure to nurture democratic institutions.

416. Mello Franco, Afonso Arinos. *The Chamber of Deputies of Brazil: A Historical Synthesis.* Tr. G.A. Chauret and J.S. Morris. Brasília: Chamber of Deputies, 1977.

Emphasizes the positive role of the Chamber of Deputies in achieving social change and political reform. Exaggerated.

417. Morazé, Charles. *Les trois âges du Brésil.* Paris: Fondation Nationale Sciences Politiques, 1954.

Offers a provocative but occasionally inaccurate overview of modern Brazilian political events from 1889 to the urban-based presidential campaign of 1950.

418. Nichols, Glenn A. "Party Failure in Pre-1964 Brazil." *Luso-Brazilian Review*, 4 (Winter 1977), 185-194.

Criticizes political analysts for emphasizing personalities of Brazilian leaders rather than the structure of the system itself.

419. Nichols, Glenn A. "Toward a Theory of Political Party Disunity: The Case of the National Democratic Party of Rio de Janeiro, Brazil." Diss. Tulane University, 1974.

Focuses on the profound divisions within the UDN and its penchant for personalism and inter-party rivalry.

420. Parahyba, Maria Antonieta de A.G. "Abertura social e participação política no Brasil." *Dados*, 7 (1970), 89-101.

Contends that increased political participation has not been accompanied by wider opportunities for political and social expression.

421. Pendle, George. *A History of Latin America.* Middlesex, England: Penguin Books, 1976.

Offers useful comparisons of events in Brazil with those in Spanish America.

422. Raine, Philip. *Brazil: Awakening Giant.* Washington, D.C.: Public Affairs Press, 1974.

Predicts future greatness for Brazil.

423. Roett, Riordan, ed. *Brazil in the Sixties.* Nashville: Vanderbilt University Press, 1972.

Collected essays by specialists on political developments, the economy, agriculture, higher education, the Church, and literature. Contains items 552, 636, 654, 703, 894, 1203, 1535, 1694.

424. Rowe, James. "The 'Revolution' and the 'System.'" *Latin American Politics*. Ed. R.D. Tomesek, 2nd ed. Garden City, N.Y.: Doubleday-Anchor, 1970, pp. 491-515.

Analyzes the "system," the term denoting the ruling elite which has, according to belief, dominated every Brazilian government regardless of political coloration.

425. Sampaio, Consuelo Novais. *Os partidos políticos da Bahia na primeira república.* Salvador: Universidade Federal de Bahia, 1978.

Assays the "politics of accommodation" in the state of Bahia under federalism. The 1930 Revolution did not change very much; rather, it squelched representative government, paving the way for total repression in 1937.

426. Schwartzman, Simon. "Patterns of Emergence and Participation in Brazil." Paper presented to Department of Political Science, University of California, Berkeley, December 1968.

Categorizes the structure of participation during six periods, from the Empire (closed) through the "Second Republic" (1945-1964; open) and after 1964 (closed).

427. Schwartzman, Simon. "Representação e cooptação política no Brasil." *Dados*, 7 (1970), 9-41.

Argues that the process of co-optation has dominated the political system and in turn is responsible for the inability of São Paulo, the strongest state, to carry its full political weight within the federation.

428. Silva, Celson José da. "Marchas e contramarchas do mandonismo local." Masters Thesis, Universidade de Minas Gerais, 1972.

Examines the *município* of Caeté as a case study in local *coronelismo*, focusing on the period since 1947 and analyzing the process of decision-making with the rise of political parties.

429. Skidmore, Thomas E. *Politics in Brazil, 1930-1964: An Experiment in Democracy*. New York: Oxford University Press, 1969.

Originally intended as a short piece explaining the background to 1964, the book skillfully analyzes the political events from 1930 to the fall of Goulart. Subsequent revelations have shown greater United States complicity in the coup than the author suggests.

430. Skidmore, Thomas E. "Politics and Economic Policy Making in Authoritarian Brazil, 1937-71." *Authoritarian Brazil* (item 431), pp. 3-46.

Contends that the 1964 coup saved the Vargas administrative state, despite the introduction of drastically new economic policies based on foreign participation in national development and the maintenance of an unusually high economic growth rate.

431. Stepan, Alfred C., ed. *Authoritarian Brazil: Origins, Policies, and Future*. New Haven: Yale University Press, 1973.

Essays of high quality from an interdisciplinary conference at Yale in 1971, ranging from economic analysis to speculation about the political future. Contains items 272, 430, 578, 646, 709, 859, 867.

432. Worcester, Donald E. *Brazil: From Colony to World Power*. New York: Charles Scribner's Sons, 1973.

A brief, interpretive synthesis of Brazil's evolution.

2. 1930 to the 1964 Coup

433. Almeida, José Américo de. *A palavra e o tempo: 1937-1945-1950.* Rio de Janeiro: José Olympio, 1965.

Excerpts speeches, essays and other documents from the career of the northeastern politician and writer whose own populist campaign for the presidency was squelched by the Estado Nôvo coup in 1937.

434. Amaral, Azevedo. *O estado autoritário e a realidade nacional.* Rio de Janeiro: José Olympio, 1938.

Explains and defends the authoritarian principle as embodied in the newly imposed Estado Nôvo constitution of 1937.

435. Anonymous. "Que e o adhemarismo?" *Cadernos de Nosso Tempo* (São Paulo), 2 (January-June 1954), 139-149.

Uses the administration of São Paulo's governor Adhemar de Barros to examine the process of populism at the state level.

436. Arraes, Miguel. *Palavra de Arraes.* Rio de Janeiro: Civilização Brasileira, 1965.

The collected speeches and writings of the deposed populist governor of Pernambuco, Miguel Arraes.

437. Bakota, Carlos Steven. "Getúlio Vargas and the Estado Nôvo: An Inquiry into Ideology and Opportunism." *Latin American Research Review*, 14 (1979), 205-215.

Reviews the literature for the 1937-1945 period and concludes that Vargas's reputation as a pragmatic opportunist must be examined in depth and from a non-partisan perspective.

438. Bandeira, Moniz. *O governo João Goulart: as lutas socias no Brasil, 1961-1964.* Rio de Janeiro: Civilização Brasileira, 1977.

Describes the atmosphere of conflict over social issues which prevailed during the Quadros and Goulart administration.

439. Bemis, George W. *From Crisis to Revolution: Monthly Case Studies.* Los Angeles: University of Southern California Press, 1964.

Offers detailed narrative accounts of the events preceding the 1964 coup. Written by a team of public administration consultants from the University of Southern California working at the Getúlio Vargas Foundation.

440. Beiguelman, Paula. "O processo político-partidário de 1945 ao plebescito." *Brasil em perspectiva*. Ed. Carlos Guilherme Mota. São Paulo: DIFEL, 1969, pp. 318-338.

Relates the chronology of political events from 1945 to the 1963 plebiscite which affirmed public opposition to parliamentarism.

441. Berson, Theodore M. "A Political Biography of Dr. Oswaldo Aranha of Brazil." Diss. New York University, 1971.

A narrative biography focusing on the Vargas period (1930 to 1937) and based on the Oswaldo Aranha papers.

442. Boito Júnior, Armando. "O populismo em crise (1953-1955)." Master's Thesis. Departamento de Ciências Sociais, Universidade Estadual de Campinas, 1976.

Examines the events which led to the death of Vargas in 1954 and to less-active populism under Vargas's successor, Café Filho.

443. Bonilla, Frank. *Jânio vem aí: Brazil elects a president: a review of the intricacies of Brazilian politics as related to the election of Jânio Quadros, Oct. 3, 1960*. New York: American Universities Field Staff, 1960.

Describes the Brazilian voting process during the turbulent 1960 national elections.

444. Borba Filho, Hermílo. *Margem das lembranças*. Rio de Janeiro: Civilização Brasileira, 1967.

A romance set in Pernambuco in the 1930's in the midst of the Liberal Alliance interventorship and the rising influence of Integralism.

445. Bourne, Richard. *Getúlio Vargas of Brazil, 1883-1954: Sphinx of the Pampas*. London: Tonbridge and Knight, 1974.

A breezy, superficial narrative portrait of a dictator-president who was not a sphinx and not really from the pampas.

446. *O Brasil na guerra*. [Special issue of] *Cultura Política*, 3 (August 1943).

Describes Brazil's war effort, its alliance with the United States, and the relationship between Vargas's social programs and the crusade to preserve democratic freedoms.

447. Café Filho, João. *Do sindicato ao Catete: memórias políticas e confissões humanas*. 2 vols. Rio de Janeiro: José Olympio, 1966.

The autobiography of the man who rose from an obscure political career in Rio Grande do Norte, when he espoused faintly left-wing causes, to the presidency after Vargas's suicide, when he represented the center-right.

448. Campos, Francisco. *O estado nacional: sua estructura, seu conteudo ideológico*. 3rd ed. Rio de Janeiro: José Olympio, 1941.

The Estado Nôvo's author explains its ideological and structural underpinnings, arguing that only through hierarchy and discipline can "liberty" be guaranteed.

449. Carneiro, Glaucio. *Lusardo: O último caudilho*. 2nd ed. Rio de Janeiro: Nova Fronteira, 1977.

Offers a sympathetic biography of João Baptista Lusardo, the "last caudillo" of Rio Grande do Sul, and a major figure of the Old Republic and the early Vargas years.

450. Carone, Edgard. *O Estado Nôvo (1937-1945)*. São Paulo: DIFEL, 1976.

Provides a comprehensive study of Vargas's corporatist dictatorship.

451. Carone, Edgard. *A República Nova (1930-1937)*. São Paulo: DIFEL, 1974.

Documents the turbulent years following the opposition victory in 1930 which saw the imposition of national government under military authoritarianism.

452. Carrazzoni, André. *Getúlio Vargas*. Rio de Janeiro: José Olympio, 1939.

Credits Vargas with reforming the decaying governmental apparatus and restoring good feeling and national pride.

453. Carvalho, Menelick de. "Democracia objectiva e liberalismo romântico." *Cultura Política*, 2 (June 1942), 29-37.

Contrasts Vargas's so-called "political humanism" with the failures of democracy around the world.

454. Conniff, Michael L. "Populism in Brazil, 1925-1945." Paper presented to the American Historical Association, San Francisco, December 1978.

Sees the roots of populism in the coalition politics of the 1920's in the city of Rio de Janeiro. Vargas, borrowing from the Rio experience, first cultivated his image through use of radio and propaganda, then created a populist party, the P.T.B., in 1945.

455. Conniff, Michael L. "Rio de Janeiro during the Great Depression, 1928-1937." Diss. Stanford University, 1976.

Argues that the administration of Pedro Ernesto Baptista provided a model for Vargas's later experiments with mass-centered populism.

456. Cony, Carlos Heitor. *Quem matou Vargas*. Rio de Janeiro: Ed. Bloch, 1974.

Speculates on the pressures and forces which contributed to the events surrounding Vargas's suicide in 1954. Blames foreign influences as a major factor.

457. Cortés, Carlos. *Gaúcho Politics in Brazil: The Role of Rio Grande do Sul in National Politics*. Albuquerque: University of New Mexico Press, 1974.

Presents a largely descriptive history of the fortunes of Brazil's southernmost state from the free-wheeling days of the Old Republic through the Vargas years.

458. Davis, Horace B. "Brazil's Political and Economic Patterns." *Foreign Policy Reports*, 11 (March 13, 1935), 1-12.

Suggests that Vargas's liberal-democratic promises were made out of expediency and that they were not fulfilled.

459. Dell, E. "Brazil's Partly United States." *Political Quarterly*, 33 (July 1962), 282-293.

Argues that the Vargas-imposed centralization of power produced inefficiency and threatened the political equilibrium.

460. Dines, Alberto et al. *Os idos de março e a queda em abril*. Rio de Janeiro: Civilização Brasileira, 1964.

The first Brazilian account of the fall of the Goulart regime, published in mid-1964 by progressive journalists.

461. Doria, Seixas. *Eu, réu sem crime*. Rio de Janeiro: Ed. Equador, 1965.

The deposed governor of the State of Sergipe proclaims his innocence of the charges of corruption and subversion which led to his ouster.

462. Duarte, Paulo. *Memórias*. 8 vols. São Paulo: Ed. Hucitec, 1973-1978.

Recounts the life and career of a leading *paulista* attorney, *bacharel*, and political figure whose public career spanned the Vargas years and the period beyond the 1964 coup.

463. Dulles, John W.F. *Unrest in Brazil: Political-Military Crises, 1955-1964*. Austin: University of Texas Press, 1970.

Shows that the open electoral system produced political figures who the military considered dangerous and unstable, thus giving the military officers an excuse to overturn the civilian government.

464. Dulles, John W.F. *Vargas of Brazil: A Political Biography*. Austin: University of Texas Press, 1967.

Contends that Vargas's genius lay in knowing what changes were inevitable (and how to implement them with minimal disruption).

465. Faust, J.J. *A revolucão devora os seus presidentes*. Rio de Janeiro: Ed. Saga, 1965.

A French journalist assigned to Brazil chronicles the events leading to the fall of the Goulart regime and warns that Brazil's lack of a "tradition of public administration" threatens further instability.

466. Fontoura, João Neves da. *Memórias: a Aliança Liberal e a Revolucão de 1930*. Vol. 2. Pôrto Alegre: Ed. Globo, 1962.

Narrates the author's role in the events which led to the successful 1930 Revolution, which he calls "popular and just."

467. Francis, Paulo. "Tempos de Goulart." *Revista Civilização Brasileira*, 1 (May 1966), 75-91.

Contends that the Goulart regime really did not differ much from earlier presidencies. The Parliamentary experiment merely emerged out of a national alliance of oligarchies with small openings for the left on foreign policy matters.

468. Freyre, Gilberto. "O Estado Nôvo e o seu presidente." *Cultura Política*, 1 (July 1941), 123-125.

Offers glowing testimony to President Vargas and his social programs.

469. Freyre, Gilberto. "Personalities Versus Parties for the Presidency of Brazil." *The Reporter*, 21 (July 23, 1959), 28-30.

Blames the Brazilian electorate for putting personality and demagoguery over more serious national issues in electoral campaigns.

470. Hambloch, Ernest. *His Majesty the President of Brazil: a Study of Constitutional Brazil*. New York: Dutton, 1935.

Attacks Vargas for using democratic language while building an authoritarian framework for his regime.

471. Harding, Timothy. "Revolution Tomorrow: the Failure of the Left in Brazil." *Studies on the Left*, 4 (Fall, 1964), 30-54.

Offers a post-mortem of the Quadros-Goulart years, helping to explain the preconditions for the 1964 military coup.

472. Henriques, Affonso. *Ascensão e queda de Getúlio Vargas*. 3 vols. São Paulo: Palácio do Livro, 1966.

A hostile biography by a former partisan of the left-wing A.N.L. attributing "Machiavellian" powers to Vargas, who is portrayed as selfish, dishonest, and manipulative.

473. Horowitz, Irving Louis. *Revolution in Brazil: Politics and Society in a Developing Nation.* New York: Dutton, 1964.

Provides a provocative analysis of pre-1964 Brazil and attempts by the left to shake the foundations of the old socio-economic order.

474. Krieger, Daniel. *Desde as missões: saudades, letras, esperanças.* 2nd ed. Rio de Janeiro: José Olympio, 1977.

Chronicles the early career of one of the founders of the national UDN in 1945. Krieger, a *gaúcho* politician of immigrant parents, became one of the civilian leaders of the coup which deposed João Goulart in 1964.

475. Lacerda, Maurício de. *Segunda República.* 2nd ed. São Paulo: Freitas Bastos, 1931.

Criticizes the newly victorious authors of the 1930 Revolution for implementing a "Second Republic," the simple substitution of one oligarchy for another.

476. Leite, Aureliano. "Bibliografia da revolução constitucionalista." São Paulo: Academia Paulista de Letras, 1962.

Lists articles, pamphlets, newspapers and general studies of the 1932 Constitutionalist Revolution. Includes works on the 1930 Revolution, which the author considers the "first act" in the drama.

477. Levine, Robert M. *Pernambuco in the Brazilian Federation, 1889-1937.* Stanford: Stanford University Press, 1978.

Provides a case study of a once-important state in political, social, and economic decline. This resulted from competition from foreign sugar growers, a shift of economic activity southward, and the resistance of the elite to reforms.

478. Levine, Robert M. *The Vargas Regime: the Critical Years, 1934-1938.* New York: Columbia University Press, 1970.

Analyzes Brazil's political life under Vargas, the failure of the far left and the far right to mobilize support, and the fate of dissenters and reformers under the growing cloud of authoritarianism.

479. Levine, Robert M., John D. Wirth and Joseph L. Love. "O poder dos estados: análise regional." *História geral da civilização brasileira. Tomo III. O Brasil republicano, estrutura de poder e economia, 1° vol.* (item 166), pp. 53-151.

Shows that while São Paulo aggregated economic and industrial strength, Minas Gerais skillfully maintained its political influence and Pernambuco found itself stripped of its former influence and autonomy.

480. Lewin, Linda. "Politics and *Parentela* in Paraíba: A Case Study of Oligarchy in Brazil's Old Republic (1889-1930)." Diss. Columbia University, 1975.

Analyzes patronage and political relationships in the rural northeastern backlands. Illustrates how governance operated on the basis of reciprocal understandings between local bosses, family clans, and state and national political machines.

481. Lima Sobrinho, Alexandre José Barbosa. *A verdade sôbre a revolução de outubro*. São Paulo: Ed. Unitas, 1933.

Offers an early analysis of the 1930 Liberal Alliance coup and the meaning of the fall of the Old Republic. Still a major source.

482. Lipson, Leslie. "Government in Contemporary Brazil." *Journal of Economics and Political Science*, 22 (1956), 183-198.

Provides a detailed examination of the post-war political system culminating in the Vargas presidency of the early 1950's.

483. Loewenstein, Karl. *Brazil under Vargas*. New York: Macmillan, 1942.

Analyzes the Estado Nôvo constitution and the Vargas dictatorship, emphasizing its juridical underpinnings and borrowings from corporatist theory.

484. Love, Joseph L. *Rio Grande do Sul and Brazilian Regionalism, 1882-1930*. Stanford: Stanford University Press, 1971.

Illustrates the mechanics of Brazilian republicanism, the relations between modernization and political centralization, and state initiative in the social and economic sphere, through an examination of Rio Grande do Sul's role in the federation.

485. Love, Joseph L. *São Paulo in the Brazilian Federation, 1889-1937*. Stanford: Stanford University Press, 1979.

Examines in depth the dynamics of regionalism from the perspective of São Paulo, Brazil's leading state in agriculture, foreign trade, and manufacturing, and its role as innovator in the political process.

486. McCann, Frank D. "Vargas and the Destruction of the Integralista and Nazi Parties." *The Americas*, 26 (July 1969), 15-34.

Attributes Vargas's decision to suppress the rising groups on the political right primarily to pragmatism and his sense that they represented threats to his power.

487. Martins, Wilson. "Brazilian Politics: Dialectic of a Revolution." *Luso-Brazilian Review*, 3 (May 1966), 3-18.

What happened to Quadros, Goulart, and the left, the author contends, is that they thought they could deal with the emotional and unstable climate generated by their demands.

488. Mello Franco, Afonso Arinos de. "The Tide of Government: from Colony to Constitutional Democracy." Tr. Richard M. Morse. *The Atlantic Monthly*, 197 (February 1956), 152-156.

Calls Vargas a public figure who took his own life in 1954 as an act of personal redemption. Blames his lust for power for distorting his values and outlook.

489. Meneghello, Ludovico. *Eu sou Artur Arão*. Pôrto Alegre: Ed. Garatuja, 1976.

The biography of Artur Arão, the son of a political chieftain from the state of Rio Grande do Sul, stressing the extreme violence that swept the state through the mid-1930's.

490. Moraes, Clodomir. "Peasant Leagues in Brazil." *Agrarian Problems and Peasant Movements in Latin America*. Ed. Rodolfo Stavenhagen. Garden City, N.Y.: Doubleday, 1970.

Discusses the rise and fall of Francisco Julião's grass-roots movement.

491. Nasser, David. *João dem mêdo.* Rio de Janeiro: Ed. *O Cruzeiro*, 1965.

Profiles Deputy João Calmon, whose debates with ex-deputy Lional Brizola exemplified the conflict between Goulart and his opponents before 1964.

492. Page, Joseph A. *The Revolution that Never Was: Northeast Brazil, 1955-1964.* New York: Grossman, 1972.

Chronicles the failure of efforts to marshall resources and mass mobilization to overthrow the stagnant social order in impoverished northeast Brazil in the decade preceding the military coup of 1964.

493. Peixoto, Alzira Vargas do Amaral. *Getúlio Vargas, meu pai.* Pôrto Alegre: Ed. Globo, 1960.

Getúlio Vargas's daughter narrates his biography through her own eyes. Alzira served her father as his closest aide from the mid-1930's until his death in 1954.

494. Pereira, Astrojildo. "Notas e reflexões de um capítulo de memórias." *Revista Civilização Brasileira*, 1 (May 1965), pp. 300-313.

Analyzes the fall of the Goulart administration. Accuses the "new lords of power" of being "possessed" with a horror of culture, learning, and informed public debate.

495. Pereira, Nilo. *Agamenon Magalhães: uma evocação pessoal.* Recife: Ed. Dialgraf, 1973.

Attempts to soften the brusque and emotionless image attributed to the 1930's Labor Minister (and Pernambuco Interventor).

496. Peterson, Phyllis J. "Brazilian Political Parties: Formation, Organization and Leadership, 1945-1959." Diss. University of Michigan, 1962.

Analyzes the three national parties created in 1945: the PSD, UDN, and PTB.

497. Pimpão, Hirosê. *Getúlio Vargas e o direito social trabalhista.* Rio de Janeiro: Ed. Guarany, 1942.

Lauds Vargas's contribution to federal social legislation during the 1930's and into the Estado Nôvo period.

498. Putnam, Samuel. "The Vargas Dictatorship in Brazil." *Science and Society*, 5 (Spring 1941), 97-116.

Warns of the dangers inherent in Vargas's flirtation with fascist ideology.

499. *Revista Brasileira de Estudos Políticos*, 16 (January 1964), 1-391.

A special issue devoted to a detailed analysis and critique of the 1962 elections and voter reaction to populist appeals.

500. Santa Rosa, Virgínio. *A desordem*. Rio de Janeiro: Schmidt Editôra, 1932.

Credits the 1930 Revolution with unmasking the incongruities, polarizations, and conflicts unresolved in Brazilian society.

501. Saunders, John V.D. "A Revolution of Agreement among Friends: the End of the Vargas Era." *Hispanic American Historical Review*, 44 (May 1964), 197-213.

Accounts the attempted assassination of journalist Carlos Lacerda, Vargas's subsequent suicide, and his controversial final letter to the Brazilian people.

502. Sharp, Walter R. "Brazil 1940: Whither the New State?" *Inter-American Quarterly*, 2 (October 1940), 5-17.

Emphasizes the quasi-fascist structure of the Estado Nôvo.

503. Silva, Hélio. *O ciclo de Vargas. 1930: A revolução traida*. Rio de Janeiro: Civilização Brasileira, 1966.

Recounts the events of 1930. One of Silva's "Vargas Cycle," a multi-volume history comprised of excerpts from archival sources without synthesis but useful for their detail.

504. Silva, Hélio. *O ciclo de Vargas. 1931: Os tenentes no poder*. Rio de Janeiro: Civilização Brasileira, 1966.

Documents the first year of the "tenentes" in power.

505. Silva, Hélio. *O ciclo de Vargas. 1932: A guerra paulista*. Rio de Janeiro: Civilização Brasileira, 1967.

Recounts the events of the 1932 São Paulo constitutionalist rebellion.

506. Silva, Hélio. *O ciclo de Vargas. 1933: A crise do tenentismo.* Rio de Janeiro: Civilização Brasileira, 1968.

Calls 1933 the year of "crisis" for *tenentismo.*

507. Silva, Hélio. *O ciclo de Vargas. 1934: A constituinte.* Rio de Janeiro: Civilização Brasileira, 1969.

Recounts the events surrounding the 1933-34 Constituent Assembly and the efforts of interest groups to influence the deliberations.

508. Silva, Hélio. *O ciclo de Vargas. 1935: A revolta vermelha.* Rio de Janeiro: Civilização Brasileira, 1969.

Documents the 1935 "communist" insurrection.

509. Silva, Hélio. *O ciclo de Vargas. 1937: Todos os golpes se parecem.* Rio de Janeiro: Civilização Brasileira, 1970.

Documents the events which led to the promulgation of the corporatist Estado Nôvo dictatorship in November 1937.

510. Silva, Hélio. *O ciclo de Vargas. 1938: Terrorismo em campo verde.* Rio de Janeiro: Civilização Brasileira, 1971.

Documents the attempted coup by the Integralists against Vargas.

511. Silva, Hélio and Maria Cecilia Ribas Carneiro. *O ciclo de Vargas. 1939: Véspera de guerra.* Rio de Janeiro: Civilização Brasileira, 1972.

Discusses the prewar atmosphere in 1939.

512. Silva, Hélio. *O ciclo de Vargas: 1945, por que depuseram Vargas.* Rio de Janeiro: Civilização Brasileira, 1976.

Explains why Vargas was deposed by the military in 1945.

513. Silva, Hélio. *1964: golpe ou contragolpe?* Rio de Janeiro: Civilização Brasileira, 1975.

Chronicles the events leading to the 1964 coup.

514. Skidmore, Thomas E. "Failure in Brazil: From Popular Front to Armed Revolt." *Journal of Contemporary History,* 15 (1970), 137-157.

Synthesizes the history of Comintern-led militant activity in the 1930's which led to the November 1935 insurrection.

515. Sodré, Nelson Werneck. *A verdade sobre o ISEB*. Rio de Janeiro: Ed. Avenir, 1978.

Chronicles the rise and fall of the Superior Institute of Brazilian Studies, the leading research organization of the 1950's with the "honor" of being the target of the first repressive decree of the military government in 1964.

516. Sola, Lourdes. "O Golpe de 37 e o Estado Nôvo." *Brasil em perspectiva* (item 205), pp. 257-284.

Traces events from the advent of the Estado Nôvo to the reopening of the political system in 1945 with the creation of three national parties.

517. Tiller, Ann Q. "The Igniting Spark: Brazil 1930." *Hispanic American Historical Review*, 45 (August 1965), 384-392.

Narrates the event surrounding the successful Liberal Alliance coup d'état which brought Vargas and the *tenentes* to power.

518. Vargas, Getúlio. *A campanha presidencial*. Rio de Janeiro: José Olympio, 1951.

Contains speeches from Vargas's 1950 successful presidential campaign. Key topics include economic nationalism, social legislation, and development.

519. Vargas, Getúlio. *O govêrno trabalhista do Brasil*. Rio de Janeiro: José Olympio, 1952.

Further speeches and statements on the President's social and working class legislation.

520. Vargas, Getúlio. *A nova política do Brasil*. 10 vols. Rio de Janeiro: José Olympio, 1938-1944.

Vargas's presidential speeches from the years of the Estado Nôvo and the wartime alliance with the United States.

521. Vargas, Getúlio. Suicide Note, in *New York Times*, Aug. 25, 1954, 2.

The cryptic last statement blaming foreign "forces," probably not penned by Vargas but by his confidant, publisher and industrialist J.S. Maciel Filho.

522. Vergara, Luiz. *Fui secretário de Getúlio Vargas*. Pôrto Alegre: Ed. Glôbo, 1960.

Relates the personal side of Vargas's career. Vergara was the chief executive's personal aide from the early 1930's until his suicide in 1954.

523. Vidal, Adhemar. *João Pessôa e a Revolução de 30*. Rio de Janeiro: Ed. Graal, 1978.

Places João Pessôa, the assassinated vice-presidential candidate of the Liberal Alliance, at the center of the events which precipitated the 1930 insurrection.

524. Vidal, Barros. *Um destino a serviço do Brasil*. Rio de Janeiro: n.p., 1945.

A little-known but very useful biography of Getúlio Vargas which emphasizes his political origins in Rio Grande do Sul.

525. Waddell, Agnes S. "The Revolution in Brazil." *Foreign Policy Association Information Service*, 6 (1931), 489-506.

Finds Vargas's 1930 provisional government vulnerable to the manipulations of political opponents and to corruption.

526. Weffort, Francisco C. "Estado e massas no Brasil." *Revista Civilização Brasileira*, 1 (May 1966), 137-158.

Considers the 1964 Revolution to signify the end of the long process of democratization which collapsed under Goulart under the weight of its internal conflicts.

527. Weffort, Francisco C. *O Populismo na política brasileira*. Rio de Janeiro: Paz e Terra, 1978.

Explains how Vargas sought legitimacy through his use of populist methods after the 1930 Revolution, and how the failure of populism to deal with the expectations it raised helped precipitate political crisis in 1964.

528. Wells, Henry, Charles Daugherty, James Rowe, and Ronald Schneider, eds. *Brazil: Election Factbook*. Washington,

D.C.: Institute for the Comparative Study of Political Systems, 1962.

Analyzes voting pattern. Notes that from 1945 to 1960 the national electorate grew from over 7 million (16% of the total population) to over 15 million (23%).

529. Wirth, John D. *Minas Gerais in the Brazilian Federation, 1889-1937*. Stanford: Stanford University Press, 1977.

Analyzes the phenomenon of regionalism and national integration from the vantage point of the Center-South state. While the Mineiro elite wielded great political influence in the end the state found its influence subordinated to a more powerful national government.

530. Worsnop, R.L. "Brazil in Ferment." *Editorial Research Report* (Jan. 15, 1962), 23-40.

Summarizes Brazil's political and economic troubles under Quadros and Goulart.

531. Wycoff, T. "Brazilian Political Parties." *South Atlantic Quarterly*, 56 (Summer 1957), 281-298.

Surveys the programs and membership of the three national political parties of the 1950's, the PSD, UDN, and PTB.

532. Young, Jordan M. *The Brazilian Revolution of 1930 and the Aftermath*. New Brunswick, N.J.: Rutgers University Press, 1967.

A brief book describing the Liberal Alliance coup, stressing personalities and the significance of changes swept in with new Vargas coalition.

3. Since 1964

533. Alarcón, Rodrigo. *Brasil: represión y tortura*. Santiago, Chile: ORBE, 1971.

A Chilean writer describes examples of repression and torture by Brazilian officials against dissidents and political prisoners.

534. Alcantara de Camargo, Aspásia. "Autoritarismo e populismo bipolaridade no sistemo político brasileiro." *Dados*, 12 (1976), 22-45.

Shows that unlike other Latin American dictatorships, Brazil's military government has permitted a dual party system to exist although under severe restrictions.

535. Almeida Filho, Hamilton. *A sangue quente: a morte do jornalista Vladimir Herzog*. São Paulo: Ed. Alfa-Omega, 1978.

Denounces São Paulo's military officials for the death by torture of the writer and television journalist whose death provoked deep public anger.

536. Álves, Márcio Moreira. *A Grain of Mustard Seed*. Garden City, N.Y.: Doubleday Anchor, 1973.

A wistful, eloquent autobiographical account of events since 1964 written by an opposition ex-Congressman in European exile from 1968 to 1979 who predicts eventual return to popular rule.

537. Álves, Márcio Moreira. *A velha classe*. Rio de Janeiro: Ed. Artenova, 1964.

The title, "The Old Class," parodies the work by Milovan Djilas. The book comprises Álves's writing on the 1964 coup.

538. Alvim, João Carlos. *A revolução sem rumo*. Rio de Janeiro: Edições do Val, 1964.

Argues that the price of the 1964 coup will be the eclipse of freedom.

539. Amnesty International. *Report on Torture*. London: Amnesty International, 1975.

Offers documentary evidence to support allegations that the regime systematically tortures political prisoners.

540. Ayres Filho, Paulo. "The Brazilian Revolution," *Latin America: Politics, Economics and Hemisphere Security*. Ed. Norman A. Bailey. New York: Praeger, 1965, pp. 239-60.

Summarizes the political events comprising the 1964 "Revolution."

541. "Black Book: Terreur et Torture au Brésil." *Croissance des Jeunes Nations*, 94 (December 1969), 19-34.

One of the many exposés of torture and brutality in Brazil under the military regime published in Europe after the intensification of repression in 1968.

542. Bolton, R.H. "Brazilian Torture." *Christian Century*, 83 (April 1, 1970), 387-388.

Reveals some of the brutal methods used to extract confessions from political prisoners in Brazilian jails.

543. Brasil. Congresso. Câmara dos Deputados. Biblioteca. "Revolução de 31 de março, Bibliografia." *Boletim da Biblioteca da Câmara dos Deputados* (Brasília), 13 (July-December 1964), 499-514.

A bibliography on the 1964 military insurrection.

544. *Brazil: Who Pulls the Strings?* Chicago: Anti-Imperialist Collective, 1972.

Presents a collection of short articles on repression in Brazil, the role of the Church, and the education contracts between the government and USAID (United States Agency for International Development).

545. *Brésil 69: Torture et Repression.* Brussels: Association Internationale des Juristes Démocrates, 1969.

Summarizes allegations of torture and brutality by the military and police against dissidents and suspected subversives.

546. Britto, Luiz Navarro de. "O federalismo na constituição de 1967." *Revista Brasileira de Estudos Politicos* (Belo Horizonte), 28 (January 1970), 47-59.

Argues that the definition of federalism in the 1967 Constitution reflects the contradictory nature of the military regime: on the one hand, less-developed states seem to be favored; on the other, rigid centralization governs national administration.

547. Brossard, Paulo. *É hora de mudar.* São Paulo: L & PM Editôres, 1977.

An outspoken opposition senator demands that the slow process of redemocratization be accelerated.

548. Callado, Antonio. *Quarup*. Tr. by Barbara Shelby. New York: Alfred A. Knopf, 1970.

A major tragi-comic novel set against the tawdry political events leading to the 1964 coup, emphasizing social injustice and foreign meddling. It has been called a "novel about national self-discovery."

549. Capuano, Thomas M. "Acts against Humanity." *Journal of Current Social Issues*, (Summer 1978), 18-21.

Describes violations of human rights by the military regime.

550. Castello Branco, Carlos. *Os militares no poder: O Ato 5*. 3rd ed. Rio de Janeiro: Ed. Nova Fronteira, 1978.

Analyzes the impact of the Institutional Act No. 5, the regime's major repressive instrument between 1968 and 1978.

551. Cavalcanti, Pedro Celso Uchôa and Jovelino Ramos, eds. *Memórias do exílio*. São Paulo: Ed. Livramento, 1978.

Collected essays by some of the intellectual leaders of the approximately 10,000 Brazilians exiled from the military regime. First published in Portugal in 1976.

552. Chalmers, Douglas A. "Political Groups and Authority in Brazil: Some Continuities in a Decade of Confusion and Change." *Brazil in the Sixties* (item 423), pp. 51-76.

Contends that the military government represents a logical extension of major trends and characteristics of Brazilian politics.

553. Cony, Carlos Heitor. *O ato e o fato*. 3rd ed. Rio de Janeiro: Civilização Brasileira, 1964.

Collected newspaper articles from the pen of an outspoken critic of the military regime, published in the months which followed the coup prior to the hardening of censorship.

554. Costa, Fernando José Leite and Lúcia Gomes Klein. "Um ano de governo Médici." *Dados*, 9 (1972), 156-221.

Narrates the events of the period between October 1969 and October 1970, the first year of the military presidency of Garrastazú Médici.

555. Della Cava, Ralph. "Democratic Stirrings." *Journal of Current Social Issues* (Summer 1978), 22-28.

Emphasizes signs toward liberalization within the Brazilian military regime in the midst of the presidential campaign of 1978 and comments on the impact of President Carter's stand on human rights in Brazil.

556. Della Cava, Ralph. "Torture in Brazil." *Commonweal*, 92 (April 24, 1970), 135-141.

One of the first detailed exposés of the use of torture by the military government.

557. *Dossier Brésil*. Brussels: Association Internationale des Juristes Démocrates, April 1971.

Chronicles forty-two cases of torture of political prisoners.

558. Dye, David R. and Carlos Eduardo de Souza e Silva. "A Perspective on the Brazilian State." *Latin American Research Review*, 14 (1979), 81-98.

Rejects the view that authoritarian rule has brought "Portugalization" to Brazil, since it rests on the isolation of the political sphere from the realm of economics and class structure.

559. Emert, Harold. "Cidade Maravilhosa: What is the Meaning of Lerfá Mú?" *Times of Brazil* (Rio de Janeiro), July 1-2, 1978, 1.

Attributes to political frustration the (presumably) nonsense slogans appearing on walls as graffiti thorughout Rio's residential South Zone in mid-1978.

560. Fiechter, Georges-André. *Brazil since 1964: Modernization Under a Military Regime*. Tr. Alan Bradley. New York: Holsted Press, 1975.

Methodically analyzes the post-1964 regime, stressing economic and management issues, the threat from urban guerrillas, and the participation of non-military elements in the emerging power structure.

561. Franco, Cid. *Anotações de um cassado*. São Paulo: Ed. Martins, 1965.

A former Socialist Party deputy from São Paulo writes of his political "banishment" after 1964.

562. Freire, Marcos. *Nação oprimida.* Rio de Janeiro: Paz e Terra, 1977.

An opposition party senator argues for a national constituent assembly in order to restore freedom and social justice.

563. Gall, Norman. "The Rise of Brazil." *Commentary*, 63 (January 1977), 45-55.

Contends that political "decompression" would threaten the equilibrium which allows intensive economic growth.

564. Góes, Walder de. *O Brasil do General Geisel.* Rio de Janeiro: Ed. Nova Fronteira, 1977.

A journalist's insightful account of the Geisel years, which he views as more complex and frustrating than the models available to analyze them.

565. Gomes, Lúcia Maria Gaspar. "Cronologia do govêrno Castelo Branco." *Dados*, 2/3 (1967), 112-132.

Lists the leading political events of the regime's first military presidency from April 15, 1964 to March 15, 1967, when Costa e Silva succeeded Castello Branco.

566. Gomes, Lúcia Maria Gaspar. "Cronologia do 1° ano do govêrno Costa e Silva." *Dados*, 4 (1968), 199-220.

Chronicles the most important political events during the first year of the Costa e Silva regime. Emphasis is divided between new economic programs and political activities.

567. Ianni, Otávio. *Crisis in Brazil.* Tr. Phyllis Eveleth. New York: Columbia University Press, 1970.

Calls the 1964 coup the "death knell" of popular democracy and the victory for capitalism's dependency system. Warns that the Right has become more radical since the overthrow of the civilian government.

568. Jerman, W. de. *Repression in Latin America.* London: Spokesman Books, 1977.

A report of the Bertrand Russell Tribunal held in Rome to focus the world's attention on violations against human rights in Brazil and elsewhere in the hemisphere.

569. Johnson, Peter T. "Academic Press Censorship Under Military and Civilian Regimes: The Argentine and Brazilian Cases, 1964-1975." *Luso-Brazilian Review*, 15 (Summer 1978), 3-25.

Contrasts "Brazil's poor record on censorship" with Argentina's long tradition of press freedom. Brazilian officials find themselves threatened by criticism, believing it capable of undermining national security.

570. Julião, Francisco. *Ate quarta, Isabella.* Rio de Janeiro: Civilização Brasileira, 1965.

The former head of the Peasant League explains his views on contemporary Brazil in a series of letters from prison to his daughter.

571. Lafer, Celso. "Estado e sociedade no Brasil." *Argumento* (Rio de Janeiro), 1 (November 1973), 33-44.

Contends that the Castelo Branco regime, preoccupied with administrative modernization, produced an impasse between the state and civil society by reducing popular participation in government.

572. Lago, Mário. *1° de abril: histórias para a história.* Rio de Janeiro: Civilização Brasileira, 1964.

Chooses his title ("April 1st") to ridicule the military coup, which he calls a *golpe*, not a revolution. Recounts his experience of 58 days of imprisonment.

573. Langguth, A.J. *Hidden Terrors.* New York: Pantheon Books, 1978.

Relates the story of Dan Mitrione, the Indiana police officer sent to Brazil to train police in counter-insurgency techniques, and ultimately to Uruguay, where he was kidnapped and murdered by Tupamaro guerrillas.

574. Levine, Robert M. "Brazil at the Crossroads." *Current History*, 64 (February 1973), 53-56, 86.

Reviews current events during 1972 and speculates on nationalistic options available within the authoritarian framework.

575. Levine, Robert M. "Brazil: the Aftermath of Decompression." *Current History*, 73 (February 1976), 53-81.

Discusses the events of 1975, including the controversial

nuclear reactor agreement with West Germany, news of offshore petroleum, and the debate over political *abertura* (relaxation).

576. Levine, Robert M. "Brazil: Institutionalizing Authoritarianism." *Latin American Research Review*, 14 (Spring 1979), 211-215.

Reviews recent literature on the military regime and discusses Brazilian uneasiness at the seeming monopoly of writing on Brazil by foreigners.

577. Levine, Robert M. "Brazil's Definition of Democracy." *Current History*, 76 (February 1979), 70-83.

Weighs the growing sentiment in Brazil for amnesty for persons exiled or arrested under the repressive earlier phases of the military regime and pressures from opposition groups for political relaxation. The military, for its part, holds out for "relative" democracy.

578. Linz, Juan. "The Future of an Authoritarian Situation on the Institutionalization of an Authoritarian Regime. The Case of Brazil." *Authoritarian Brazil* (item 431), pp. 233-254.

Foresees the possibility of constant and indecisive experimenting with policy accompanied by a series of military coups.

579. Machado, Cristina Pinheiro. *Os exilados*. São Paulo: Ed. Alfa-Omega, 1979.

Describes the plight of the 5,000 Brazilians still in voluntary or forced exile from the military regime.

580. Magalhães, Irene Maria, Maria Aparecida Álves Hime and Nancy Aléssio. "Segundo e terceiro ano do governo Costa e Silva." *Dados*, 8 (1971), 152-233.

Chronicles the events of the second and third years of the Costa e Silva regime.

581. Martins, Mário. *Em nossos dias de intolerância*. Rio de Janeiro: Tempo Brasileira, 1965.

Protests the punitive measures taken against dissenters in the initial months of the Revolution.

582. Martins, Roberto Ribeiro. *Liberdade para os brasileiros*. Rio de Janeiro: Civilização Brasileira, 1978.

Seeks to prepare its readers for the coming debate over political amnesty, which the author staunchly advocates.

583. Martins, Sodré. *31 de março de 1964: revolução autêntica ou simples quartelada?* Salvador: Editôra Manú, 1964.

Exhorts Brazilians to preserve the "purity" of the 1964 Revolution and combat communism.

584. Maurer, Harry. "Is Brazil on the Brink of Democracy?" *New York Review of Books*, 25 (September 28, 1978), 43-48.

Sees signs of relaxation amidst warnings that the military will resist any reforms which threaten to relinquish its near-absolute control.

585. Moniz, Edmundo. *O golpe de abril.* Rio de Janeiro: Civilização Brasileira, 1965.

Accuses the military regime of halting the social progress made during the previous eight years.

586. Montoro, Franco. *A luta pelas eleições diretas.* São Paulo: Ed. Brasiliense, 1978.

Calls for direct elections and reform of the political system. Montoro is a leading opposition member of the Senate.

587. Nobre, Freitas. *Constituinte.* Rio de Janeiro: Paz e Terra, 1978.

An opposition deputy calls for social reforms and a return to democratic constitutionalism.

588. Nunes, Adão Pereira. *Do planalto à Cordilheira.* Rio de Janeiro: Civilização Brasileira, 1979.

Recounts the experience of the author, who was forced to flee from Brasília across the Andes into exile at the height of the post-1964 repression.

589. Pedreira, Fernando. *Março 31: civís e militares no processo da crise brasileira.* Rio de Janeiro: José Álvaro, 1964.

Argues that the 1964 coup constituted both a barracks revolt and a revolutionary insurrection, but the promulgation of the Institutional Act of April 9 froze its revolutionary potential.

590. Petras, James E., ed. *Latin America: From Dependence to Revolution.* New York: John Wiley, 1973.

Suggests trouble ahead for Brazil's military dictatorship and peaceful evolution for Chile's socialist experiment under Allende.

591. Pinto, Bilac. *Guerra revolucionária.* Rio de Janeiro: Ed. Forense, 1964.

Calls the 1964 coup a vigorous reaction against the steady strangulation of the traditional order.

592. Rowe, James. "Revolution and Counterrevolution in Brazil." *Latin American Politics.* Ed. R.A. Tomasek. Garden City, N.Y.: Doubleday-Anchor, 1970, pp. 532-538.

Views the events of April 1, 1964 and casts doubts on the "communist threat" hypothesis.

593. Santos, Wanderly Guilherme dos. "Raizes de imaginação política brasileira." *Dados*, 7 (1970), 137-161.

Argues that published studies favoring the 1964 coup share a common and inflexible style of analyzing political conflict.

594. Schmidt, Augusto Frederico. *Prelúdio a revolução.* Rio de Janeiro: Edições do Val, 1964.

Argues that the 1964 coup was necessary in order to forestall chaos and disorder.

595. Sinet, Maurice. *Inteligen cia: Sine & CIA.* Rio de Janeiro: Civilização Brasileira, 1968.

Pokes fun through cartoons at United States (and C.I.A.) influence on Brazil and its support of the military government.

596. Souza, Amaury de. "Annotated Bibliography of the Brazilian Political Movement of 1964." Riverside, California: Latin American Research Program, University of California, Riverside, Report No. 2 [October 1966].

Summarizes the articles and books dealing with the 1964 coup which appeared in its aftermath.

597. Souza, Percival de. *Violência e repressão.* São Paulo: Ed. Símbolo, 1978.

Relates incidents of violence and repression by the military regime during the 1970's.

598. Stacchini, José. *Março 1964: mobilização da audácia*. São Paulo: Companhia Editôra Nacional, 1965.

Emotionally defends the 1964 coup as a necessary and "audacious" step to restore stability and defeat the left.

599. Távora, Araken. *How Brazil Stopped Communism*. Rio de Janeiro: Vida Domestica, 1964.

Offers an apologia for the 1964 coup as a defense against the imminent collapse of Brazilian democracy against a communistic onslaught.

600. United States. Senate. Committee on Foreign Relations. *United States Policies and Programs in Brazil, Hearings, May 4, 5, and 11, 1971*. Washington, D.C.: Government Printing Office, 1971.

The transcripts of hearings held under the chairmanship of Senator Frank Church. Includes testimony on police assistance programs, allegations of torture, and other acts of complicity in violations of human rights.

601. "A volta do 'ChΣfΣ.'" *Veja* (São Paulo), 88 (May 13, 1970), 20-23.

Comments on the attempted return to political life of former Integralist fuehrer Plínio Salgado, as a leader of the pro-government party, ARENA, from São Paulo State. Salgado claims that nearly 700,000 Brazilians are still loyal to Integralist leadership.

D. THE ARMED FORCES

602. Álves, Hermano. "Brazil: Martial Mythologies." *Latin American Review of Books*, 1 (Spring 1973), 89-101.

Contends that Brazil's most serious political problem is the definition of the armed forces' role in society and the regime's psychological fear of reestablishing civilian government.

603. Ames, Barry. *Rhetoric and Reality in a Militarized Regime: Brazil Since 1964*. Beverly Hills: Sage Publishing Company, 1973.

Concludes that Brazil's military has a rising level of professional skills, but these skills are not easily transferred to nonmilitary problems.

604. "Armed Resistance in Amazônia." *Brazilian Information Bulletin* (Berkeley), 9 (January 1973), 12-14.

Describes the "secret guerrilla war" being waged in the states of Goias, Matto Grosso, and Pará against the military regime and kept hidden from the world press.

605. Avelar, Romeu de. *General Góes Monteiro*. Maceió, Alagoas: Imprensa Oficial, 1949.

Provides a non-controversial view of Góes Monteiro's life and career as the power behind Vargas during the late 1930's through the years of the Estado Nôvo.

606. Barros, João Alberto Lins de. *Memórias de um revolucionário*. 2nd ed. Rio de Janeiro: Civilização Brasileira, 1954.

The memoirs of a leading member of the Prestes Column and controversial *tenente* administrator and intervenor (appointed governor) in the post-1930 Liberal Alliance government.

607. Carneiro, Glauco. "A guerra de Sorbonne." *O Cruzeiro* (Rio de Janeiro), 32 (June 24, 1967), 16-21.

Describes the conflict within military circles between moderates (the "Sorbonne" school) identified with Castelo Branco and hard-liners on the right.

608. Castello Branco Filho, Moysés. *Depoimento para a história da revolução no Piauí*. 2nd ed. Rio de Janeiro: Ed. Artenova, 1975.

Traces the *tenente* movement in the northern state of Piauí through the Liberal Alliance revolution in 1930 and beyond.

609. Centro de Pesquisa e Documentação de História Contemporânea do Brasil. *Bibliografia: tenentismo*. Rio de Janeiro: CPDOC, 1978.

The most complete bibliography on the *tenente* movement currently available.

610. Coelho, Edmundo Campos. *Em busca de identitade: o exército e a política na sociedade brasileira*. Rio de Janeiro: Ed. Forense, 1976.

Describes the army's "search for identity." Contends that the absence of strong national authority led to the collapse of the Republic in 1930 and military intervention.

611. Conniff, Michael L. "The Tenentes in Power: A New Perspective on the Brazilian Revolution of 1930." *Journal of Latin American Studies*, 10 (May 1978), 61-82.

Finds the *tenente* Clube 3 de Outubro instrumental in converting the regionalist revolt of 1930 into a national revolution under Vargas's leadership.

612. Coutinho, Lourival. *O General Góes depõe*. Rio de Janeiro: Ed. Coelho Branco, 1955.

A sympathetic memoir of General Góes Monteiro.

613. Damata, Gasparino. *Queda em ascensão*. Rio de Janeiro: Ed. *O Cruzeiro*, 1951.

A semi-memoir fictionalized account of a Brazilian seaman in the United States Navy during World War II.

614. Dean, Robert W. *The Military in Politics in Brazil*. Washington, D.C.: National War College, 1963.

Assesses the military's anxiety over political instability culminating in the rise of the "hard-line" position among officers standing in the wings to take power.

615. Dimas Filho, Nelson. *Costa e Silva: o homem e o lider*. Rio de Janeiro: Ed. *O Cruzeiro*, 1966.

An adulatory biography of the army marshal who replaced Castello Branco in 1967 as military president.

616. Dulles, John W.F. *Castello Branco: The Making of a Brazilian President*. College Station, Texas: Texas A & M Press, 1978.

Narrates, in admiring fashion, the life and career of the first military president after the 1964 coup to the date of his resignation from the Army.

617. Figueiredo, E. de, ed. *Tenentismo*. Rio de Janeiro: Zahar, 1978.

Concentrates on the ideological basis of the nationalist movement within the military which precipitated the 1930 *golpe*.

618. Flynn, Peter. "The Revolutionary Legion and the Brazilian Revolution of 1930." *Latin American Affairs*. Ed. Raymond Carr. Oxford: Oxford University Press, 1970, pp. 63-105.

    Contends that a national revolutionary party in 1931 had no chance of gaining access to the political structure. *Tenentismo*, then, failed as a consequence of its premature effort at political organization.

619. Freire, Josué. *O exército em face das luctas políticas*. Rio de Janeiro: Est. Central de Material de Intendência, 1938.

    Reviews the seditious movement within the Brazilian army which led to the ill-fated November 1935 insurrections in Rio de Janeiro, Natal, and Recife.

620. "As guerras secretas." *Veja* (São Paulo), 522 (September 6, 1978), 52-58.

    The first published account in Brazil of the 1972 campaign against rural guerrillas on the Pará-Goiás border.

621. Hilton, Stanley E. "Military Influence on Brazilian Economic Policy, 1930-1945." *Hispanic American Historical Review*. 53 (February 1973), 71-94.

    Argues that military leaders were minimally concerned with national industrial development in the 1930's.

622. IPM-709. *O comunismo no Brasil*. Rio de Janeiro: Biblioteca do Exército Editôra, 1966.

    Reveals the army's deep-seated fear of communist subversion, based on documents allegedly seized from subversives.

623. Johnson, John J. "The Military in Brazil." *The Military and Society in Latin America*. Stanford: Stanford University Press, 1964, pp. 175-243.

    Discusses the role of the military as "moderating factor" in Brazilian society. Written before the coup.

624. Keith, Henry H. and Robert A. Hayes, eds. *Perspectives on Armed Politics in Brazil*. Tempe: University of Arizona Press, 1976.

Essays on the military's role by C. Neal Ronning, Lewis A. Tambs, Dalmo Dallari, and others.

625. Levine, Robert M. "Il Brasile verso la 'rivoluzione' permanente." *Mercúrio* (Rome), 17 (March 1974), 83-90.

Agrees with a 1971 Rand Corporation study (item 647) which holds that the military regime is likely to remain in power for many years, openly or behind the scenes.

626. Lyra Tavares, Gen. A. de. *Exército e nação*. Recife: Imprensa Universitária, 1965.

One of the leaders of the military coup justifies his actions as necessary "counterrevolutionary" intervention.

627. Macaulay, Neill. *The Prestes Column: Revolution in Brazil*. New York: Quadrangle Books, 1974.

Describes the *tenente*-led guerrilla movement which dramatically revealed the weakness of the central government during the mid-1920's and which helped set the stage for the 1930 coup.

628. McCann, Frank D. "The Nation in Arms: Obligatory Military Service during the Old Republic." *Essays Concerning the Socio-Economic History of Brazil and Portuguese India*. Ed. Dauril Alden and Warren Dean. Gainesville: University of Florida Press, 1977, pp. 211-243.

Shows that universal conscription was introduced as a reformist measure seeking to create a citizen soldiery and to strengthen the national government.

629. Moraes, João Baptista Mascarenhas de. *Memórias*. Rio de Janeiro: José Olympio, 1969.

The commander of the F.E.B. describes Brazil's role in the Italian campaign and the preparations for war which preceded it.

630. Morais, Carlos Wagner, comp. *O livro dos pensamentos do general Figueiredo*. São Paulo: Ed. Alfa-Omega, 1978.

A collection of the political statements of President-designate João Baptista Figueiredo, with a brief accompanying biographic text.

631. Nunn, Frederick M. "Military Professionalism and Professional Militarism in Brazil, 1870-1970." *Journal of Latin American Studies*, 4 (May 1972), 29-54.

Considers Brazilian military professionals a "state within a state" who equate their professional well-being with Brazil's.

632. Oliveira, Eliezer Rizzo de. "As forças armadas: política e ideologia no Brasil (1964-1969)." Master's Thesis. Departamento de Ciências Sociais, Universidade Estadual de Campinas, 1976.

Places the Escola Superior de Guerra (the Military War College) at the center of the changing ideology of the armed forces and its new authoritarian-nationalist orientation.

633. Rachum, Ilan. "The Brazilian Revolution of 1930: A Revision." *Inter-American Economic Affairs*, 29 (Fall 1975), 59-84.

Argues that the depression did not cause the fall of the Old Republic, as is commonly held, although it hastened the old regime's demise. Calls the 1930 Revolution "the major defeat of the Brazilian military in this century."

634. Rachum, Ilan. "Brazil's *Tenentes*: Military Protest and Radicalization." *Scripta Hierosolymitana*, 26 (1974), 93-119.

Argues that *tenentismo* failed because the exit of Prestes and Siqueira Campos left the movement leaderless and ideologically divided.

635. Rachum, Ilan. "From Young Rebels to Brokers of National Politics: The *Tenentes* of Brazil (1922-1967)." *Boletin de Estudios Latinoamericanos y del Caribe*, 23 (December 1977), 41-60.

Analyzes the reasons for *tenente* political longevity in Brazilian life: the demand for new solutions, the persistence of national problems over four decades, and the underlying atmosphere of political instability.

636. Roett, Riordan. "A Praetorian Army in Politics: The Changing Role of the Brazilian Military." *Brazil in the Sixties* (item 423), pp. 3-50.

Argues that military leaders oppose social change, are

wary of an independent political system, and fear open civilian participation in government.

637. Santos, Davino Francisco dos. *A marcha vermelha*. São Paulo: Ed. Saraiva, 1948.

An anti-communist diatribe in the form of a memoir-biography by an army captain who joined the Communist Party in 1935 and left it in 1942.

638. Schmitter, Philippe C., ed. *Military Rule in Latin America: Functions, Consequences and Perspectives*. Beverly Hills: Sage Publications, 1973.

Seven essays including an interesting analysis of the role of the armed forces by Manfred Kossok.

639. Silva, Hélio and Maria Cecilia Ribas Carneiro. *O ciclo de Vargas. 1942: Guerra no continente*. Rio de Janeiro: Civilização Brasileira, 1972.

Documents Brazil's entry into World War II.

640. Silva, Hélio and Maria Cecilia Ribas Carneiro. *O ciclo de Vargas. 1944: O Brasil na guerra*. Rio de Janeiro: Civilização Brasileira, 1974.

Describes the role of the Brazilian Expeditionary Force in Italy and the homefront in wartime.

641. Sodré, Nelson Werneck. *A coluna Prestes*. Rio de Janeiro: Civilização Brasileira, 1978.

Analyzes the role of the ill-fated Prestes Column as precurser of *tenente* nationalism and symbol of resistance against social injustice.

642. Sodré, Nelson Werneck. *História militar do Brasil*. Rio de Janeiro: Civilização Brasileira, 1965.

Blames the military for using the 1964 coup to block the efforts by the ousted regime to reform the structural organization of Brazil in order to achieve authentic democracy.

643. Sodré, Nelson Werneck. *Memórias de um soldado*. Rio de Janeiro: Civilização Brasileira, 1967.

An insightful narrative autobiography by the retired army general and neo-Marxist polymath. Especially valuable for its portrait of cadet life during the heady days which preceded the eruption of the *tenente* movement.

644. Steiner, H.J. and D.M. Truebeck. "Brazil: All Power to the Arsenals." *Foreign Affairs*, 49 (April 1971), 464-479.

Emphasizes the success of the military in modernizing itself and the Brazilian nation.

645. Stepan, Alfred C. *The Military in Politics: Changing Patterns in Brazil*. Princeton: Princeton University Press, 1971.

Asserts that the Brazilian armed forces are divided internally, principally into two groups, "liberal internationalists" (identified with Castello Branco) and "authoritarian nationalists."

646. Stepan, Alfred C. "The New Professionalism of Internal Warfare and Military Role Expansion." *Authoritarian Brazil* (item 431), pp. 47-68.

Examines the shift of emphasis within the Latin American armies from external concerns to combatting internal subversion, to some extent a by-product of close cooperation with United States military missions in the 1960's.

647. Stepan, Alfred C. and Luigi R. Einaudi. *Latin American Institutional Development: Changing Military Perspectives in Peru and Brazil*. Santa Monica: California: Rand Corporation, 1971.

Contends that the Brazilian military regime has entrenched itself and is likely to remain in power indefinitely.

648. Távora, Juarez. *Uma vida e muitas lutas: memórias*. 2 vols. Rio de Janeiro: José Olympio, 1973-74.

Narrates the *tenente* hero's early career and his central role in the 1930 Revolution, the elaboration of the *tenente* ideology, and the administration of the northeastern states under the provisional government.

649. United States Army. Forces South Atlantic. Historical Section. *The Final Campaign across Northwest Italy, 14 April - 2 May 1945*. Milan: Pizzi and Pizio, 1945.

Relates the story of the closing day of the war in Italy, during which time the Brazilian Expeditionary Force played an important role at Montese and Collecchio.

650. Viana Filho, Luis. *O governo Castelo Branco*. Rio de Janeiro: José Olympio, 1975.

One of the first analyses of the Castelo Branco military presidency to be published in Brazil.

651. Walters, Vernon. *Silent Missions*. Garden City, N.Y.: Doubleday, 1978.

A personal memoir by the man who served as liaison officer with the Brazilian Expeditionary Force in Italy and who held a close friendship with General Castelo Branco in 1964, when he served as military attaché. Walters admires Castelo Branco and defends the coup.

652. Wirth, John D. "*Tenentismo* in the Brazilian Revolution of 1930." *Hispanic American Historical Review*, 44 (May 1964), 161-179.

Emphasizes the authoritarian nationalist undercurrent within the movement which exploded among young military officers in 1922 and which greatly influenced Vargas's Liberal Alliance.

653. Young, Jordan M. "Military Aspects of the 1930 Brazilian Revolution." *Hispanic American Historical Review*, 44 (May 1964), pp. 180-196.

Recounts the events surrounding the fall of the Old Republic.

E. FOREIGN POLICY

654. Bell, Peter D. "Brazilian-American Relations." *Brazil in the Sixties* (item 431), pp. 77-104.

Agrees with Hélio Jaguaribe that American-Brazilian relations in the 1960's were governed by "the unchallenged, self-styled concern of the United States" and its self-interest.

655. Black, Jan Knippers. *United States Penetration of Brazil*. Philadelphia: University of Pennsylvania Press, 1977.

Criticizes the United States for strengthening the hand of non-progressive groups in Brazil and reinforcing authoritarian tendencies in the military command.

656. Burns, E. Bradford. "Tradition and Variation in Brazilian Foreign Policy." *Journal of Inter-American Studies*, 9 (April 1967), 195-212.

Points out the conflict over Brazil's foreign policy between nationalists and conservatives. Nationalists see the world as Brazil's stage, and advocate a strong, anti-American posture.

657. Carvalho, Delgado de. *A história diplomática do Brasil*. Rio de Janeiro: José Olympio, 1959.

Provides the standard interpretation of the history of diplomatic relations between Brazil and the Atlantic powers.

658. Cooke, Morris L. *Brazil on the March: A Study in International Cooperation*. New York: McGraw Hill, 1944.

The chief of the World War II technical aid mission to Brazil praises the Brazilians and describes projects underway.

659. Costa, Licurgo. *Uma nova política para as Americas*. São Paulo: Ed. Martins, 1960.

Explains the so-called "Kubitscheck Doctrine," Brazil's effort, in the late 1950's, to play an independent role in foreign affairs within the boundaries of Pan Americanism.

660. Couto e Silva, Golbery do. *Geopolítica do Brasil*. Rio de Janeiro: José Olympio, 1966.

Argues the case for Brazil's geopolitical destiny. The author, an army general, played a major role in the 1964 coup and after.

661. Dantas, Francisco C. de San Tiago. *Política externa independente*. Rio de Janeiro: José Olympio, 1962.

Excerpts documents and speeches on the Goulart "regime's independent" diplomatic policy.

662. Davis, Harold Eugene et al. *Latin American Foreign Policies: An Analysis*. Baltimore: Johns Hopkins University Press, 1975.

Contends that Brazil has taken the foreign policy role of a bridge between the United States and Spanish America, interpreting the one to the other.

663. Fontaine, Roger W. *Brazil and the United States: Toward a Maturing Relationship*. Stanford: Hoover Institution on War, Revolution, and Peace, 1974.

Argues that the United States should accept Brazil's new international aspirations as a future world power in order to maintain its traditional friendship.

664. Francis, Michael J. "The United States at Rio, 1942: the Strains of Pan-Americanism." *Journal of Latin American Studies*, 6 (May 1974), 77-95.

Shows that despite Brazil's public pro-United States stance, its leaders privately kept open lines of communication with Nazi Germany.

665. Frye, Alton. "Nazi Germany and the American Hemisphere, 1933-1941." Diss. Yale University, 1967.

Bases analysis on unpublished German records, stressing Nazi efforts to woo Brazil from its traditional role of economic dependence on the United States.

666. Giffin, Donald Warren. "The Normal Years: Brazilian-American Relations, 1930-1939." Diss. Vanderbilt University, Nashville, Tenn., 1962.

A narrative study based mostly on diplomatic records from the United States side of U.S.-Brazilian relations.

667. Goldhamer, Herbert. *The Foreign Powers in Latin America*. Princeton: Princeton University Press, 1972.

Surveys the contemporary foreign policies of the major powers toward Latin America, including Japan, the Soviet Union, and Great Britain.

668. Harms-Baltzer, Käte. *Die Nationalisierung der deutschen Einwanderer und ihrer Nachkommen in Brasilien als Problem der deutsch-brasilianischen Beziehungen, 1930-1938*. Berlin: n.p., 1970.

Offers a detailed study of German-Brazilian relations during the Vargas period based entirely on German sources.

669. Hill, Lawrence F. *Diplomatic Relations between the United States and Brazil*. Durham, N.C.: Duke University Press, 1932.

Provides an overview of the history of Brazilian-U.S. relations, including a description of the opening of the Amazon region to international penetration.

670. Hilton, Stanley E. *Brazil and the Great Powers, 1930-1939: The Politics of Trade Rivalry*. Austin: University of Texas Press, 1975.

Uses extensive diplomatic sources to examine the competition between Germany and the United States for economic preeminence in Brazil as the war neared.

671. Hilton, Stanley E. *Suástica sôbre o Brasil: a história da espionagem alemã no Brasil, 1939-1944*. Rio de Janeiro: Civilização Brasileira, 1977.

Probes the extent of German espionage in Brazil during the Estado Nôvo.

672. Holanda, Nestor de. *Diálogo Brasil-URSS*. 2nd ed. Rio de Janeiro: Civilização Brasileira, 1962.

Advocates improved relations between Brasília and Moscow.

673. Landry, David M. "Brazil's New Regional and Global Roles." *World Affairs*, 137 (Summer 1974), 23-37.

Concludes that Brazil's nationalistic ambitions will likely supersede any desire to see authority shift from nation-state toward supranational institutions.

674. Linhares, Maria Y. Leite. "Brazilian Foreign Policy and Africa." *The World Today* (London), 18 (December 1962), 532-540.

Advocates a positive role in Lusophone Africa by which Brazil would, allied to local elites, help the Africans integrate themselves into the new continental realities.

675. Luddeman, Margarete K. "Nuclear Technology from West Germany. A Case of Disharmony in U.S.-Brazilian Relations." Washington, D.C.: Georgetown University Latin American Studies Program, Occasional Paper No. 1 [April 1978].

Warns that the Carter administration's efforts to stop the West German-Brazilian nuclear agreement promise to "do good but destroy harmony in the process."

676. McCann, Frank D., Jr. "Aviation Diplomacy: the United States and Brazil, 1939-1941." *Inter-American Affairs*, 21 (Spring 1968), 35-50.

Uses diplomatic sources as well as the Pan American Airways archive. Shows how the goal of establishing air links with South America helped prepare the way for Brazilian-United States cooperation.

677. McCann, Frank D., Jr. *The Brazilian-American Alliance, 1937-1945.* Princeton: Princeton University Press, 1973.

Shows how the U.S. sought to impose its influence over Brazil in the military as well as economic sphere. Includes a valuable description of the Brazilian Expeditionary Force in Italy.

678. Maia, Jorge. *O Brasil no terceiro mundo.* Rio de Janeiro: Ed. Bloch, 1968.

Calls for Brazil to modify its foreign policy and to identify with Third World interests.

679. Maia Neto. *Brasil: Guerra quente na América Latina.* Rio de Janeiro: Civilização Brasileira, 1965.

Blames the United States for complicity in the 1964 coup and defends the record of the Goulart administration.

680. Martins, Carlos Estêvam. "Brazil and the United States from the 1960's to the 1970's." *Latin America and the United States: The Changing Political Realities.* Ed. Júlio Cotler and Richard R. Fagen. Stanford: Stanford University Press, 1974, pp. 269-301.

States the nationalist case for an independent Brazilian foreign policy free from the United States orbit.

681. Morel, Edmar. *O golpe comecou em Washington.* Rio de Janeiro: Civilização Brasileira, 1965.

Argues that foreign multinational interests, notably the oil companies and Hanna Mining Corporation, helped bring about Goulart's downfall.

682. Morris, Michael. "Trends in U.S. Brazilian Maritime Relations." *Inter-American Economic Affairs*, 27 (Winter 1973), 3-24.

Foresees a revival of the "independent" foreign policy which characterized the 1950's and 1960's, especially under President Quadros.

683. Odália, Nilo. "O Brasil nas relações internacionais: 1945-1964 " In *Brasil em perspectiva* (item 205), pp. 358-370.

Outlines Brazilian foreign policy from 1945 through the Cold War, the Kubitscheck, Quadros, and Goulart administrations, and 1964.

684. Parker, Phyllis R. *1964: O papel dos Estados Unidos no golpe de estado de 31 de março.* Tr. Carlos Nayfield. Rio de Janeiro: Civilização Brasileira, 1977.

Shows that the United States government played a more definable role in the 1964 military coup than it earlier admitted. Based on research in the Lyndon B. Johnson Presidential Library.

685. Pereira, Astrojildo. *URSS-Itália-Brasil.* Rio de Janeiro: Ed. Alba, 1935.

Urges Brasília to move to the left and ally with the Soviet Union.

686. Perry, William. *Contemporary Brazilian Foreign Policy: the International Strategy of an Emerging Power.* Beverly Hills: Sage Publications, 1976.

Shows that Geisel's policy of "responsible pragmatism" is really a direct descendant of the "política externa independente" of the populist early 1960's.

687. Pinsky, Jaime. "O Brasil nas relações internacionais, 1930-1945." *Brasil em perspectiva* (item 205), pp. 339-351.

Argues that Vargas's decision to back the Allied cause undermined his government's own viability once the war ended.

688. Quadros, Jânio. "Brazil's New Foreign Policy." *Foreign Affairs*, 40 (October 1961), 19-27.

Brazil's president proposes that Brazil strengthen ties to the developing world, particularly Africa, and to oppose colonialism.

689. Rodrigues, José Honório. *Brazil and Africa.* Berkeley: University of California Press, 1965.

Calls for Brazil to cultivate relations with black Africa.

690. Rodrigues, José Honório. *Interesse nacional e política externa.* Rio de Janeiro: Civilização Brasileira, 1966.

Advocates an independent foreign policy stressing Brazil's national interest.

691. Rosenbaum, H. Jon. "A Critique of the Brazilian Foreign Service." *Journal of Developing Areas*, 2 (April 1968), 377-392.

Discusses the military regime's diplomatic options under Castello Branco and Costa e Silva and the problems posed by Brazil's authoritarian model of development.

692. Santos, Ralph G. "Brazilian Foreign Policy and the Dominican Crisis: The Impact of History and Events." *The Americas*, 29 (July 1972), 62-77.

Contends that Brazil's participation in the Johnson administration's intervention in the Dominican Republic in 1965 represented a critical departure from Brazil's tradition of independent, nationalist foreign policy.

693. Schneider, Ronald M. *Brazil: Foreign Relations of a Future World Power*. Boulder, Colorado: Westview Press, 1977.

Analyzes the expectations and achievements of Brazil's foreign policy makers. Contends that the military government has created a "jet-age Bismarckianism" to exploit international events to their advantage.

694. Schröder, Hans-Jurgen. "Hauptprobleme der deutschen Lateinamerikapolitik." *Jahrbuch für Geschichte von Staat, Wirtschaft und Gesellschaft Lateinamerikas*, 12 (1975), 408-433.

Reviews the various hypotheses about Nazi territorial aspirations in the Western Hemisphere, downgrading possible designs on Brazil.

695. Selcher, Wayne A. *The Afro-Asian Dimension of Brazilian Foreign Policy 1956-1972*. Gainesville: University of Florida Press, 1974.

Surveys Brazil's growing concern with Africa, and Asia, and the Middle East after World War II, describing a subtle and complex consensus with Third World nations based on convergence of economic and political interests. The study stops at 1968 despite the book's title.

696. Storrs, Keith Larry. "Brazil's Independent Foreign Policy, 1961-1964." Diss., Cornell University, 1973.

Traces Brazil's efforts to adopt a Third World orientation in foreign policy under Quadros and Goulart and its return to its "special relationship" with the United States after the coup.

697. Trask, David F., Michael C. Meyer, and Roger R. Trask, eds. *A Bibliography of United States-Latin American Relations Since 1810*. Lincoln: University of Nebraska Press, 1968.

Includes 11,000 entries, some annotated.

698. Trask, Roger R. "George F. Kennan's Report on Latin America (1950)." *Diplomatic History*, 12 (Summer 1978), 307-311.

Reveals Kennan's feelings of condescension toward Latin Americans during his visit; his report to Dean Acheson calls Rio de Janeiro "repulsive" and excessively divided between rich and poor.

699. Tyson, Brady. "O sistema interamericano depois de Santo Domingo." *Politica Externa Independente*, 1 (1966), 83-95.

Reviews Brazil's hemispheric foreign policy after the U.S.-Brazilian collaboration in the 1965 military intervention in the Dominican Republic.

IV.
Economics

A. ECONOMIC DEVELOPMENT

1. Theoretical Studies

700. Almeida, Cândido Mendes de. *Nacionalismo e desenvolvimento*. Rio de Janeiro: Instituto Brasileiro de Estudos Afro-Asiaticos, 1963.

Surveys Brazil's dependent-colonial status. The study has been compared by some to Frantz Fanon's *Les Damnés de la Terre*.

701. Bacha, Edmar. "Princípios econômicos a avaliação governmental de projetos de investimento." *Dados*, 9 (1972), 92-101.

Argues that the federal government frequently fails to evaluate the relationships between investment decisions and development goals.

702. Baer, Werner and Isaac Kerstenetzky. "The Brazilian Economy." *Brazil in the Sixties* (item 423), pp. 105-145.

Contends that Brazil's military leaders have been more concerned with structural/growth problems than with stability or efficiency.

703. Basbaum, Leôncio. *Caminhos brasileiros do desenvolvimento*. São Paulo: Ed. Fulgor, 1960.

Analyzes Brazil's role in the international economic order and points to its vulnerability.

704. Bastos, Humberto. *A marcha do capitalismo no Brasil*. São Paulo: Ed. Martins, 1944.

Discusses the evolution of capitalism in Brazil and Brazil's place within the international marketplace. Contrasts the economic differences from region to region within Brazil.

705. Bhatra, Sarvan K. *Democracy, Development and Planning.* Savannah, Ga.: Armstrong College Commission, 1970.

Compares Brazil and India as developing nations seeking to spur economic growth.

706. Braga, Cincinato. *Brasil novo.* 4 vols. Rio de Janeiro: Imprensa Nacional, 1930-31.

Suggests economic policies for the new provisional government and advocates the creation of a central bank, agricultural modernization, agrarian credit, and other reforms.

707. Bresser Pereira, L.C. *Desenvolvimento e crise no Brasil, 1930-1967.* Rio de Janeiro: Zahar, 1968.

Criticizes the concept of capitalist developmentalist nationalism and argues that only a socialist solution promises success for Brazil.

708. Buescu, Mircea and Vicente Tapajós. *História do desenvolvimento econômico do Brasil.* Rio de Janeiro: Casa do Livro, 1969.

Divides Brazil's economic history into periods based on cycles of economic production and exportation.

709. Cardoso, Fernando Henrique. "Associated-Dependent Development: Theoretical and Practical Implications." *Authoritarian Brazil* (item 431), pp. 142-178.

Views Brazil as part of the new division of labor in the capitalist world. The national Brazilian bourgeoisie, in consequence, may only hope to integrate itself into the scheme of international capitalism, to make the most of it in spite of its lack of independent technology.

710. Cardoso, Fernando Henrique. "Dependency and Development in Latin America." *New Left Review*, 74 (July-August 1972), 83-95.

Summarizes the author's dependency theories, specifically linking the concept with imperialism, which he sees as practically obligatory for capitalist expansion.

711. Chilcote, Ronald H. "A Question of Dependency." *Latin American Research Review*, 13 (Spring 1978) 55-68.

Discusses the work of dos Santos and Cardoso, theories of development and underdevelopment emphasizing imperialism and the role of capital formation.

712. Cohn, Gabriel. *Petróleo e nacionalismo.* São Paulo: DIFEL, 1968.

Identifies and discusses the role of groups which advocated a nationalist petroleum policy and which contributed, in the 1950's, to the ultimate creation of a state oil monopoly, Petrobrás.

713. Cooperation in Documentation and Communication. *The Brazilian Model: Political Repression and Economic Expansion.* Washington, D.C.: CODOC, 1974.

Claims a direct relationship between Brazil's economic health and the strengthening of the apparatus of repression.

714. Costa, Rubens Vaz. *Crescimento populational e desenvolvimento econômico.* Fortaleza: Banco do Nordeste do Brasil, 1970.

Argues that population growth is necessary for economic development although it requires that adjustments be made to better distribute resources.

715. Dos Santos, Theotônio. "The Structure of Dependence." *American Economic Review*, 60 (May 1970), 231-36.

Defines dependency in terms of economic subjection, not class relations, emphasizing, consequently, the role of capitalism as imperialism.

716. Duarte, Sérgio Guerra. *Por que existem analfabetos no Brasil?* Rio de Janeiro: Civilização Brasileira, 1963.

Blames Brazil's dependent economic status for hindering land reform and national-based industrialization, and, in turn, for the high rate of illiteracy among the Brazilian people.

717. Figueiredo, Vilma. *Desenvolvimento dependente brasileiro.* Rio de Janeiro: Zahar, 1978.

Restates the argument that Brazil's industrial evolution fits within the model of dependent development.

718. Flynn, Peter. "The Brazilian Development Model." *The World Today*, 29 (November 1973), 481-494.

Considers Brazil's model for authoritarian economic development to be a major selling point to the Third World nations.

719. Frank, André Gunder. *Capitalism and Underdevelopment in Latin America: Historical Studies of Chile and Brazil.* New York: Monthly Review Press, 1967.

Perceives a hierarchy of metropolis-satellite relationships in underdeveloped countries and across international borders. For Brazil, São Paulo plays the role of intermediate metropolis, dominating the Northeast but dominated at the same time by New York.

720. Frank, André Gunder. *Lumpenbourgeoisie, Lumpendevelopment: Dependence, Class, and Politics in Latin America.* New York: Monthly Review Press, 1978.

Argues that external dependency acts to shape a bourgeoisie whose interests serve the foreign metropolis, and who perpetuate continuing underdevelopment and pauperization.

721. Frank, André Gunder. "On the Mechanics of Imperialism: the Case of Brazil." *Readings in U.S. Imperialism.* Ed. K.T. Fann and Donald C. Hodges. Boston: Porter Sargent Publisher, 1971, pp. 237-248.

Points out that much of the capital on which Americans "earn" profits in Brazil is Brazilian in origin and American only in ownership, control, and earnings.

722. Furtado, Celso. *Análise do "modelo" brasileiro.* Rio de Janeiro: Civilização Brasileira, 1972.

Points to the Brazilian economy's tendency to underconsumption and warns that the absence of an automatic mechanism for linking gains in productivity to rewards for workers spells danger for the system's long-term equilibrium.

723. Furtado, Celso. *Development and Underdevelopment.* Tr. Ricardo E. De Aguiar and Eric Charles Drysdale. Berkeley: University of California Press, 1964.

Argues that Brazilian development has resulted from external forces, not conscious national choice rooted in an awareness of Brazil's underdevelopment. Furthermore, the state bureaucracy has steadfastly resisted attempts to implement social change.

724. Furtado, Celso. *Dialéctica do desenvolvimento.* Rio de Janeiro: Fundo de Cultura, 1964.

Argues that Brazil has failed to overcome its structural

obstacles to change and has been unable to create an independent entrepreneurial class committed to national development.

725. Furtado, Celso. "Political Obstacles to the Economic Development of Brazil." *Obstacles to Change in Latin America*. Ed. Claudio Veliz. London: Oxford University Press, 1965, pp. 145-161.

Warns that Brazil has not yet succeeded in creating an institutional system capable of permitting "the transformation of its basic aspirations into positive and viable operational projects."

726. Furtado, Celso. *Um projeto para o Brasil*. 2nd ed. Rio de Janeiro: Ed. Saga, 1968.

Three essays seeking to find the causes of Brazil's "paralyzed economic system." Contends that development will only proceed if accompanied by structural change and a redistribution of income within the country.

727. Gilbert, Alan. *Latin American Development: A Geographic Perspective*. New York: Penguin Books, 1974.

Reviews the literature of development and argues that developmental economists fail to ask the question "development for whom?" Advocates broad-range studies of transportation needs, land use, and population distribution.

728. Ianni, Octávo. "O Estado e a acumulação capitalista: projeto de pesquisa sobre as relações entre o Estado e a economia no Mexico (1934-40) e no Brasil (1937-45)." *Debate e Crítica*, 3 (1974), 121-129.

Compares the role of the state in the economy in Vargas's Brazil and Cardenas's Mexico.

729. Ianni, Otavio. "O Estado e o desenvolvimento econômico do Brasil." *América Latina*, 7 (January-March 1964), 39-56.

Written before the 1964 coup. Argues that Brazil's economy is undergoing a transition from colonial agricultural capitalism to formative capitalist-industrialism.

730. Kahil, Raouf. *Inflation and Economic Development in Brazil*. London: Oxford University Press, 1973.

Agrees with the structuralist view that Brazil's backward agriculture, its deteriorating terms of trade, and the crush of its urban problems all contributed to its inflation problem.

731. Kahl, Joseph. *Modernization, Exploitation, and Dependency in Latin America: Germani, González Casanova, and Cardoso.* New Brunswick, New Jersey: Transaction Books, 1976.

Analyzes the works of three Latin American sociologists, one of them the Brazilian Fernando Henrique Cardoso, who is evaluated both as a dependency theorist and as a writer on entrepreneurship and stratification.

732. Malan, Pedro and José Eduardo de Carvalho Pereira. "A propôsito de uma reinterpretação do desenvolvimento brasileiro desde os anos 30." *Dados*, 9 (1972), 126-145.

Criticizes the Marxist view of Brazilian capitalist development which argues that economic development is incompatible with social advancement.

733. Martins, Leôncio. *Industrialização, burguesia nacional e desenvolvimento.* Rio de Janeiro: Ed. Saga, 1968.

Analyzes the role of entrepreneurs in a development process increasingly linked to international factors.

734. Mericle, Kenneth S. "Corporatist Control of the Working Class: Authoritarian Brazil Since 1964." *Authoritarianism and Corporatism in Latin America.* Ed. James M. Malloy. Pittsburgh: University of Pittsburgh Press, 1977, pp. 303-338.

Argues that sustained economic growth offers the regime opportunities to expand its popularity among the upper strata of the working class.

735. Oliveira, Francisco de. *A economia da dependencia imperfeita.* Rio de Janeiro: Ed. Graal, 1977.

A Marxist discussion of the nature of Brazilian capitalist development, asserting that foreign interests have gained the upper hand and imposed a captive national economy.

736. Pokshishevsky, V.V. "The Major Economic Regions of Brazil." *Soviet Geography*, 1 (January-February 1960), 48-68.

An interesting description by a Soviet geographer using Lenin's "New Data on the Laws of Development of Capitalism in Agriculture" as a methodological model.

737. Rangel, Ignácio. *A inflação brasileira.* 2nd ed. Rio de Janeiro: Tempo Brasileiro, 1963.

Argues that inflation, carefully monitored, can aid developing economies.

738. Rosenbaum, H. Jon and William G. Tyler, eds. *Contemporary Brazil: Issues in Economic and Political Development.* New York: Praeger, 1972.

Articles by specialists on planning, agriculture, taxation, politics, the Church, and urban issues.

739. Serra, José, ed. *America Latina: Ensaios de interpretação econômico.* Rio de Janeiro: Paz e Terra, 1976.

A collection of essays on economic development in Brazil and Latin America, capped by a discussion of the problems accruing from the analysis of developmental processes.

740. Simonsen, Mário H. *Brasil 2002.* Rio de Janeiro: APEC Editôra, 1972.

Views Brazil's high post-1968 growth rate as a result of rationalized economic activity and the emergence of a dynamic and modern capital market.

741. Singer, Paul I. *O "Milagre Brasileiro": causas e consequências.* São Paulo: CEBRAP, 1972.

Warns that the burdens created as by-products by the "economic miracle" will be borne by lower-class groups and may well harm prospects for long-term economic health.

742. Skidmore, Thomas E. "The Years Between the Harvests: the Economics of the Castello Branco Presidency, 1964-1967." *Luso-Brazilian Review*, 15 (Winter 1978), 153-177.

Shows that the corporatist structure adopted by the military government made it easy to prevent serious worker mobilization against steps which forced down real wages in the interest of economic growth.

743. Sodré, Nelson Werneck. "Nationalism and Development." Paper presented to the University of California Project

"Brazil-Portuguese Africa," UCLA and University of California, Riverside, January 1968.

Advocates a nationalistic economic policy as a way out of the "structural crisis" caused by the imposition of dictatorship in 1964. Asks that inflation be combatted by improving Brazil's position taken in commercial relations with the exterior.

744. Syurud, Donald E. *Foundations of Brazilian Economic Growth*. Stanford: Hoover Institute, 1974.

Attributes present economic successes to political stability, sound management, and quick mobilization of policy instruments by the government.

745. Toledo, Caio Navarro de. *ISEB: Fábrica de ideologias*. São Paulo: Ática, 1977.

Attempts to reconstruct the ideological climate which characterized the I.S.E.B. research center in the late 1950's through an analysis of the writing of its leading contributors. Argues that developmentalism prevailed despite stirrings of unrest against Brazil's dependent status.

746. Vargas, Getúlio. *A política nationalista do petróleo no Brasil*. Rio de Janeiro: Tempo Brasileiro, 1964.

States the President's views during the 1950's favoring national control over petroleum reserves.

747. Wells, John. "The 'Miracle' as Model." *Latin American Review of Books*, 1 (Spring 1973), 111-116.

Analyzes Furtado's model of Brazilian economic development, which he considers cyclical rather than secular in approach. Criticizes Furtado's failure to consider the investment process.

748. Wish, John R. *Economic Development in Latin America: An Annotated Bibliography*. New York: Praeger, 1965.

Lists studies on development without specific reference to individual countries. Entries are extensively annotated.

2. International Economic Relations

749. Abreu, M. "Brazilian Foreign Economic Policy Under Vargas, 1930-1945." Diss. Cambridge University, 1977.

Uses consular reports and other primary courses to examine the political climate which influenced Brazil's foreign trade policies during the provisional government and the Estado Nôvo.

750. Ackerman, Frank. "Industry and Imperialism in Brazil." *The Review of Radical Political Economics*, (Ann Arbor, Michigan) 3 (Spring 1971), 1-39.

Credits the Brazilian government's willingness to make concessions to multinational investors and its use of repression to insure a stable work force with creating the pre-conditions for the "economic miracle."

751. American Chamber of Commerce for Brazil. *São Paulo, Brazil: The Take-Off Is Now*. São Paulo: American Chamber of Commerce, 1971.

States the Chamber of Commerce's view of the "New Brazil," inviting foreign investment and praising the new economic order.

752. Arruda, Marcos et al. *Multinationals and Brazil: The Impact of Multinational Corporations in Contemporary Brazil*. Toronto: Latin American Research Group, 1975.

Marxist-oriented study by the Brazilian exile research group LARU, condemning the multinationals' presence.

753. Baer, Werner and Mário Henrique Simonsen. "American Capital and Brazilian Nationalism." *Yale Review*, 53 (1964), 192-198.

Argues that foreign capital investment in Brazil can be beneficial, and that nationalistic warnings are one-sided. Wonders why Brazilian nationalists focus their attacks solely on United States businesses.

754. "Bibliografia sôbre desenvolvimento econômico." *Boletim da Biblioteca da Sudene* (Recife), 6 (April 1967), 11-26.

A bibliography on economic development and efforts to attract foreign technology and investment, especially to the Northeast.

755. Black, Edie and Fred Goff. *The Hanna Industrial Complex.* New York: North American Congress for Latin America, 1969.

Warns that economic concessions given to the Ohio-based corporation will yield virtual control of Amazonian mineral resources.

756. Brasil. Congresso. Câmara dos Deputados, Biblioteca. "Aliança para o Progresso, Bibliografia." *Boletim da Biblioteca da Câmara dos Deputados* (Brasília), 12 (January-June 1963), 287-299.

Lists articles and studies on the Alliance for Progress's Brazilian programs.

757. "Brazil: A Major Contender in the Arms Business." *Business Week* (July 31, 1978), 45-46.

Predicts that by the 1980's Brazil will be marketing $500 million in arms annually, equal to the military exports of France or Great Britain in the 1970's. Brazil's arms are especially attractive to non-aligned nations because "they are free of ideological ties."

758. "The Brazilian Gamble: Why Bankers Bet on Brazilian Technocrats." *Business Week* (December 5, 1977), 72-81.

Explains that investors are confident that Brazilian planners can sustain its "sizzling" growth rate, maintain domestic stability, and avoid serious political strains.

759. Brown, Douglas Allen. "Three Perspectives on U.S. Foreign Aid: Explaining the Alliance for Progress." Diss., University of Oregon, 1974.

760. Canabrava Filho, Paulo. *Militarismo y imperialismo en el Brasil.* Buenos Aires: Tiempo Contemporâneo, 1970.

Links the Brazilian military regime with the interest of foreign imperialism.

761. Carvalho, Getúlio, ed. *Multinacionais: os limites da soberânia.* Rio de Janeiro: Fundação Getúlio Vargas, 1977.

A collection of essays on the impact of multinational investment in developing countries, focusing not on the nature of the process itself but on methods of "coexisting" with them.

762. Dell, Sidney. *A Latin American Common Market?* London: Royal Institute of International Affairs, 1966.

Contends that regional economic integration is impossible without basic political and social change.

763. Doellinger, Carlos von. "Foreign Trade Policy and Its Effects." *Brazilian Economic Studies*, 1 (1975), 39-96.

Contends that Brazil's economy has grown increasingly vulnerable to outside influences. Its foreign trade policy has benefitted its national productive system, but society has had to pay a high price for its economic development.

764. Galeano, Eduardo. "The De-Nationalization of Brazilian Industry." *Monthly Review*, 21 (1969), 11-30.

A Uruguayan journalist of the left blames international capitalism for undermining Brazil's industrial potential.

765. Garg, Ramesh C. "Brazilian External Debt: A Study in Capital Flows and Transfer of Resources." *Journal of Interamerican Studies and World Affairs*, 20 (August 1978), 341-351.

Warns that Brazil must reduce its dependence on imports and, thereby, on foreign capital to finance its trade deficits. Advocates import substitution as an alternative course.

766. Gauld, Charles A. *The Last Titan: Percival Farquar, American Entrepreneur in Latin America.* Stanford: Institute of Latin American Studies, 1964.

A laudatory biography of the Quaker railroad and mining entrepreneur responsible, indirectly, for arousing early Brazilian economic nationalism.

767. Gomes, Severo. *Tempo de mudar.* Pôrto Alegre: Ed. Glôbo, 1977.

A former cabinet minister argues for a nationalist position on trade and industrialization and relaxed political restrictions.

768. Great Britain. Board of Trade/Overseas Trade Department. *Economic Surveys, 1921-1961.* London: Somerset/ Chadwyck Healey, 1979. Series ES 95-112.

Reports by the British Commercial Secretaries attached to the Embassy and consulates in Brazil, on the economic climate. Covers 31 microfiche cards dealing with, for Brazil, the years between 1921 and 1953.

769. Grunwald, Joseph, ed. *Latin America and World Economy: A Changing International Order*. Beverly Hills: Sage Publications, 1978.

An anthology of essays examining the tension created by the desire of Latin American nations to integrate with the world economy yet at the same time preserve their self-reliance.

770. Gudin Filho, Eugênio. *Câmbio e café, 1933-1934*. Rio de Janeiro: Ed. Laemmert, 1934.

A brief (21p.) study of the new regime's policies towards the coffee sector and agricultural exports.

771. Hayter, Teresa. *Aid as Imperialism*. Harmondsworth, Middlesex: Penguin Books, 1971.

Argues that foreign aid has amounted to no more than an attempt to preserve capitalistic domination of developing nations.

772. Ingles, Jerry L. and Loretta Fairchild. "Evaluating the Impact of Foreign Investment: Methodology and the Evidence from Mexico, Colombia, and Brazil." *Latin American Research Review*, 12 (August 1977), 57-70.

Notes that each major business group--domestic and foreign-owned--feels that the other is favored by the government, thereby fueling distrust and hindering national development.

773. Jacobina, Alberto Pizarro and Tácito Líbio Reis de Freitas. "A Amazônia em fôco." *Revista Civilização Brasileira*, 4 (January-February 1968), 19-48.

Warns that Brazil's control of the Amazon is faced with serious external threats, including "imperialist" takeover under the orchestration of the "300-pound Dr. Strangelove, Dr. Hermann Kahn" of the Hudson Institute.

774. Love, Joseph L. "External Financing and Domestic Politics: The Case of São Paulo, Brazil, 1889-1937." *Latin American Modernization Problems*. Ed. Robert E. Scott.

Urbana, Illinois: University of Illinois Press, 1973, pp. 239-259.

Examines the effects of foreign borrowing on republican-era São Paulo; shows that domestic affairs in under-developed countries cannot be understood without considering external influences.

775. Mangabeira, Francisco. *Imperialismo, petróleo, Petrobrás.* Rio de Janeiro: Zahar, 1964.

Warns that foreign interests threaten to dominate Petrobrás and Brazil's petroleum reserves.

776. Mass, Bonnie. *Political Economy of Population Control in Latin America.* Montreal: Editions Latin America, 1972.

Charges that the United States is seeking to limit hemispheric population growth as a weapon in its imperialist apparatus of control.

777. Metzger, Eduard. *Die Besteurung von Tochterunternehmen in brazilian nach deutschem und brasilianischen Richt.* Hamburg: Institut für Iberamerika-Kunde, 1974.

Offers an extensive compilation of Brazilian laws on the taxation of foreign subsidiaries.

778. Monteiro, Sylvio. *Como atua o imperialismo ianque?* Rio de Janeiro: Civilização Brasileira, 1963.

Attacks United States interventionism, profit making, and investment activities which, the author charges, strangle national economic interests.

779. Morley, Samuel A. and Gordon W. Smith. "Import Substitution and Foreign Investment in Brazil." *Oxford Economic Papers*, 23 (March 1971), 120-135.

Argues that, given Brazil's relatively weak private sector, economists must choose between a heavy governmental role or provide a free hand to multinational investors.

780. Normano, John F. *The Struggle for South America.* London: George Allen & Unwin, 1931.

Analyzes the economic rivalries for Latin American markets among European commercial powers and the United States.

781. North American Congress on Latin America. "Brazil: Development for Whom?" *NACLA's Latin American and Empire Report*, 7 (April 1973), 1-33.

Blames multinational interests for pillaging Latin American resources in the name of economic development.

782. Onody, Oliver. *História dos direitos alfandegários no Brasil, 1808-1954*. Rio de Janeiro: unpublished, c. 1954.

A manuscript, located in the Roberto Simonsen Library, exhaustively summarizing Brazilian trade and tariff policy from the arrival of the Portuguese Court in 1808 to 1953.

783. Phelps, Dudley Maynard. *Migration of Industry to South America*. New York: McGraw-Hill, 1936.

Contends that foreign investment in Latin America (including Brazil) is beneficial, in spite of cries to the contrary from nationalists and other voices of alarm.

784. Ribeiro, Darcy. *The Americas and Civilization*. Tr. L.T. Barrett and M.M. Barrett. New York: Dutton, 1971.

Seeks to explain the differences between modes of development in North and South America. Blames multinational corporations for holding industrializing nations in a state of backwardness.

785. Rocha, Euzébio. *Brasil: país ameaçado*. São Paulo: Ed. Fulgor, 1965.

Warns against the pernicious influence of foreign economic domination.

786. Roett, Riordan. *The Politics of Foreign Aid in the Brazilian Northeast*. Nashville: Vanderbilt University Press, 1972.

Synthesizes the history of efforts to revive the region's economy through both domestic and foreign investment culminating in the establishment of SUDENE.

787. Sodré, Nelson Werneck. *Quem matou Kennedy*. Rio de Janeiro: Ed. Gernasa, 1964.

Warns that the same military-industrial interests responsible for the death of John F. Kennedy seek to dominate Brazil.

788. Tendler, Judith. *Inside Foreign Aid.* Baltimore: Johns Hopkins University Press, 1975.

A brief (140 pp.) but cogent analysis based on experience as a former U.S. AID official in Brazil, suggesting that procedures sometimes retard development rather than promote it.

789. Tyler, William G. "A polîtica norte-americana e o impasse do cafê soluvel." *Revista Civilização Brasileira*, 3 (March-April 1968), 87-98.

Testifies to the coercive economic power of the United States in international trade, using the International Coffee agreement as a case study.

790. Whitaker, Josê Maria de Aguiar. *Relatôrio da administração financeira do Governo Provisôrio.* Rio de Janeiro: Revista dos Tribunais, 1937.

States and defends Vargas's provisional government's policy towards agricultural price supports, especially for coffee, and its fiscal program.

3. The Domestic Economy

a. *General Studies*

791. Aartsen, J.P.V. "Northeastern Brazil: Present Status and Possibilities of Development." In *Nederlandsch Asdrijksundig Genootschap* (Amsterdam), 76 (1959), 228-242.

Advocates regional development to forestall social unrest.

792. Andrade, Manuel Correia de. *Acceleração e freios ao desenvolvimento brasileiro.* Petrôpolis: Ed. Vozes, 1973.

Seven essays by a leading geographer on the disparity in patterns of economic development in Brazil. Most are regional case studies.

793. Baranson, Jack. *Automotive Industries in Developing Countries.* Baltimore: Johns Hopkins Press, 1969.

Demonstrates that factory costs in Argentina, Mexico, and Brazil were significantly higher than in the

United States owing to the difficulty of creating economies of large-scale production.

794. Buescu, Mircea. *História econômica do Brasil; pesquisas e análises.* Rio de Janeiro: A.P.E.C., 1970.

Collected articles by the author on various aspects of Brazilian economic history, including exchange, national income, and inflation.

795. Buescu, Mircea. *300 anos de inflação.* Rio de Janeiro: A.P.E.C., 1973.

Differentiates among the several varieties of economic inflation which afflicted Brazil since the seventeenth century.

796. De Carli, Gileno. *Política de desenvolvimento do Nordeste.* Recife: SUDENE, 1971.

A brief history of the origins of SUDENE, the regional development agency for Northeast, written in quasi-memoir form by a specialist whose life has been devoted to understanding the roots of economic and agricultural backwardness in his native region.

797. Ellis, Howard S., ed. *The Economy of Brazil.* Berkeley: University of California Press, 1969.

Essays by Brazilian and foreign authors on a variety of economic themes. Contains items 856, 870.

798. Furtado, Celso. *The Economic Growth of Brazil. A Survey from Colonial to Modern Times.* Tr. Ricardo W. de Aguiar and Eric C. Drysdale. Berkeley: University of California Press, 1963.

An interpretive history by one of Brazil's most notable economists, since 1964 a professor at the Sorbonne. Before his exile he headed SUDENE and served as Finance Minister.

799. Iglésias, Francisco. "Situação de história econômica no Brasil." *Anais de história* (Assis, São Paulo), 2 (1970), 9-64.

Reviews the literature on Brazilian economic history and finds it understudied and insufficiently separated from political and social history in its methodology.

800. Joslin, David. *A Century of Banking in Latin America.* London: Oxford University Press, 1963.

Utilizes the archives of the Bank of London & South America Ltd. to survey the centenary of the bank in 1962. Two subsidiaries (London and Brazilian Bank; Brazilian and Portuguese Bank) operated exclusively in Brazil.

801. Lobo, Eulália Maria Lahmeyer, et al. "Evolução dos preços e do padrão de vida no Rio de Janeiro, 1820-1930." *Revista Brasileira de Economia*, 25 (October-December 1971), 235-265.

Presents a carefully-devised cost of living index for the city of Rio de Janeiro for a period of 110 years based on the day-to-day prices of thirteen basic consumer commodities.

802. Lobo, Eulália Maria Lahmeyer. *História do Rio de Janeiro (do capital comercial do capital industrial e financiera)*. 2 vols. Rio de Janeiro: Instituto Brasileiro de Mercado de Capitais, 1978.

A massive, detailed economic study of Rio de Janeiro from 1760 to 1945 representing the best uses of quantitative history. Includes a thirty-page bibliography organized topically.

803. Luz, Nícia Villela and Carlos Manuel Peláez. "Economia e história, o encontro entre dois campos do conhecimento." *Revista Brasileira de Economia*, 25 (July-September 1972), 273-302.

Criticizes the cost-of-living table constructed by Eulália Maria Lahmeyer Lobo and her collaborators (item 801) for not taking into account prices paid for exported goods.

804. Magalhães Júnior, Sérgio Nunes de. "Os ciclos econômicos." *Revista Brasileira de Estatística* (Rio de Janeiro), 8 (October-December 1947), 807-814.

Estimates yearly totals for national income from 1901 to 1946.

805. Normano, João Frederico. *Brazil, a Study of Economic Types*. Chapel Hill, N.C.: University of North Carolina Press, 1935.

Surveys the economic history of Brazil from discovery to the 1930 Revolution and its first five years.

806. Onody, Oliver. *A inflação brasileira, 1820-1958*. Rio de Janeiro: n.p., 1960.

Reviews the history of inflation in Brazil and official means adopted to counteract its effects. Estimates the real cost-of-living index between 1829 and 1959.

807. Overholt, William H. *The Future of Brazil.* Boulder, Colorado: Westview Press, 1978.

Six articles on investments, economic development, political prospects, and foreign policy.

808. Peláez, Carlos Manuel and Wilson Suzigan. "Bases para a interpretação monetária da história econômica brasileira." *Revista Brasileira de Economia*, 26 (October-December 1972), 57-93.

Estimates an annual rate of economic growth for Brazil between 1870 and 1970 of 11.7%, more than double that of the United States during the same period.

809. Pelaez, Carlos Manuel and Wilson Suzigan. *História monetária do Brasil: análise da política, comportamento e instituições monetárias.* Rio de Janeiro: IPEA, 1976.

Provides a detailed monetary history of Brazil.

810. Sahota, Gian Singh. *Brazilian Economic Policy: An Optimal Control Theory Analysis.* New York: Praeger, 1975.

An econometrician's detailed study of growth, taxation, income distribution, and public policies in Brazil since 1950.

811. Simonsen, Roberto Cochrane. *Brazil's Industrial Evolution.* São Paulo: Escola Livre de Sociologia e Política, 1939.

Asserts that the role of the First World War was less than is usually thought in influencing the growth of Brazilian industrial capacity.

812. Suzigan, Wilson. "A política cambial brasileira, 1889-1946." *Revista Brasileira de Economia*, 25 (July-September 1971), 93-111.

Surveys the history of Brazilian monetary policy.

813. Vieira, Dorival Teixeira. "A evolução do sistema monetário brasileiro." *Revista de Administração* (São Paulo), 1 (June 1947), 1-334.

A book-length article on the history of Brazil's monetary system and fiscal evolution.

814. Vilela, Anibal and Wilson Suzigan. *Política do governo e crescimento da economia brasileira, 1889-1945*. Rio de Janeiro: IPEA, 1973.

A major, sophisticated economic history of the period of the Old Republic through the first Vargas regime.

815. Von Gersdorff, Ralph. *Saving, Credit and Insurance in Brazil: Their Contribution to Economic Development*. Barbados, W.I.: Government Printing Office, 1962.

Provides the only work in English on this subject.

b. 1930 to the 1964 Coup

816. Abreu, Macedo de Paiva. "A dívida pública externa do Brasil, 1931-1943." *Pesquisa e Planejamento Econômico*, 5 (1975), 37-88.

Explores the Vargas government's efforts to absorb state debts and renegotiate Brazil's foreign loan during the depression years and beyond to the coming of the war.

817. Bouças, Valentim F. *Brasil: esclarecimentos econômicos, 1928-1932*. London: Waterlow & Sons, 1933.

Explains Brazil's position on payment of international debts, tariffs, and the costs of government.

818. Bouças, Valentim F. *Brazil. Economic Data, 1928-1932*. London: International Monetary Congress, 1933.

Reviews Brazil's fiscal position under Vargas's provisional government. Offers data on banking, the public debt, exchange rates, cost of living, and revenues and expenditures of the union and states.

819. Bouças, Valentim F. *Estudos econômicos e financeiros; meio século de trabalho*. 3 vols. Rio de Janeiro: Edições Financeiras, 1953-55.

A collection of studies and commentaries by Vargas's chief fiscal advisor on the economic policies of the 1931-42 period.

820. Campos, Roberto de Oliveira. *Economia, planejamento e nacionalismo*. Rio de Janeiro: APEC Editora, 1963.

Surveys the economic development policies of the 1950's culminating in Kubitschek's program of massive public works.

821. Courtin, René. *Le probleme de la civilisation économique au Brésil*. Paris: Librairie de Medicis, 1941.

Provides an overview of Brazil's economic progress during the 1930's, when the author, an economist, resided in Brazil. Notes the persistence of colonial forms of economic activity and land tenure.

822. Duncan, J.S. *Public and Private Operation of Railways in Brazil*. New York: Columbia University Press, 1932.

Surveys the history of foreign and nationally-owned railroads since 1835.

823. Galey, John H. "The Politics of Development in the Brazilian Amazon, 1940-1950." Diss., Stanford University, 1977.

Examines Amazonian development during the period of cooperation with United States military personnel.

824. Gauthier, Howard L. and Robert K. Semple. "Tendências nas desigualidades regionais da economia brasileira, 1947/1966." *Dados*, 9 (1972), 103-113.

Analyzes regional economic differences after World War II, blaming official policies for increasing the distance between the haves and have-nots.

825. Harvard University. Bureau for Economic Research in Latin America. *Economic Literature for Latin America; a Tentative Bibliography*. 2 vols. Cambridge, Mass.: Harvard University Press, 1935-1936.

A "tentative" bibliography of 12,520 items including books, pamphlets, and periodical articles arranged by country and subdivided by subject. Compiled by Clarence Haring, Miron Burgin, J.F. Normano, and others.

826. Hirschman, Alberto O. *Journeys Toward Progress: Studies of Economic Policy-Making in Latin America*. New York: Twentieth Century Fund, 1963.

Summarizes the history of efforts to combat the Northeast's terrible periodic droughts, following a predictable formula: major efforts are launched with fanfare, but long-term problems are ignored.

827. Kroetz, Lando Rogério. "As estradas de ferro de Santa Catarina (1910-1960)." Master's Thesis, Departamento de História, Universidade Federal do Paraná, 1976.

Credits the emerging railroad network in the state of Santa Catarina with creating the preconditions for economic growth and diversification.

828. Leff, Nathaniel H. *The Brazilian Capital Goods Industry, 1929-1964*. Cambridge: Harvard University Press, 1968.

Finds that the growth of a domestic capital goods industry has reduced Brazil's dependence on foreign trade but has not acted to remove import restraints.

829. Leff, Nathaniel H. *Economic Policy-Making and Development in Brazil, 1947-1964*. New York: John Wiley, 1968.

Studies coffee policy, investment and foreign exchange, attitudes towards direct foreign investment, and export policy.

830. Love, Joseph L. "External Financing and Domestic Politics: the Case of São Paulo, Brazil, 1889-1937." *Latin American Modernization Problems*. Ed. Robert E. Scott. Urbana: University of Illinois Press, 1972, pp. 236-259.

Demonstrates the ease with which the state of São Paulo was able to secure foreign loans under the Republic, given the ability of its political machine to guarantee conditions of stability attractive to foreign investors.

831. Mendes de Oliveira, Geraldo de Beauclair. "A evolução do sistema financeiro na época Vargas." Master's Thesis, Instituto de Ciências Humanas e Filosofia, Universidade Federal Fluminense, 1974.

Shows that Vargas's financial advisors translated their "intense preoccupation" with Brazil's credit system into revisions of the national banking structure.

832. Monteiro, Jorge Viana and Luiz Roberto Azevedo Cunha. "Alguns aspectos da evolução do planejamento econômica no Brasil (1934-1963)." *Pesquisa e Planejamento Econômico*, 4 (1974), 1-24.

Traces the history of federal-level economic planning from the mid-Vargas regime to the end of the Goulart years.

833. Neuhaus, Paulo. *História monetária do Brasil, 1900-45.* Rio de Janeiro: IBMEC, 1975.

Summarizes Brazilian monetary policy through the end of World War II.

834. Niemeyer, Otto E. *Rapport ... au gouvernement fédéral du Brésil.* Paris: Chambre de Commerce Franco-Brésilienne, 1931.

A report produced at the request of the Brazilian government on Brazil's fiscal status, making suggestions about taxation, budgeting, shipping, and the liquidation of state debts.

835. Pinheiro Neto, João. *Salário é causa de inflação?* Rio de Janeiro: Civilização Brasileira, 1963.

Calls for legislative action to curtail inflation. Salaries, the author notes, help finance development; subsidies to large agricultural producers prejudice the majority.

836. Pires do Rio, José. *A moeda brasileira e seu perene caráter fiduciário.* Rio de Janeiro: José Olympio, 1947.

Studies the state of the Brazilian currency through periods of growth and stagnation. Touches also on foreign trade, tariff, and banking policies.

837. Robock, Stefan H. *Brazil's Developing Northeast: A Study of Regional Planning and Foreign Aid.* Washington, D.C.: Brookings Institution, 1963.

Reviews the needs of the drought-stricken region at the height of the Alliance for Progress.

838. Simonsen, Roberto Cochrane. *As crises no Brasil.* São Paulo: Ed. Limitada, 1930.

A brief but influential pamphlet (57p.) written in response to the shock of the 1929 economic crisis worldwide on the national economy. Reviews efforts by earlier Brazilian administrations to deal with economic difficulties.

839. Skidmore, Thomas E. "The Politics of Economic Stabilization in Postwar Latin America." *Authoritarianism and Corporatism in Latin America.* Ed. James Malloy.

Pittsburgh: University of Pittsburgh Press, 1976, pp. 149-190.

Compares Argentina, Brazil, and Mexico for the period between 1945 and 1970.

840. Smith, Peter Seaborn. "Bolivian Oil and Brazilian Economic Nationalism." *Journal of Inter-American Studies and World Affairs*, 13 (April 1971), 166-81.

Argues persuasively that the upsurge of nationalism in the 1950's prevented Brazil from effectively exploiting previously granted petroleum concessions in Bolivia, diverting resources, instead, to the Brazilian state petroleum monopoly, Petrobrás.

841. Smith, Peter Seaborn. *Oil and Politics in Modern Brazil*. Toronto: University of Toronto Press, 1976.

Examines Petrobrás and the popular myths which accompanied its creation that Brazil harbored great petroleum reserves, and that foreigners would exploit them if not restrained. The army, concerned with development, encouraged national control.

842. Wirth, John D. *The Politics of Brazilian Development, 1930-1954*. Stanford: Stanford University Press, 1970.

Analyzes the motives of economic policy-making through three case studies: foreign trade, petroleum, and steel, and Vargas's role in fostering national development.

843. Wythe, George. *Brazil: An Expanding Economy*. 2nd ed. New York: Greenwood Press, 1968.

A detailed and still useful introduction to Brazil's economy and its major strengths and weaknesses. First published in 1949 by the Twentieth Century Fund.

c. Since 1964

844. Bacha, Edmar L. "Recent Brazilian Economic Growth and Some of Its Main Problems." *Textos Para Discussão*, No. 25. Brasília: Departamento de Economia, Universidade de Brasília, April 1975.

Discusses Brazil's debt, income distribution, and economic development.

845. Baer, Werner. "The Brazilian Economic Miracle: The Issues and the Literature." *Bulletin of the Society for Latin American Studies* (Glasgow), 24 (March 1976), 3-23.

Speculates that the drastic curtailment of imports, the unprecedented expansion of the foreign debt, and the world oil crisis may force Brazilian authorities to alter their basic economic policies as the "miracle" fades.

846. Baer, Werner. "The Recent Development of the Brazilian Economy." *Brazilian Economic Studies*, 1 (1975), 7-38.

Summarizes Brazilian economic policies which contributed to the post-1968 boom and reflects on the uniqueness of the flexible "Brazilian model."

847. Baer, Werner, Isaac I. Kerstenstzky and Mário H. Simonsen. "Transportation and Inflation: A Study of Irrational Policy-Making in Brazil." *Economic Development and Cultural Change*, 13 (January 1965), 188-202.

Demonstrates that short-run inflation (sometimes called "corrective inflation") tended to produce deficits in various sectors, such as transportation, thereby reducing the need for government subsidies and helping to reduce budget deficits.

848. Barnet, Richard. "Letter from Rio." *Harper's*, 245 (September 1972), 16-21.

Charges that the regime's programs for economic development come at the cost of social progress and personal freedoms.

849. Barros, José Roberto Mendonça and Douglas H. Graham. "The Brazilian Economic Miracle Revisited: Private and Public Sector Initiative in a Market Economy." *Latin American Research Review*, 13 (Spring 1978), 5-38.

Argues that despite the professed goals of strengthening the private sector, the growth of state enterprises has overshadowed them.

850. "Brazil's 'Economic Miracle'?" *Brazilian Information Bulletin* (Berkeley), 4 (July 1971), 1-8.

Condemns "the rulers of Brazil and their foreign backers" for trying to counter charges of political repression with "a massive campaign about the so-called 'Brazilian Economic Miracle.'"

851. "Brazil's Military-Industrial Complex." *Brazilian Information Bulletin* (Berkeley, California), 9 (January 1973), 1-4.

Shows how the armed forces are constructing an arms-export industry as well as building highways for military use as part of its blueprint to dominate South America.

852. Campbell, Gordon. *Brazil Struggles for Development.* London: Charles Knight, 1973.

Deals with the implications of opening the Amazon region to development, demographic pressures, and other factors related to modernization.

853. Carneiro, Ricardo. "A distribuição de renda na região metropolitana de Recife." *Revista Pernambucana de Desenvolvimento* (Recife), 2 (1975), 195-210.

Analyzes income distribution in the Recife area, finding real income, overall, to have fallen between 1960 and 1970.

854. Cooper, Richard N. "Novel Exchange Rate System Supports the Economic Surge." *The Americana Annual, 1974.* New York, 1974, pp. 55-57.

Praises the regime's innovative "crawling peg" system of variable credit which is credited with reducing the level of inflation.

855. Duarte, João Carlos. *Aspectos da distribuição da renda no Brasil em 1970.* Piricicaba, São Paulo: Imprensa Universitária, 1971.

Shows that the top five percent of income earners improved their position between 1960 and 1970 while the share of the lower eighty percent fell.

856. Ellis, Howard S. "Corrective Inflation in Brazil, 1964-66." *The Economy of Brazil* (item 797), pp. 177-212.

Shows how "corrective inflation" as a conscious government policy was used to reduce budget deficits after the 1964 coup.

857. "End of the Miracle: Geisel and Repression." *Brazilian Information Bulletin* (Berkeley), 14 (Summer 1974), 1-20.

Claims that repression and human rights violations have

increased in direct proportion to national economic advances.

858. Fishlow, Albert. "Brazilian Size Distribution of Income." *American Economic Review*, 62 (May 1972), 391-402.

Summarizes the view which holds that the military's program of guided economic growth has increased the disparity between the affluent and the non-affluent.

859. Fishlow, Albert. "Some Reflections on Post-1954 Brazilian Economic Policy." *Authoritarian Brazil* (item 431), pp. 69-118.

Analyzes the impact of the "economic miracle" on wages. Concludes that the masses have become further impoverished although merely a five-percent income redistribution would bring the poorest up to a minimum standard of living.

860. Fundação Getúlio Vargas. "A economia brasileira em 1977." *Conjuntura Econômica*, 32 (February 1978), 1-340.

A special issue devoted to the current state of the national economy. Offers detailed statistics on prices, revenues, employment, production, imports and exports, and overall conditions.

861. Hoffmann, Helga. "Wage Indexation and Anti-Inflationary Incomes Policy in Brazil." *Bulletin of the Society for Latin American Studies* (Glasgow), 26 (March 1976), 81-100.

Claims that the burden of Brazil's anti-inflation campaign has been unfairly placed on the shoulders of the non-affluent and that wage policies worsen the inequities.

862. Jackman, Richard and Kurt Klapholz. *Taming the Tiger: An Essay in the Economic History and Political Economy of Indexation*. London: International Economics Association, 1975.

Praises Brazil's pioneering role in using flexible mortgage rates and other forms of monetary correction to deal with inflation and to encourage investment.

863. Langoni, Carlos. *Distribução da renda e desenvolvimento econômico no Brasil.* Rio de Janeiro: Ed. Expressão e Cultura, 1973.

Argues that economic growth since 1964 has benefitted the population at large, an interpretation which has "officially" been endorsed by the military government.

864. Levine, Robert M. "Booming Brazil." *The Americana Annual*, 1974, New York, 1974, pp. 46-53; 57.

Examines the paradox of economic growth amidst political repression on the tenth anniversary of the coup.

865. Link, Max. *Stand und Zukenftsperspektiven der Industrialisierung Brasiliens.* Stuttgart: Verlag Paul Haupt, 1972.

Argues that the economic "miracle" is overrated but has forged ahead nonetheless, setting the stage for subsequent economic development from a more mature and stable base.

866. Morley, Samuel A. "Growth and Inequality in Brazil." *Luso-Brazilian Review*, 15 (Winter 1978), 244-271.

Characterizes post-1964 growth as regressive, with the bulk of benefits going to the skilled and well-educated. But new members were able to enter the labor force, and on the whole employment expanded at a rapid pace.

867. Morley, Samuel A. and Gordon W. Smith. "The Effect of Changes in the Distribution of Income on Labor, Foreign Investment, and Growth in Brazil." *Authoritarian Brazil* (item 431), pp. 119-141.

Argues that variations in income distribution have had little effect on the pattern of economic growth. Neither would progressive redistribution necessarily jeopardize Brazil's growth goals or unduly penalize large industries.

868. Ness, Walter L. "Financial Markets Innovation as a Development Strategy: Initial Results from the Brazilian Experience." *Economic Development and Cultural Change*, 22 (April 1974).

Sees such reforms in the financial sector as indexed debt instruments as a major factor behind the post-1964 economic boom.

869. Robock, Stefan H. *Brazil: A Study in Development Progress*. Lexington, Mass.: Lexington Books, 1975.

Examines the performance of the "economic miracle" of 1968-1974 and predicts unparalleled future growth.

870. Simonsen, Mário H. "Inflation and the Money and Capital Markets of Brazil." *The Economy of Brazil*. Ed. Howard S. Ellis. Berkeley: University of California Press, 1969, pp. 136-161.

Describes the mechanisms developed after 1964 to revalue the capital of firms in accordance with price changes.

871. Soares, Glaúcio Ary Dillon. "After the Miracle." *Luso-Brazilian Review*, 15 (Winter 1978), 278-301.

Finds that the military regime has based its legitimacy on high growth and the predicted consequences of such economic progress. Change from within the State depends on the balance of power among the groups that control resources, particularly the central government itself.

872. Superintendência do Desenvolvimento do Nordeste (SUDENE). Departamento de Industrialização. *Incentivos para a indústria e agricultura do Nordeste*. Recife: SUDENE, 1968.

Lists the fiscal and tax incentives given to investors in the Northeast by the federal government.

B. INDUSTRIALIZATION

873. Almeida, Hugo. "A SUDENE e o desenvolvimento industrial do nordeste." *Estudo de problemas brasileiros*. Recife: Universidade Federal de Pernambuco, 1971, pp. 203-213.

States the official view of the tasks of SUDENE, the Northeast's regional development agency, in promoting industrial development through incentive planning.

874. Baer, Werner. *The Development of the Brazilian Steel Industry*. Nashville: Vanderbilt University Press, 1969.

The major study of steel production from the establishment of Volta Redonda in the Paraiba Valley in the 1940's.

875. Baer, Werner. "Evaluating the Impact of Brazil's Industrialization." *Luso-Brazilian Review*, 15 (Winter 1978), 178-190.

Warns that Brazil's petroleum dependency may outweigh the otherwise positive picture of economic growth achieved since 1964. In other areas the government seems to be moving toward reduced "dependency" in awarding contracts and sponsoring joint industrial ventures.

876. Baer, Werner. "Import Substitution and Industrialization in Latin America: Experience and Interpretations." *Latin American Research Review*, 7 (Spring 1972), 95-122.

Describes the policy of Import Substitution Industrialization and reviews the problems which developed as ISI reached maturity. By the 1960's industry had become the dominant sector in Brazil.

877. Baer, Werner. *Industrialization and Economic Development in Brazil*. Homewood, Illinois: Richard D. Irwin, 1965.

Argues that regional and sectoral imbalances have made the management of the Brazilian economy increasingly unwieldy.

878. Barquin, Ramon C. "Computation in Latin America." *Latin American Research Review*, 11 (Spring 1976), 75-102.

Notes that Brazil has one of the best aggregations of computer facilities for industrial and commercial use in Latin America, anchored by a strong IBM affiliate.

879. Bastos, Humberto. *O pensamento industrial no Brasil*. São Paulo: Ed. Martins, 1952.

Credits protectionism and nationalism as the two forces most responsible for Brazil's industrial growth. A good source of comparative statistical data.

880. Bergsman, Joel. *Brazil: Industrialized Trade Policies Since 1940*. London: Cambridge University Press, 1970.

A pioneering analysis on the measurement of industrial protection in two dozen Brazilian industrial sectors.

881. "Bibliografia sôbre indústria brasileira." *Boletim da Biblioteca da Sudene* (Recife), 6 (September 1966), 14-29.

A bibliography on industrial production, growth, and prospects for future expansion.

882. Bougeard, Robert. *A indústria química no Brasil.* 2 vols. São Paulo: Editôra Banas, 1961.

A history of the chemical industry in Brazil.

883. Brandão, Octávio. *Combates e batalhas: memórias.* São Paulo: Ed. Alfa-Omega, 1978.

The autobiography of the leader of the movement to regain national control of the petroleum industry, finally achieved in the 1950's with the creation of Petrobrás.

884. Brandão Lopes, Juárez Rubens. *A crise do Brasil arcáico.* São Paulo: DIFEL, 1967.

Finds that industrialization has acted to erode traditional employer-employee paternalism and created a major new set of frustrations and conflicts.

885. Cardoso, Fernando Henrique. *Empresário industrial e desenvolvimento econômico no Brasil.* São Paulo: DIFEL, 1964.

Challenges earlier assumptions that a dynamic and independent entrepreneurial class has been developing within Brazil's industrial sector.

886. Cardoso, Fernando Henrique. "The Industrial Elite in Latin America." *Underdevelopment and Development: The Third World Today.* Ed. Henry Bernstein. Middlesex, England: Penguin Books, 1973, pp. 191-204.

Argues that the hold of the traditional dominant classes can be broken only through social change and redirected national development.

887. Cardoso, Fernando Henrique. "The Structure and Evolution of Industry in São Paulo: 1930-1960." *Studies in Comparative International Development*, (1965). St. Louis: Washington University Press, 1965, pp. 43-47.

Notes the contribution of foreign-owned industry to São Paulo's economic growth, and comments on such new forms of entrepreneurship as investment holding companies and mutual funds.

888. Cohn, Gabriel. "Problemas da industrialização no século XX." *Brasil em perspectiva* (item 205), pp. 285-318.

Characterizes the economic spurt as having been non-integrated and relatively spontaneous. As a result, no cohesive industrial elite emerged.

889. Collier, David. "Industrial Modernization and Political Change: A Latin American Perspective." *World Politics*, 30 (July 1978), 593-614.

Measures "perception of threat" to the status quo as a sign of political stability. Brazil is found to rank at the intermediate part of the scale; its system has not only survived but is more or less "successful" in its own terms.

890. Dean, Warren. *The Industrialization of São Paulo, 1880-1945.* Austin: University of Texas Press, 1969.

A major study of industrialists and industrialization in São Paulo during its most dramatic period of economic growth.

891. Dickenson, John P. *Brazil: An Industrial Geography.* Boulder, Colorado: Westview Press, 1978.

Measures the impact of the Brazilian government's policy of subsidizing industrial development through tax incentives and ventures designed to encourage investment.

892. Gasparian, Fernando. "A situação da economia brasileira." Paper presented to Columbia Seminar on Brazil. New York, March 1971.

The former director of the Brazilian National Confederation of Industry calls for greater flexibility in trade policy and efforts to develop an independent entrepreneurial elite and adequate research technology.

893. Giroletti, Domingos Antônio. "A industrialização de Juiz de Fora, 1850 a 1930." Master's Thesis. Departamento de Ciência Política, Universidade Federal de Minas Gerais, 1976.

Traces the rise of industrialization in the city of Juiz de Fora and the surrounding *zona da mata* region and acknowledges the importance of the growth of a local market for manufactured products.

894. Goodman, David E. "Industrial Development in the Brazilian Northeast: An Interim Assessment of the Tax Credit Scheme of Article 34/18." *Brazil in the Sixties* (item 423), pp. 231-272.

Discusses the tax-initiatives promulgated by the military government to spur heavy capital investment in infrastructure construction in the Northeast.

895. Goodman, David E., Júlio F. Ferreira Sena and Roberto Cavalcanti de Albuquerque. "Fiscal Incentives for the Industrialization of the Northeast of Brazil, and the Choice of Techniques." *Brazilian Economic Studies*, 1 (1975), 201-226.

Contends that the timid attempts to modify industrial policy associated with incentive for the economic development of the Northeast resulted not from unawareness of the distortions introduced but from reluctance to induce political investors to diversify their investment activity.

896. Gordon, Lincoln and Englebert Grommers. *United States Manufacturing Investment in Brazil.* Cambridge: Harvard University Press, 1962.

Maintains that industrial development was retarded by the historical survivals of plantation society but that recent decades have demonstrated Brazil's vast industrial potential.

897. Ianni, Octávio. "Democracia e progresso." *Revista Civilização Brasileira*, 1 (May 1965), 5-13.

Contends that the pressures contributing to the 1964 military movement may have been fueled by the regime's inability to sustain industrial growth.

898. Kahl, Joseph A. *The Measurement of Modernism, A Study of Values in Brazil and Mexico.* Austin: University of Texas Press, 1968.

Argues that industrialization creates a new value structure, tending to recognize individual achievement. The poor, who are less affected by modernization than the affluent, hold to traditional values.

899. Lima, Heitor Ferreira. *3 industrialistas brasileiros: Mauá, Rui Barbosa, Roberto Simonsen.* São Paulo: Ed. Alfa-Omega, 1976.

Offers biographies of three Brazilian industrialists, including Roberto Simonsen, a main figure in São Paulo's economic life in the 1930's.

900. Loeb, G.F. *Industrialization and Balanced Growth with Special Reference to Brazil.* New York: Gregory Lounz, 1958.

Blames Brazilian fiscal speculation and resultant inflation for producing economic instability.

901. Luz, Nícia Vilela. *A luta pela industrialização no Brasil.* São Paulo: DIFEL, 1964.

Traces the emergence of industrial groups from early twentieth century stirrings of industrialization, mostly in São Paulo.

902. Makler, Harry M. "Labor Problems of Native, Migrant, and Foreign Born Members of the Recife Industrial Elite." *The Journal of Developing Areas*, 9 (October 1974), 27-52.

Finds that non-Pernambucanos who enter the industrial elite tend to be more bureaucratic, more critical of performance, and more career oriented, according to interviews with a stratified sample of 96 heads of Recife manufacturing enterprises.

903. Makler, Harry M. "SUDENE and the Industrial Elite of the Brazilian Northeast: The Bahia and Pernambuco Cases." Paper presented to the Conference on the Brazilian Northeast, Racine, Wisconsin, November 1974.

Posits that the Northeast is falling increasingly dependent upon outside economic influences. SUDENE, the regional development agency, has monopolized public power, enabling, in turn, southern and multi-national corporations to penetrate the Northeast.

904. Peláez, Carlos Manuel. "A balança comercial, a grande depressão e a industrialização brasileira." *Revista Brasileira de Economia* (March 1968), 15-47.

Studies trade and industrialization as influenced by the Depression, examining Celso Furtado's writings on the impact of the government's coffee policies upon economic recovery, and arguing that resources were shifted not from coffee to industry but to other agricultural commodities.

905. Quirino, Tarcizio Rêgo. "The Industrial Job Structure of University-Trained Personnel in São Paulo, Brazil. Diss., University of Wisconsin, 1975.

906. Rady, Donald Edmund. *Volta Redonda: A Steel Mill Comes to a Brazilian Coffee Plantation. Industrial Entrepreneurship in a Developing Economy*. Albuquerque: University of New Mexico Press, 1973.

A descriptive history of Brazil's first large-scale steel center from its inception in the 1940's through the 1960's.

907. Sanders, Thomas G. "Development and Environment: Brazil and the Stockholm Conference." *American Universities Field Staff Reports*, 17 (June 1973).

Summarizes the Brazilian position that industrialization and economic growth must be given priority over any other considerations, even efforts to curtail pollution.

908. Shirley, Robert W. "Legal Institutions and Early Industrial Growth." *Manchester and São Paulo: Problems of Rapid Urban Growth* (item 1010), pp. 157-176.

Finds that São Paulo elites were better equipped to deal with social problems produced by industrialization than their economic liberal counterparts in Manchester.

909. Spiegel, Henry William. *The Brazilian Economy: Chronic Inflation and Sporadic Industrialization*. Philadelphia: Blakiston Press, 1949.

Points to the difficulties of attempting to industrialize a society which remains socio-economically traditional.

910. Stein, Stanley J. *The Brazilian Cotton Manufacture; Textile Enterprise in an Underdeveloped Area, 1850-1950*. Cambridge, Mass.: Harvard University Press, 1957.

An important study of the evolution of textile manufacturing, Brazil's first major industrial activity, touching on social issues, dependency economics, and the role of technology.

911. Tendler, Judith. *Electric Power in Brazil: Entrepreneurship in the Public Sector*. Cambridge, Mass.: Harvard University Press, 1968.

Examines the interplay between foreign-owned power companies (Light, S.A. and others) and evolving nationalistic efforts by the government to regulate them.

912. Tyler, William G. *Manufactured Export Expansion and Industrialization*. Tübingen, West Germany: J.C.B. Mohr, 1976.

Agrees with the revisionists that import substitution did not boost industrialization as much as previously believed.

913. Vieira, Dorival Teixeira. "The Industrialization of Brazil." *Brazil: Portrait of a Half a Continent* (item 1275), pp. 244-264.

Surveys the growth of textile and other manufacturing activity.

914. Winpenny, J.T. *Brazil, Manufactured Exports and Government Policy*. London: Grant & Cutler, 1972.

Surveys industrialization since 1939, commenting on the state of the economy, manufactured exports, government incentives, and post-1964 changes.

C. LABOR

915. Alexander, Robert J. *Labor Relations in Argentina, Brazil and Chile*. New York: McGraw-Hill, 1962.

Offers a general survey of Brazilian trade union organization and history.

916. Berlinck, Manuel T. *Marginalidade social e relações de classes em São Paulo*. Petrópolis: Ed. Vozes, 1975.

Studies relations between rich and poor in the city of São Paulo, examining the impact of capital expansion and urban growth on social marginality.

917. "Bibliografia sôbre mulheres no trabalho." *Boletim da Biblioteca da Fundação Getúlio Vargas* (Rio de Janeiro), 3 (April-September 1961), 141-148.

A bibliography relating to women in the work force.

918. Brandão Lopes, Juárez Rubens. *Sociedade industrial no Brasil*. São Paulo: DIFEL, 1964.

Finds greater labor stability in Minas Gerais than in more heavily industrialized São Paulo owing to a stronger paternalistic tradition among *mineiros*.

919. Corrêa e Silva, Armando. "Estrutura e mobilidade social do prolitariado urbano em São Paulo." *Revista Civilização Brasileira*, 3 (May 1967), 57-90.

Profiles the urban worker in São Paulo and analyzes the restricted process of social mobility. Higher wages allow workers to choose their zone of residence in contrast to unemployed or subsistence urban persons who must settle wherever possible.

920. Davis, Horace B. and M.R. Davis. "Scale of Living of the Working Class in São Paulo, Brazil." *Monthly Labor Review* (January 1937), 245-53.

Examines working-class conditions and finds real wages to be extremely low, even in the industrial sector.

921. Dias, Everardo. *História las lutas sociais no Brasil*. São Paulo: Ed. Edaglit, 1962.

Traces the evolution of socialist ideas in Brazil and their impact on incipient labor organizations, especially in São Paulo.

922. Erickson, Kenneth Paul. *The Brazilian Corporative State and Working Class Politics*. Berkeley: University of California Press, 1977.

Demonstrates that labor unions failed to encourage mass political mobilization but they have consistently prevented that mobilization. Sheds light on the allegation by conservatives in 1964 that President João Goulart and his administration had been mobilizing the masses to establish a left-wing dictatorship.

923. Erickson, Kenneth Paul. "Populism and Political Control of the Working Class in Brazil." *Proceedings of the Pacific Coast on Latin American Studies*, 4 (1975), 117-144.

Contends that the Vargas regime established a classical paternalistic relationship between the government and the urban masses, and that further populist impulses surfaced in 1953 and 1963.

924. Erickson, Kenneth P. and Patrick V. Peppe. "Dependent Capitalist Development, U.S. Foreign Policy, and Repression of the Working Class in Brazil and Chile." *Latin American Perspectives*, 3 (Spring 1976), 19-74.

Compares the treatment of workers under the Brazilian and Chilean military regimes and argues that the international economic system favors suppression of labor militancy.

925. Fausto, Bóris. *Trabalho urbano e conflicto social*. São Paulo: DIFEL, 1976.

A major theoretical contribution to Brazilian labor history emphasizing the role played by immigrant anarcho-syndicalists.

926. Garcia, Ronaldo Coutinho. "Sobreviver para trabalhar: salário e alimentação do trabalhador brasileiro." *Cadernos do Centro de Estudos e Ação Social* (Salvador, Bahia), 48 (1977), 33-40.

Documents the gnawing difficulty faced by lower-class wage earners to provide sustenance for their families.

927. Goodman, David E. "The Brazilian Economic 'Miracle' and Regional Policy: Some Evidence from the Urban Northeast." *Journal of Latin American Studies*, 8 (May 1976), 1-27.

Shows that the urban population of the region has failed to partake of the benefits of recent expansion, especially the "working poor," who comprise two-thirds of the urban labor force.

928. Goodman, David E. "The Brazilian Economic 'Miracle' and Urban Labour Markets: A Regional Perspective." London: University College and the Institute of Latin American Studies, University of London, mimeographed [1975].

Criticizes official overemphasis of efficiency objectives in regional economic policy for the Northeast. As such, the mainstream of the population has failed to benefit from recent economic expansion.

929. Harding, Timothy F. "The Political History of Organized Labor in Brazil." Diss., Stanford University, 1973.

A massive (690 pp.) history emphasizing structural and ideological aspects of labor since 1930.

930. Hardman, Francisco Foot. *O trabalhador urbano no Brasil, 1889-1945: um levantamento bibliográfico.* Campinas: Departamento de Ciências Sociais, Universidade Estadual de Campinas, 1975.

A bibliography on the history of the Brazilian urban working class.

931. Hoffmann, Helga. *Desemprêgo e subemprêgo no Brasil.* São Paulo: Ed. Ática, 1977.

Contends that although a scarcity of labor persisted through the expansion of coffee production, subsequent industrialization and urbanization generated conditions for unemployment, hidden as well as open.

932. Humphrey, John. "The Brazilian State, the Working Class and the Economic Miracle." *Bulletin of the Society for Latin American Studies* (Glasgow), 24 (March 1976), 59-80.

Links the position of the working class in political life to relations with the elite and to economic health.

933. Ianni, Octavio. *Industrialização e desenvolvimento social no Brasil.* Rio de Janeiro: Civilização Brasileira, 1963.

Argues that working-class militancy has been obstructed by the retention of paternalist social relations publicly and privately.

934. Leitão, Evaristo, et al. "O custo da vida do trabalhador rural no Brasil." Brasil. Ministro do Trabalho, Indústria e Comércio. *Boletim* (Rio de Janeiro), 3 (July 1937), 89-103.

An invaluable early analysis of real wages among rural agricultural workers, a group normally bypassed by studies of the labor market prior to the Second World War.

935. Maram, Sheldon L. "Anarcho-Syndicalism in Brazil." *Proceedings of the Pacific Coast Council on Latin American Studies*, 4 (1975), 101-116.

Notes that syndicalists helped construct Brazil's first labor movement but their tactical failings eventually crippled organized labor.

936. Martins, Rodrigues, et al. "Bibliografia sôbre trabalhadores e sindicatos no Brasil." São Paulo: Estudos CEBRAP, No. 7, 1974.

A comprehensive bibliography of works on the history of the Brazilian labor movement.

937. Niemeyer, Waldyr. *Movimento sindicalista no Brasil.* Rio de Janeiro: n.p., 1933.

Collected articles from Rio de Janeiro's *Correio da Manhã* on the evolution of the Brazilian labor movement from 1907 through the early 1930's. Includes information on the syndicates formally recognized by the Vargas administration in 1931--the first so recognized in Brazilian history.

938. O, Manuel de. *100 anos de suor e sangue.* Petropólis: Ed. Vozes, 1971.

Recounts a lifetime of worker struggles of a labor militant who died a few days short of his hundredth birthday, and who worked as a mechanic until his early nineties. Offers valuable insights into early efforts at labor organization, especially along the route of the hated, English-owned Great Western Railway of Brazil.

939. Pastore, José and Archibald Haller. "The Socioeconomic Status of the Brazilian Labor Force." *Luso-Brazilian Review*, 14 (Summer 1977), 1-28.

Shows that vertical mobility remains extremely difficult for Brazilians of the lower class, despite economic advances after 1964: "Brazil is doing well but the people are doing badly."

940. Poblete-Troncoso, Moisés. "Recent Advances in Labour Legislation in Latin America (1928-1934)." *International Labor Review* (Geneva), 30 (1934), 58-80.

Includes a discussion of the first efforts of the Vargas administration to normalize labor organization and create an apparatus for government supervision.

941. Rodrigues, Araky Martins. *Operário, operária.* São Paulo: Ed. Símbolo, 1978.

Explores the behavior of *paulista* industrial workers, their aspirations and perceptions of reality. Finds that several factors inhibit potential rebelliousness.

942. Rodrigues, Leôncio Martins. *Industrialização e atitudes operárias*. São Paulo: Ed. Brasiliense, 1970.

A treatise on industrialization and working-class attitudes and values, based on the model developed by the French sociologist Alain Touraine.

943. Sampaio, Yoni. "Sharecropping Agriculture in Northeast Brazil: A Transition Phase." Paper presented to the Conference on the Brazilian Northeast, Racine, Wisconsin, November 1974.

Contends that the rural labor force is becoming increasingly proletarianized.

944. Senne, José Júlio de Almeida. "Schooling, Job Experience and Earnings in Brazil." Diss., The Johns Hopkins University, 1975.

945. Soares Leite, José Sérgio. *O vapor do diabo*. Rio de Janeiro: Paz e Terra, 1977.

Surveys the values and attitudes of sugar refining workers, finding two distinct types: "professionals" (line workers) and "artists" (maintenance and repairmen).

946. Sobrinho, Barbosa Lima. "Ação sindical e desenvolvimento econômico." *Encontros com a Civilização Brasileira*. Rio de Janeiro: Civilização Brasileira, 1978, pp. 65-75.

Argues that lasting economic development depends upon the creation of a strong, autonomous sector of organized labor.

947. Springer, Frank. *A Brazilian Factory Study, 1966*. Cuernavaca: CIDOC, 1969.

Studies São Paulo worker attributes. Attributes lack of labor militancy to fear of unemployment in an oversaturated labor market.

948. Telles, Jover. *O movimento sindical no Brasil*. Rio de Janeiro: Ed. Vitória, 1962.

Reviews the history of the Brazilian labor movement from the perspective of the Left. Emphasizes advances made during the period between 1946 and 1962.

949. Vianna, Luiz Werneck. "Estudos sobre sindicalismo e movimento operário: resenha de algumas tendências." *Dados*, 17 (1978), 9-24.

Considers the historiography of labor organization in Brazil to reflect a tendency to view its subject in the broader context of Brazilian social change.

950. Vianna, Luiz Werneck. *Liberalismo e sindicato no Brasil*. Rio de Janeiro: Paz e Terra, 1976.

Argues that Brazil had achieved "political liberalism and labor corporatism" by the end of the Estado Nôvo in 1945.

951. Weffort, Francisco C. "Democracia e movimento operário." *Revista de Cultura Contemporânea*, 1 (July 1978), 7-14.

Laments the fact that during the entire period between 1935 and 1951 organized labor enjoyed relative freedom of action for one and a half years (during 1945 and 1946).

952. Weffort, Francisco C. *Participação e conflito industrial: Contagem e Osasco, 1968*. São Paulo: CEBRAP, 1972.

Analyzes two major strikes, in Minas Gerais and São Paulo, suppressed by force before they could spread.

953. Weffort, Francisco C. "Sindicatos e política." Faculty Thesis, Universidade de São Paulo, 1974.

Shows the pre-1964 populist coalition was based on a pro-capitalist alliance between the working class, the State, and the national bourgeoisie.

954. Wyer, J. "Economic Organization and Ideology of Rural Laborers in Brazil." Diss., London School of Economics, University of London, 1978.

V.
Urban Brazil

A. URBANIZATION AND PLANNING

955. Abreu, Sílvio F. *O Distrito Federal e seus recursos naturais*. Rio de Janeiro: Conselho Federal de Geografia, 1957.

Offers a physical and historical survey of the evolution of the city of Rio de Janeiro.

956. Adelman, Jeffry. "Urban Planning and Reality in Republican Brazil: Belo Horizonte, 1890-1930." Diss., Indiana University, 1974.

Analyzes the growth of the planned capital city of Minas Gerais during the Old Republic.

957. Amado, Jorge. *Bahia de Todos os Santos; guia das ruas e dos mistérios da cidade do Salvador*. São Paulo: Ed. Martins, 1945.

A sentimental guide to the city of Salvador, the novelist's home.

958. Arblaster, D. "Spatial Aspects of Urban Development in Pernambuco, Brazil." Diss., University of Leicester, 1978.

959. Arnau, Frank. *Brasília: Phantasie und Wirklichkeit*. Munich: Prestel-Verlag, 1960.

Recalls the history of the idea to create Brasília, stressing Getúlio Vargas's role in the mid-1930's and the inclusion of plans in the 1934 Constitution to transfer the capital to the interior.

960. Barbosa, Raul de Sá. "Brasília, evolução." *Módulo*, 18 (June 1960), 28-42.

A bi-lingual (Portuguese and English) analysis of the new city, tracing the history of plans for an inland capital back to 1789, calling it "not an improvisation but a maturation."

961. Bazzanella, Waldemiro. *Problemas de urbanização na America Latina.* Rio de Janeiro: CLAPCS, 1960.

A 121-page annotated bibliography of 547 entries on urban development in Brazil.

962. Cole, J.P. *Latin America: An Economic and Social Geography.* New York: Plenum Press, 1965.

Finds Brazil to differ from its Latin American neighbors because its population lives on a continuous belt stretching across its coastline and because of its sub-continental size.

963. Cooper, Donald. "Oswaldo Cruz and the Impact of Yellow Fever on Brazilian History." *The Bulletin of the Tulane University Medical Faculty*, 26 (February 1967), 49-52.

Narrates the history of Cruz's campaign to eradicate yellow fever and to establish a systematic campaign to introduce sanitary technology to Brazilian cities.

964. Cornelius, Wayne A. and Robert V. Kemper, eds. *Metropolitan Latin America: The Challenge and the Response.* Beverly Hills: Sage Publications, 1978.

Surveys the critical problems faced by modern Latin American cities, including Rio de Janeiro.

965. Cowell, Bainbridge, Jr. "Defining 'Urban' and 'Rural' in Brazil." *Latin American Research Review*, 14 (1979), 193-200.

A useful historiographical article lamenting that intellectuals link cities to "modern" Brazil, while rural society represents the past and its backwardness.

966. Doxiadis Associates. *Guanabara--A Plan for Urban Development.* Rio de Janeiro: Ed. CEDUG, 1965.

Outlines a master plan for the urban redevelopment of the city of Rio de Janeiro, based on new arterial highways and tunnels to improve intra-city mobility.

967. Duarte, Aluízio C., comp. *A área central da cidade do Rio de Janeiro.* Rio de Janeiro: Instituto Brasileiro de Geografia e Estatística, 1967.

Shows that "downtown" Rio de Janeiro monopolizes all of the administrative, cultural, commercial, and managerial functions of the city and its metropolitan area.

968. Eckardt, Wolf von. "Brasília: Symbol in the Mud." *American Institute of Architects Journal*, 36 (November 1960), 126-33.

Reviews the hopes and goals for Brasília's role as Brazil's new national center.

969. Epstein, David G. *Brasília, Plan and Reality: A Study of Planned and Spontaneous Urban Development*. Berkeley: University of California Press, 1973.

Examines Brasília not only from the planning standpoint but in terms of the lives of its inhabitants, including the slum dwellers of the jerry-built satellite cities ringing the federal capital.

970. Evenson, Norma. *Two Brazilian Capitals: Architecture and Urbanism in Rio de Janeiro and Brasília*. New Haven: Yale University Press, 1973.

Contrasts the modern evolution of the old capital, Rio de Janeiro, with the new capital, Brasília, in terms of urban design, architecture, and symbolism.

971. Faissol, Speridião. "Typology of Cities and Regionalization of Economic Development." Paper presented to the International Geographic Union, London, July 1971.

Studies urban spatial patterns in Rio de Janeiro, Recife, Pôrto Alegre, and Salvador. Suggests that geographers use clustering techniques to better analyze regional connections.

972. Foland, Frances M. "Recife, False Gem of the Northeast." *Institute of Current World Affairs* (New York), Publication FMF-9 [November 1967].

Describes the impoverished northeastern part of Recife and its human burden of migrants and poor.

973. France, Centre d'Études de Géographie Tropicale. *La Regionalisation de l'espace au Brésil*. Paris: CEGT, 1972.

Articles by French and Brazilian regional planners and historians, including Pedro Geiger, Pierre Monbeig, and Milton Santos, touching on economic development as well as regionalism and demographic expansion.

974. Freyre, Gilberto. *Brasis, Brasil, Brasília*. Lisbon: Edição Livros do Brasil, 1960.

Attacks Brasília's design as sterile and insufficiently

rooted in national cultural themes. Echoes the complaints of many observers that the city was built by architects, not by planners.

975. Freyre, Gilberto. "A Brazilian's Critique of Brasília." *The Reporter*, 22 (March 31, 1960), 31-32.

Calls Brasília cramped, conventional, and old-fashioned in its use of spaces designed presumably for a "caste of high-priests, all-powerful and omniscient."

976. Freyre, Gilberto. *Guia prático, histórico e sentimental da cidade do Recife*. Recife: Typ. 'The Propagandist,' 1934; rpt. Rio de Janeiro: José Olympio, 1942.

Offers a loving guide to Freyre's birthplace.

977. Geiger, Pedro Pinchas. *Evolução da rede urbana brasileira*. Rio de Janeiro: Ministério da Educação e Cultura, 1963.

Examines Brazilian urbanization and the formation of urban demographic networks as a by-product of modernization.

977a. *Guia Quatro Rodas do Brasil: 1978*. São Paulo: Ed. Abril, 1978.

A 543-page road guide to Brazilian cities and major towns, including detailed street maps and information about population and local economic activity.

978. Holford, William. "Brasília: A New Capital City for Brazil." *Architectural Review*, 122 (December 1957), 394-402.

Describes the architects' competition for the design of Brasília, and the final selection from among the twenty-six entries submitted.

979. Katzman, Martin T. *Cities and Frontiers in Brazil: Regional Dimensions of Economic Development*. Cambridge, Mass.: Harvard University Press, 1977.

Interprets differing themes dealing with demographic expansion and urban growth over time. A valuable contribution which cuts across geography, economics, and social issues.

980. Kent, Hollister. "Vera Cruz: Brazil's New Federal Capital." Diss., Cornell University, 1956.

Describes the early stages of planning of Brasília.

981. Le Corbusier. *Précisions sur un état présent de l'architecture et de l'urbanisme*. Paris: Editions Crès et Cie, 1930.

Describes the author's first visit to Rio de Janeiro to propose architectural innovations for its redesign.

982. Leeds, Anthony. *The Anthropology of Cities: Some Methodological Issues*. Austin: University of Texas, Institute of Latin American Studies, 1968.

Compares Rio de Janeiro and São Paulo as case studies in dealing with the multiple variables in the city system. Notes the differences in intensity between the cities and their highly differentiated roles.

983. Lima Cavalcanti, Arthur. "Política urbana e habitacional: reforma urbana." *Revista Civilização Brasileira*, 1 (May 1965), 338-360.

A blueprint for urban reform, part of a decree to have been signed into law by President Goulart on April 2, 1964. The plan calls for extensive federal investment in urban housing construction.

984. Ludwig, Armin K. "The Kubitchek Years, 1956-61: A Massive Undertaking in a Big Rush." *Cultural Change in Brazil*. Muncie, Indiana: Ball State University, 1969, pp. 101-113.

A geographer analyzes Brasília's planning and construction from the point of view of its location, problems, and promise.

985. Ludwig, Armin K. "The Planning and Creation of Brasília: Toward a New and Unique Regional Environment?" *New Perspectives of Brazil* (item 385), pp. 179-204.

Reviews Brasília's early impact and its failings.

986. Machado, Roberto. *Apontamentos para uma bibliografia carioca*. Rio de Janeiro: Centro Carioca, 1943.

A 112-page bibliography of works on the city of Rio de Janeiro.

987. Magalhães, Aloisio and Eugene Feldman. *Doorway to Brasília*. Philadelphia: Falcon Press, 1959.

Includes an English translation of the Costa Report on the design of Brasília, considered by planners a model although it made no social projections and made no suggestions for regional development.

988. Mandell, Paul I. "The Rise and Decline of Geography in Brazilian Development Planning: Some Lessons to Be Learned." *Luso-Brazilian Review*, 10 (Winter 1973), 187-196.

Laments the substitution of the geographer by the economist in planning circles favored by the Brazilian government.

989. Merrick, Thomas W. and Douglas H. Graham. *Population and Economic Development in Brazil: 1800 to the Present*. Baltimore: The John Hopkins University Press, 1979.

Examines in depth the demographic history of urban Brazil, treating such themes as population trends, the impact of immigration, the growth of the labor force, and urban poverty. A major study.

990. "Metropolis Made to Order." *National Geographic Magazine*, 117 (May, 1960), 704-24.

The standard *National Geographic* treatment with exquisite photographs of Brasília's stark architecture and landscape.

991. Morse, Richard M. "A Framework for Latin American Urban History." *Urbanization in Latin America: Approaches and Issues*. Ed. Jorge E. Hardoy. Garden City, N.Y.: Anchor/Doubleday, 1975, pp. 57-108.

Argues that industrialism reworks rather than obliterates pre-existing urban life and institutions.

992. Morse, Richard M. *From Community to Metropolis: A Biography of São Paulo, Brazil*. rev. ed. New York: Octagon Books, 1974.

A major study of the urban growth of São Paulo first published in 1958, reprinted with an updated final chapter and discussion of the literature.

993. Morse, Richard M. "A Prolegomenon to Latin American Urban History." *Hispanic American Historical Review*, 52 (August 1972), 359-394.

Explores the cultural roots of the prevalent attitude among Latin American intellectuals that cities symbolize prestige, authority, and wealth despite the fact that population and productivity have traditionally been located in the countryside.

994. Morse, Richard M. "Trends and Issues in Latin American Urban Research, 1965-1970." *Latin American Research Review*, Part I: 6 (Spring 1971), 3-52; Part II: 6 (Summer 1971), 19-76.

Urges that scholars not permit themselves to be limited by traditional methodological boundaries in reconstructing and explaining the historic course and regional patterns of urbanization.

995. Morse, Richard M., et al., eds. *The Urban Development of Latin America, 1750-1920*. Stanford: Institute of Latin American Studies, 1973.

A provocative and wide-ranging overview of population data on the large cities of eight Latin American nations, including Brazil, from a 1970 Stanford University seminar.

996. Natal e Silva, Colemar. "A capital do Brasil e o planalto central." *Cultura Política*, 2 (July 1942), 30-40.

Advocates that the national capital be moved to the central plateau (the site of present-day Brasília) in order to achieve greater socioeconomic integration.

997. Niemeyer, Oscar. *Minha experiência em Brasília*. Rio de Janeiro: Ed. Vitória, 1961.

Autobiographical reminiscences by one of the planners of Brasília.

998. Oliven, R. "Urbanisation and Social Change in Brazil: A Case Study of Porto Alegre." Diss., University of London, 1978.

999. "Opiniões sobre Brasília." *Habitat*, 58 (January-February 1960).

An entire issue devoted to the newly opened capital city, calling it a bold gesture, but at the same time Kafkaesque, almost sterile and inhumane.

1000. Pyle, Gerald F. "Approaches to Understanding the Urban Roots of Brazil." *Geographic Research on Latin America*. Ed. Barry Lentrek. Muncie, Indiana: Ball State University Press, 1971, pp. 378-396.

Analyzes the spatial organization of Brazilian urban society, seeking to identify those aspects unique to urban growth in Brazilian and Luso-Brazilian history.

1001. Richardson, Ivan L. *Urban Government for Rio de Janeiro*. New York: Praeger, 1973.

Describes Rio's government, finances, and political organization. One in a series of studies of urban administration around the world.

1002. Rodell, Michael Joseph. "City Growth and Regional Development: Salvador and Bahia in Northeastern Brazil, 1940 to 1970." Diss., University of California, Los Angeles, 1975.

Considers the impressive physical growth of Salvador as a by-product of industrialization and planned regional development.

1003. Sable, Martin H. *Latin American Urbanization: A Guide to the Literature, Organizations and Personnel*. Metuchen, N.J.: Scarecrow Press, 1971.

Lists nearly seven thousand entries on the literature of urbanization.

1004. Silva, Janice Theodora da. *Raizes da ideologia de planejamento: Nordeste, 1889-1930*. São Paulo: Ed. Ciências Humanas, 1978.

Traces regional planning policy in the Northeastern drought region from the beginning of the Republic to federal recognition of the problem by 1930.

1005. Singer, Paul I. *Desenvolvimento econômico e evolução urbana*. São Paulo: Editôra da Universidade, 1968.

Compares urban-economic development in five Brazilian cities: Blumenau, Santa Catarina, Pôrto Alegre, Recife, Belo Horizonte, and São Paulo. Links urbanization to the expansion of foreign trade. The cities themselves become internal markets to support expanded commerce and business activity.

1006. Staubli, Willy. *Brasília*. New York: Universe Books, 1965.

Illustrates the unique aspects of Brasília from the perspective of city planning and architecture.

1007. Tolosa, Hamilton C. "Macroeconomics of Brazilian Urbanization." *Brazilian Economic Studies*, 1 (1975), 227-274.

Notes a close association between the cost-differential

and the semiprivate structure of the Brazilian urban system.

1008. Vaitsman, Maurício. *Quanto custou Brasília.* Rio de Janeiro: Ed. Pôsto de Serviço, 1968.

One of Brasília's technical planners analyzes the costs of building the new capital.

1009. Wilhelm, Jorge. *São Paulo Metropole 65.* São Paulo: DIFEL, 1965.

Proposes urban renewal for São Paulo based on the premise that the "radiocentric" model of urban growth is inadequate. The author prefers a model which views São Paulo as one among a number of commercially linked urban nuclei.

1010. Wirth, John D. and Robert L. Jones, eds. *Manchester and São Paulo: Problems of Rapid Urban Growth.* Stanford: Stanford University Press, 1978.

Compares the two cities as examples of rapid urbanization, industrialization, and economic diversification. Contains items 908, 1033, 1559, and 1697.

B. DEMOGRAPHY AND NATIONAL INTEGRATION

1011. Almeida, Vicente Unzer de and Otávio Teixeira Mendes Sobrinho. *Migração rural-urbana: aspectos da convergência de população do interior e outras localidades para a capital do Estado de São Paulo.* São Paulo: Universidade de São Paulo, 1951.

Concludes that the large metropolis receives disproportionately more rural migrants than secondary cities.

1012. Andrade, Eduardo Lage de. *Sertões do noroeste.* São Paulo: n.p., 1945.

Explores the penetration of the Northwest by railroad and river travel. Documents the brutality of the incursions against the land and people of the region.

1013. Avellar, Sônia Maria de. "Desenvolvimento e tensões sócio-politícas." Masters thesis, Universidade Federal de Minas Gerais, 1971.

Examines internal migration and population mobility in terms of the stress produced on migrants. Emphasizes the psychological isolation of regions beyond the Center-South.

1014. Ávila, Fernando Bastos de. *Economic Aspects of Immigration: The Brazilian Immigration Problem.* The Hague: Martinus Nijhoff, 1954.

The author, a priest, advocates accelerated immigration from Europe despite Brazil's problems at home with its burgeoning birthrate.

1015. Balán, Jorge. *Centro e períferia no desenvolvimento brasileiro. Textos de Antônio Octávio Cintra, Simon Schwartzman, Jorge Balán, Fábio Wanderley Reis, e Edmar Lisbôa Bacha.* São Paulo: Universidade de São Paulo, 1974.

Papers from a 1972 Belo Horizonte conference on center/periphery relations, regionalism, internal migration, political development, and industrial growth.

1016. Balán, Jorge. "Migrações e desenvolvimento capitalista no Brasil." *Estudos CEBRAP* (São Paulo), 5 (July-September 1973), 7-79.

Reviews the literature on immigration to Brazil, comparing Brazil's experience with Mexico and Argentina. Discusses the Northeast's failure to attract European settlers in contrast with the successful experience of the Center-South and South.

1017. Blakemore, Harold and Clifford T. Smith, eds. *Latin America: Geographical Perspectives.* London: Methuen, 1971.

Nine country studies. The Brazilian section is by J.H. Galloway, who offers a historical synthesis of demographic expansion and the rise of urban life.

1018. Borges, T. Pompeu Accioly. *Migracões internas no Brasil.* Rio de Janeiro: Comissão Nacional de Polîtica Agrária, 1955.

A short (42 pp.) but important study of routes of population migration within Brazil.

1019. Cândido, Antônio. "Literature and the Rise of Brazilian National Self-Identity." *Luso-Brazilian Review*, 5 (June 1968), 27-44.

Cites Sérgio Buarque de Holanda and others to show the remarkable imagery which accompanied Brazil's initial colonization and the rise of national consciousness.

1020. Carneiro, José Fernando. *Imigração e colonização no Brasil.* Rio de Janeiro: Faculdade Nacional de Filosofia, 1950.

Divides the history of immigration to Brazil into three periods: 1808-1886; 1887-1930; and 1930-1949. Surveys the impact of agricultural colonization by immigrants, especially in Santa Catarina and Rio Grande do Sul.

1021. Costa Godolphim, Waldir da. "Amazônia e seus problemas." *Brasil: realidade e desenvolvimento.* São Paulo: Brasiliana, 1972, pp. 133-149.

Reveals that government officials planned to use selected cities as "growth poles" to support migrant population which would result from Transamazonian settlement.

1022. Diffie, Bailey W. "Some Foreign Influences in Contemporary Brazilian Politics." *Hispanic American Historical Review*, 20 (1940), 402-429.

Discusses German, Japanese, and Italian immigration to Brazil in the context of the coming international conflict and the rise of fascist influence in Brazil.

1023. Graham, Douglas H. "Divergent and Convergent Regional Economic Growth and Internal Migration in Brazil, 1940-1960." *Economic Development and Cultural Change*, 18 (April 1970), 362-382.

Shows that internal migration exacerbated the widening divergence between the richer and poorer states after 1940, and was accelerated by the increased pace of industrialization in the south and by improved transportation facilities.

1024. Graham, Douglas H. "Migração estrangeira e a questão da oferta de mão-de-obra no crescimento econômico brasileiro, 1880-1930." *Estudos Econômicos*, 3 (April 1973), 7-64.

Contrasts the experience of immigration of Argentina, Brazil and the United States and links migratory patterns to international economic health. Brazil received greater numbers of immigrants when migration to the other two countries was reduced.

1025. Graham, Douglas H. and Sérgio Buarque de Holanda Filho. "Interregional and Urban Migration and Economic Growth in Brazil." Paper presented to the Symposium on Internal Migration, Belo Horizonte, University of Minas Gerais, April 1972.

Reveals that internal migration accounted for well over half of the population increase in Brazil's major cities during the 1960's.

1026. Holloway, Thomas H. "Creating the Reserve Army? The Immigration Program of São Paulo, 1886-1930." *International Migration Review*, 12 (Summer 1978), 187-209.

Shows how the onset of the depression suffocated the State of São Paulo's efforts to recruit, transport, and distribute immigrant manpower.

1027. Levine, Robert M. "Some Views on Race and Immigration During the Old Republic." *The Americas*, 27 (April 1971), 373-80.

Shows that planters strongly preferred Caucasian immigration and were especially reluctant to admit agricultural workers of African and Japanese origin.

1028. Lowrie, Samuel H. *Imigração e crescimento da população no estado de São Paulo*. São Paulo: n.p., 1938.

Compares immigration to Brazil and the United States and offers data on social mobility, intermarriage, and life expectancy for immigrant groups.

1029. Luizetto, Flávio Venâncio. "Os constituentes em face da imigração (estudo sôbre o preconceito e a discriminação racial e etnica na Constitutição de 1934)." Master's Thesis, University of São Paulo, 1975.

Finds legislators at the quasi-populist 1933-34 Constituent Assembly to have been hostile to immigration of non-whites.

1030. Marcílio, Maria Luiza, ed. *Demografia histórica: orientações técnicas e metodológicas*. São Paulo: Liv. Pioneira, 1977.

A collection of articles suggesting new approaches to urban history through studies of demographic change, mortality, and other indices.

1031. Mata, M. da, et al. *Migrações internas no Brasil*. Rio de Janeiro: I.P.E.A., 1973.

Identifies adverse land tenure conditions, poverty, and rural-urban income differentials as the causes for the rural exodus to industrialized urban centers, mostly in the Center-South.

1032. Monbeig, Pierre. *Pionniers et planteurs de São Paulo*. Paris: A. Colin, 1952.

Examines the conditions which accompanied the expansion of São Paulo's agricultural frontier from 1900 to the 1940's.

1033. Morse, Richard M. "Manchester Economics and Paulista Sociology." *Manchester and São Paulo: Problems of Rapid Urban Growth* (item 1010), pp. 7-34.

Suggests that the *paulistas*, on the periphery of the Atlantic world, had to create a new concept of nationality out of an agricultural tradition.

1034. Mortara, Giorgio. *Os estudos demográficos no Brasil*. Rio de Janeiro: Biblioteca Nacional, 1959.

Reviews the history of Brazilian censuses, and the literature on Brazil's population and criticizes each from the standpoint of modern demographic methodology.

1035. Rosenbaum, H. Jon and William G. Tyler. "Policymaking for the Brazilian Amazon." *Journal of Inter-American Studies and World Affairs*, 13 (July-October 1971), 416-33.

Argues that if the Amazon is to be developed as a solution to old problems of national integration, new ones may emerge, such as the need for political realignment and redefined principles by which to distribute social and political resources.

1036. São Paulo. Diretoria Administrativa de Hospedaria dos Imigrantes. *Registro de imigrantes*. 65 vols. Manuscript.

The complete record of immigration to São Paulo from 1860, averaging 600 pages per volume, with information on each immigrant and his or her age, nationality and place of former residence. Located in São Paulo.

1037. Saunders, John V.D. *Differential Fertility in Brazil*. Gainesville: University of Florida Press, 1958.

Notes widening differences in regional levels of fertility in inverse relation to affluence.

1038. Smith, Anthony. *Mato Grosso, Last Virgin Land.* New York: Joseph, 1972.

Describes the Royal Geographic Society's expedition to Central Brazil in 1967-69. The author is a zoologist aware of the destruction which "civilization" has brought.

1039. Smith, Nigel. "Transamazon Highway: A Cultural-Ecological Analysis of Colonization in the Humid Tropics." Diss., University of California, Berkeley, 1976.

Discusses the human and ecological problems caused by the abrupt opening of the Amazon basin to settlers, prospectors, and developers in the early 1970's.

1040. Stepan, Alfred C. "The Continuing Problem of Brazilian Integration." *Latin American History; Select Problems.* Ed. Frederick B. Pike. New York: Harcourt, Brace and World, 1969, pp. 260-297.

A collection of readings which deal, for the republican period, with the creation of SUDENE, the Northeast's regional development agency, the Estado Nôvo, and the structural origins of the 1964 crisis.

1041. Tenório, Oscar. *Imigração.* Rio de Janeiro: Ed. Pimenta de Mello, 1936.

Summarizes the debate at the 1933-34 constituent assembly which led to quota restrictions on immigration, and points out the likely impact on the labor market, especially in the agricultural sector.

1042. "The Transamazon Highway." *Brazilian Information Bulletin* (Berkeley), 1 (February 1971), 4-5.

Charges that the purpose of constructing the highway is to open the Amazon for foreign investors, attracted by Rondônia's tin, Pará's iron, and Amazonian rubber.

1043. Velloso, João Paulo dos Reis. "A estratégia de desenvolvimento e o programa de integração nacional." *Revista do Serviço Público*, 105 (May-August 1970), 15-30.

Discusses the underpopulated Amazon region as a potential site for the resettlement of impoverished surplus population from the Northeast.

1044. Vidal, Adhemar. "Os movimentos nordestinas de emigração." *Cultura Política*, 3 (January 1943), 51-56.

An early study tracing the exit routes of migrants from the rural Northeast to the coast and Center-South.

1045. Wagley, Charles, ed. *Man in the Amazon*. Gainesville: University of Florida Press, 1974.

Fifteen essays by scholars who, for the most part, are optimistic about prospects for the future. One author, Betty Meggers, calls current Amazonian development "maladaptive"; Wagley, the dean of anthropologists specializing in Brazil, advocates caution and asks that the lessons of the past be considered with care.

1046. Willems, Emílio. "Immigrants and the Assimilation in Brazil." *Brazil: Portrait of Half a Continent* (item 1275), pp. 209-266.

Examines patterns of immigrant acculturation in the south of Brazil.

1047. Willems, Emílio. "Some Aspects of Culture Conflict and Acculturation in Southern Rural Brazil." *Rural Sociology*, 7 (1942), 375-385.

An essay on the adaptation of European immigrants, mostly Italians and Germans.

C. URBAN LIFE

1048. Almeida, Suely Kofes de. "Entre nós, os pobres, eles os negros." Master's Thesis, Departamento de Ciências Sociais, Universidade Estadual de Campinas, 1976.

A case study of a lower-class housing tract constructed by the national housing agency. Finds that racial differences are accentuated by the community's structure.

1049. Amman, Safira Bezerra. "Participação social: o Distrito Federal, un estudo de caso." Master's Thesis, Universidade de Brasília, 1976.

Finds barriers to social interaction and popular participation in meaningful social exchange posed by structural conditions of *carioca* urban life.

1050. Azevedo, Aloísio de. *A Brazilian Tenement*. Tr. Harry Brown. New York: Robert McBride, 1926.

Translation of the novel *O Cortiço*, a poignant story of slum life in the city of São Paulo.

1051. Bakota, Carlos S. "Crisis and the Middle Classes: The Ascendency of Brazilian Nationalism." Diss., U.C.L.A., 1973.

An important study of the emerging middle class, focusing on São Paulo in the period preceding the explosion of *tenente* nationalism.

1052. Bilac, Elisabete Dória. *Famílias de trabalhadores; estratégias de sobrevivência*. São Paulo: Ed. Símbolo, 1978.

Analyzes the struggle of working class families in São Paulo to survive economically by reorganizing patterns of family life.

1053. Brasil. Instituto Brasileiro de Geografia e Estatística. *Tábuas de mortalidade e de sobrevivência para a capital federal e a capital de São Paulo, annos 1920-21 e 1939-40*. Rio de Janeiro: Instituto Brasileiro de Geografia e Estatistíca.

Provides life expectancy tables for the years 0-5 and decennial years for inhabitants of the cities of Rio de Janeiro and São Paulo for 1920-21 and 1939-40.

1054. Cardoso, Ruth. "Sociedade e poder: representações dos favelados de São Paulo." *Ensaios de Opinião*, 6 (1978), n.p.

Suggests that relations between different social classes are subject to manipulation, and change according to context.

1055. Comissao Censitária dos Mucambos do Recife. *Observações estatísticas sôbre os mucambos do Recife*. Recife: Imprensa Oficial, 1939.

Relates in detail the miserable conditions under which the inhabitants of Recife's waterfront slums, the *mucambos*, live. This work, published by the State of Pernambuco, provides an exception to the rule that governments during the 1930's usually ignored deep-seated social problems.

1056. Conniff, Michael L. "Voluntary Associations in Rio, 1870-1945: A New Approach to Urban Social Dynamics." *Journal of Inter-American Studies and World Affairs*, 17 (February 1975), 64-81.

Seeks insight into the study of Brazilian society through the study of voluntary associations: clubs, social organizations, professional associations, and related groups.

1057. Cony, Carlos, Heitor, ed. *Assim marcha a família*. Rio de Janeiro: Civilização Brasileira, 1965.

Presents a startling and unprecedented collection of articles dealing with the underside of Brazilian urban life, including prostitution, crime, sexual deviance, and poverty.

1058. Cordeiro, Maria Luisa. *Quando morre o outono*. Pôrto Alegre: Ed. Globo, 1949.

A novel describing middle class life in the city of São Paulo.

1059. Coutinho, Galeão. *Confidencias de Dona Marcolina*. São Paulo: Ed. Saraiva, 1949.

A chatty novel about urban *paulista* life in the 1940's.

1060. Damata, Gasparino. *Antologia da Lapa*. 2nd ed. Rio de Janeiro: Ed. Codecri, 1978.

Describes the bohemian life which characterized Rio's Lapa district before it deteriorated into a center for prostitution and transvestism.

1061. Dupré, Sra. Leandro Maria José. *Dona Lola*. São Paulo: Ed. Brasiliense, 1949.

A novel about urban middle-class life during the Second World War.

1062. Fontes, Armando. *Os corumbas*. 6th ed. Rio de Janeiro: José Olympio, 1946.

A novel of northeastern urban life, first published in 1933.

1063. Freyre, Gilberto. *Mucambos do nordeste*. Rio de Janeiro: M.E.C., 1937.

Describes *mucambo* (waterside slums) life on the coast of the Northeast's Zona da Mata. Freyre later came to defend the *mucambo* as a unique adaptation to the tropical environment.

1064. Gibson, Hugh. *Rio*. Garden City, N.Y.: Doubleday, 1937.

Provides an impressionistic picture of Rio de Janeiro in the 1930's. The author was United States Ambassador to Brazil.

1065. Gilliam, Angela M. "Language Attitudes, Ethnicity and Class in São Paulo and Salvador da Bahia." Diss., Union Graduate School, Ohio, 1975.

Discusses the social dimension of Afro-Brazilian language and the speech patterns of the lower class.

1066. Goulart, José Alípio. *Favelas do Distrito Federal*. Rio de Janeiro: Ministério da Agricultura, 1957.

Relates the history of the growth of Rio's *favelas*.

1067. Hansen, Elizabeth Riggs. "Santana: Middle Class Families in São Paulo, Brazil." Diss., New York University, 1977.

1068. Jesús, Carolina Maria de. *Child of the Dark*. New York: Mentor/New American Library, 1962.

A moving diary by a resident of a São Paulo *favela*. After brief financial success, the author was forced to return to the slums, where she resided until her death in poverty in 1977.

1069. Leeds, Anthony. "Brazilian Careers and Social Structure: A Case History and Model." *Contemporary Cultures and Societies of Latin America*. Ed. Dwight Heath and Richard N. Adams. New York: Oxford University Press, 1964, pp. 379-404.

Examines the *panelinha*, the mutual-aid alliances which serve as extended kinship groups, facilitating business relationships in urban centers.

1070. Leeds, Anthony. "The Concept of the 'Culture of Poverty.'" *The Culture of Poverty: A Critique*. Ed. Eleanor B. Leacock. New York: Simon and Shuster, 1971, pp. 249-254.

Shows how members of Brazil's urban lower class construct self-help networks among relatives, neighbors, and patrons to mobilize cash, services, and credit.

1071. Leeds, Anthony, ed. *Rio's Favelas*. Austin: University of Texas, Institute of Latin American Studies, 1969.

Articles on urban *samba* groups, problems of slum urbanization, and social reform.

1072. Leeds, Anthony and Elizabeth Leeds, eds. *A sociologia do Brasil urbano*. Rio de Janeiro: Zahar, 1978.

Rejects the notion of "urban" and "rural" values in favor of a broader system of societal values separately influenced by the urban environment.

1073. Leser, W. "Crescimento da população e nível de saúde na cidade de São Paulo." *Problemas Brasileiros*, 16 (October 1974), 17-36.

Analyzes population growth and health conditions in São Paulo, finding that unchecked migration and lower wages to the city is causing levels of health to deteriorate.

1074. Lispector, Clarice. *Family Ties*. Tr. Giovanni Ponteiro. Austin: University of Texas Press, 1972.

Short stories on psychological themes first published as *Laços de Família* in 1944 by Brazil's foremost story writer.

1075. Lobo, Eulália Maria Lahmeyer, et al. "Estudo de categorias sócio-profissionais, dos salários e do custo da alimentação no Rio de Janeiro de 1820 a 1930." *Revista Brasileira de Economia*, 27 (October-December 1973), 129-176.

Attempts to compare wages with food costs for the city of Rio de Janeiro. Finds a gradual increase in consumption levels accompanied by a slow decline in the percentage of family income spent on food.

1076. Machado, Dyonelio. *Desolação*. Rio de Janeiro: José Olympio, 1944.

An unusual novel dealing with urban labor conflict and police repression.

1077. Malloy, James M. "Social Security Policy and the Working Class in the Twentieth Century." *Journal of Inter-American Studies and World Affairs*, 19 (February 1977), 35-60.

Argues that social security agencies have often acted to postpone social change and to increase the immobility and dependency of the poor while not significantly improving living conditions.

1078. Medina, Carlos Alberto de. *A favela e o demagôgo*. São Paulo: Ed. Martins, 1964.

Calls the lower class electorate susceptible to political demagogery and manipulation.

1079. Meehan, Eugene J. *In Partnership With People: An Alternative Development Strategy*. Rosslyn, Va.: Inter-American Foundation, 1979.

Includes a description of several projects underwritten by the publicly-funded I.A.F. in Brazil, especially among migrants and other urban poor in the cities of Salvador and São Paulo.

1080. Nogueira, Oracy. "Atitudes desfavorávis de alguns anunciantes de São Paulo em relação aos empregados de côr." *Sociologia*, 4 (1942), 328-358.

Studies racial prejudice expressed in want-ads in São Paulo newspapers.

1081. Nunes, Guida. *Rio, metrópole de 300 favelas*. Petrópolis: Ed. Vozes, 1976.

Views the "other Rio," the more than a million *favela* inhabitants, praising them for their fortitude *in extremis*.

1082. Pendrell, Nan. "Squatting in Salvador." Diss., Columbia University, 1969.

An anthropologist's analysis of patterns of urban life among slum dwellers in Salvador, Bahia.

1083. Perlman, Janice E. *The Myth of Marginality: Urban Poverty and Politics in Rio de Janeiro.* Berkeley, University of California Press, 1967.

Argues persuasively that despite prevailing stereotypes, *favela* residents are neither politically alienated nor parasites on the economy nor inclined toward crime. They share middle-class values and are relatively economically productive.

1084. Pontes, Eloy. *Favela.* Rio de Janeiro: José Olympio, 1946.

A novel about slum life.

1085. Raphael, Allison. "Miracles in Brazil: A Study of the Pentecostal Movement 'O Brasil para Cristo.'" Master's Thesis, Columbia University, 1975.

Shows how Pentecostal leaders have acted as political brokers and adapted their organizations to political realities.

1086. Rubião, Murilo. "The Ex-Magician and Other Stories." New York: Harper & Row, 1979.

Offers several Kafkaesque tales dealing with the terrors of finitude and the burden of the past. Some of the stories, while fantasies, are closely rooted in contemporary political reality.

1087. Sodré, Nelson Werneck. *A história da imprensa no Brasil.* Rio de Janeiro: Civilização Brasileira, 1966.

Stresses the diversity of the Brazilian press throughout its history.

1088. Velho, Gilberto. *A utópia urbana.* Rio de Janeiro: Zahar, 1973.

An anthropologist examines the social structure of the Rio residential zone of Copacabana, finding that *cariocas* will go to almost desperate lengths to be able to boast a Copacabana address.

VI.
Rural Brazil

A. AGRICULTURE

1089. Adams, Dale W. and Joseph L. Tommy. "Financing Small Farms: The Brazilian Experience, 1965-69." *Agricultural Finance Review*, 35 (October 1974), 36-41.

Shows that the net effect of a 1965 Brazilian law designed to facilitate loans to small farmers was to increase the concentration of total loan funds held by a few.

1090. Amado, Jorge. *Cacau; romance*. Rio de Janeiro: José Olympio, 1933.

A novel set in the cocoa region of southern Bahia.

1091. Amado, Jorge. *The Violent Land*. Tr. Samuel Putnam. New York: Alfred A. Knopf, 1946.

A novel of northeastern agricultural life and conflict, published in Portuguese as *Terras sem fim*.

1092. Amaral, Luis. *História geral da agricultura brasileira*. 2nd ed. 2 vols. São Paulo: Companhia Editôra Nacional, 1958.

Analyzes the factors which have hindered agricultural growth, namely, poor transportation, harmful fiscal policies and practices, and lack of tariff protection.

1093. Andrade, Manuel Correia de. *Problemas e perspectivas de desenvolvimento do cooperativismo nordeste do Brasil*. Recife: PIMES, 1974.

Blames Pernambuco's moribund agricultural health on its outdated reliance upon monoculture. Bahia, by contrast, has diversified, selling to internal as well as foreign markets.

1094. Avni, Haim and Yoram Shapira. "Teaching and Research on Latin America and Israel." *Latin American Research Review*, 9 (Fall 1974), 39-51.

Includes data on various Israeli technical assistance programs in irrigation and agricultural development in Brazil, mostly in the Northeast.

1095. Bacha, Edmar. "A política cafeeira do Brasil, 1952-1967." *Dados*, 5 (1968), 144-161.

Argues in favor of retaining internal regulation of coffee prices in order to stabilize coffee production. Coffee growers warmly embraced the 1964 military coup and in turn were rewarded by immediate aid, although soon afterward prices fell and planters bitterly attacked the regime.

1096. Bernardes, Nilo. "Condições geográficas de colonização em Alagoas." *Revista Brasileira de Geografia*, 29 (1967), 65-83.

Shows that the lack of a suitable local market for food crops contributed to concentration of land ownership and the ultimate industrialization of food production, bypassing the rural peasantry.

1097. "Bibliografia sôbre história da cana-de-açucar." *Brasil Acucareiro* (Rio de Janeiro), 73 (June 1969), 73-76.

A bibliography on the history of sugar cane agriculture in northeastern Brazil.

1098. "Bibliografia sôbre reforma agrária." *Boletim da Biblioteca da SUDENE* (Recife), 4 (December 1965), 414-429.

Lists studies dealing with efforts at agricultural reform before and after the 1964 coup.

1099. Bonilla, Frank. "Rural Reform in Brazil: Diminishing Prospects for a Democratic Solution." New York: American Universities Field Staff [1961].

Surveys the difficulties faced by advocates of land reform in the impoverished Northeast.

1100. Carvalho, Afrânio de. *Reforma agrária*. Rio de Janeiro: Ed. *O Cruzeiro*, 1963.

Summarizes the history of government efforts to implement land reform.

1101. Cehelsky, Marta. *Land Reform in Brazil: The Management of Social Change*. Boulder, Co.: Westview Press, 1978.

Explores the significance of land reformation and the attitudes towards agrarian problems adopted before 1964 and by the military regime which followed. Contends that continued resistance to land reform attests to the resilience of traditional elites.

1102. Feder, Ernest. *The Rape of the Peasantry: Latin America's Landholding System*. Garden City, N.Y.: Doubleday, 1971.

A description of landholding conditions taken largely from published United Nations reports.

1103. Galjart, Benno. *Itaguaí: Old Habits and New Patterns in a Brazilian Land Settlement*. Wageningen, The Netherlands: Centre for Agricultural Publishing and Documentation, 1967.

Reviews the process of agricultural colonization in Brazil, and finds the results largely unsuccessful, although the immigrants did not resist technological innovation.

1104. Gross, Daniel R. "Sisal and Social Structure in Northeast Brazil." Diss., Columbia University, 1970.

Notes that new commercial elites who usurp the power of traditional members of the rural upper classes frequently are distrusted as "outsiders," while the fallen elites are viewed with nostalgia.

1105. Gross, Daniel R. and Barbara A. Underwood. "Technological Change and Caloric Costs: Sisal Agriculture in Northeastern Brazil." *American Anthropologist*, 73 (June 1971), 725-740.

Argues that the introduction of sisal as an export crop may have been deleterious for agricultural laborers although some landowning peasants were able to improve their living standard.

1106. Hall, Anthony L. *Drought and Irrigation in North-East Brazil*. London: Cambridge University Press, 1978.

Measures the effectiveness of the regime's drought-relief policy, which stresses irrigation to resolve rural poverty and unemployment. Three case studies suggest, however, that the irrigation approach exacerbates problems rather than solving them.

1107. Holloway, Thomas H. *The Brazilian Coffee Valorization of 1906: Regional Politics and Economic Dependence.* Madison: Wisconsin Historical Society, 1975.

Finds Brazil's experiment with price supports for coffee to have been initially successful but ultimately unable to solve the problem of overproduction.

1108. Homem de Mello, Fernando. "Economic Policy and the Agricultural Sector in Brazil." *Luso-Brazilian Review*, 15 (Winter 1978), 195-222.

Warns that Brazil may now have exploited all its opportunities for integrating agricultural production into the large sphere of economic development short of redirecting incentives among producers.

1109. Instituto Brasileiro de Reforma Agrária. *Cadastro de inmoveis rurais.* Rio de Janeiro: IBRA, 1967.

Shows that less than 20 percent of Brazil's land mass is effectively utilized in agriculture. More than three-quarters of Brazil's farm properties are *minifúndios*, too small to provide subsistence.

1110. Inter-American Committee for Agricultural Development. *Land Tenure Conditions and Socio-Economic Development: Brazil.* Washington, D.C.: Pan American Union, 1965.

An important report by the committee organized in 1962 after Punta del Este on agricultural conditions in Brazil. Documents the pressing need for land reform.

1111. Knight, Peter T. *Brazilian Agricultural Technology and Trade.* London: Praeger, 1971.

A study of corn, rice, soy beans and beef production in the prosperous agricultural state of Rio Grande do Sul, finding their export strongly influenced by the ratio of domestic to international prices and by direct export controls.

1112. Laclau, Ernesto. "Feudalism and Capitalism in Latin America." *New Left Review*, 67 (May-June 1971), 19-38.

Discusses the issue of whether plantation agriculture represents a feudal survival or a capitalistic adaptation to rural patrimonial-dominated social structure.

1113. Lappe, F.M. and J. Collins. *Food First*. Boston: Houghton Mifflin, 1977.

Calls the settlement of the Amazon in the 1970's a harmful event in the tradition of Brazil's "dualistic society," where a national and foreign elite dominate individual citizens, who are unprotected by special interests.

1114. Margolis, Maxine L. "The Coffee Cycle on the Paraná Frontier." *Luso-Brazilian Review*, 9 (June 1972), 3-12.

Notes the similarity of Paraná coffee experience to the Paraíba valley and to the spread of cotton in the southern and southwestern United States.

1115. Margolis, Maxine L. *The Moving Frontier: Social and Economic Change in a Southern Brazilian Community*. Gainesville: University of Florida Press, 1973.

Studies the impact of the gradual shift from coffee cultivation to cattle raising in the northeast part of the state of Paraná on the economy and demographic character of the region. Population drained from the area, and the economic value of agriculture decreased as coffee declined.

1116. Markham, Charles G. "Climatological Aspects of Drought in Northeastern Brazil." Diss., University of California, Berkeley, 1967.

Shows that regional climate follows patterns which make predictability of rainfall relatively possible, thereby offering a key to solving the drought problem.

1117. Marques, Aguinaldo N. *De que morre o nosso povo?* Rio de Janeiro: Civilização Brasileira, 1963.

A far-fetched attack on imperialism and *latifundia* as the "principal causes of disease and death in Brazil."

1118. Martins, Luciano. "Aspectos políticos da revolução brasileira." *Revista Civilização Brasileira*, 1 (May 1965), 15-37.

Suggests that the process of industrialization in Brazil did not supplant the agrarian elite; in consequence, the industrial bourgeoisie has been unable to assume hegemony over the traditional sectors.

1119. Medcalf, J.C., et al. *Experimental Programs in Brazil.* New York: IBEC Research Institute, 1955.

Describes the work of the Rockefeller Foundation-funded agricultural institute which, in collaboration with the Agronomy Institute of São Paulo, seeks to increase crop yields.

1120. Medina, Carlos Alberto de. "A estrutura agrária brasileira: características e tendências." *América Latina*, 7 (January-March 1964), 71-91.

Contends that the roots of Brazilian *latifundia*-based agriculture are sufficiently tenacious to resist any attempts at land reform.

1121. Meijer, Hendrik. *Rural Brazil at the Cross Roads.* Wageningen, Holland: Veenman, 1951.

Surveys landowning practices in the rural interior for the period up to the 1940 national census.

1122. Moran, Emílio F. *Agricultural Development in the Transamazon Highway.* Bloomington: Indiana University Latin American Studies Center, 1976.

Argues that barriers to successful tropical agricultural development are not only environmental but are influenced by the *type* of plans which are imposed on the region.

1123. Nicholls, William H. "The Agricultural Frontier in Modern Brazilian History: the State of Paraná in 1920-65." *Cultural Change in Brazil.* Muncie, Ind.: Ball State University Press, 1969, pp. 36-64.

Concludes that the agricultural frontier in Brazil, in contrast to the experience of the U.S., has played, except in the Northeast, a minor developmental role.

1124. Paiva, Ruy Miller. "Agricultural Modernization and Technological Dualism in Developing Countries." *Brazilian Economic Studies*, 1 (1975), 97-135.

Views Brazil's agricultural prospects in a promising light, assuming certain reforms were to be carried out. These increased profits in several areas, including cotton production, and should yield direct benefits for rural laborers.

1125. Palaez, Carlos Manuel. "Análise econômica do programa brasileiro de sustentação do café, 1906-45: teoria, política e medição." *Revista Brasileira de Economia*, 25 (October-December 1971), 5-211.

Presents a comprehensive overview of state and federal coffee price protection from 1906 to the end of the Estado Nôvo.

1126. Peláez, Carlos Manuel. "The State, the Great Depression, and the Industrialization of Brazil." Diss., Columbia University, 1968.

Argues that from 1898 to 1945 the effects of coffee and monetary policies did more to retard industrial growth than foreign neo-colonialism.

1127. Pereira, Potyara A.P. "Burocracia e planejamento regional na Amazônia." *Revista Brasileira de Estudos Políticos*, 46 (January 1978), 127-158.

Analyzes SUDAM, the Amazonian regional development agency, and its goals for regional development and improved land use.

1128. Perucci, Gadiel. "Estrutura e conjuntura da economia acuareira no nordeste do Brasil, 1889-1930." Paper presented to the Conference on the Brazilian Northeast, Racine, Wisconsin, November 1974.

Examines the history of sugar production in the Northeast and attendant problems of rural exodus and the continued shift of economic dynamism to the South.

1129. Perucci, Gadiel. *A república das usinas*. Petrópolis: Ed. Vozes, 1977.

Examines the transition from sugar cane plantation production to mechanized refineries, the *usinas*, and the impact on the Northeast.

1130. Prado Júnior, Caio. *A questão agrária no Brasil*. São Paulo: Ed. Brasiliense, 1979.

Assigns the blame for Brazil's agrarian backwardness to the nation's feudal-capitalist heritage of land ownership and agricultural production.

1131. Rio de Janeiro, Universidade de. Instituto de Ciências Sociais. *Bibliografia sôbre reforma agrária*. Rio de Janeiro: Universidade de Rio de Janeiro, 1962.

An extensive (84 pp.) bibliography of studies dealing with land reform.

1132. São Paulo. Instituto de Economia Agrícola. *Modernization of Agriculture in the State of São Paulo*. São Paulo: Imprensa Oficial, 1973.

Traces efforts to improve agricultural output since 1948, a process made difficult by the failure of producers elsewhere in Brazil to cooperate.

1133. Schilling, Paulo R. *O que é reforma agrária?* Rio de Janeiro: Civilização Brasileira, 1963.

Advocates land reform to "democratize" property ownership and bring social justice to the rural peasantry.

1134. Schuh, G. Edward. *The Agricultural Development of Brazil*. New York: Praeger, 1970.

Explores the trend to fragmentation of landholdings in Brazil. Some break-ups of large estates are legal fictions, divided up for tax purposes but collectively under family ownership.

1135. Smith, T. Lynn. "Aspects of the Modernization of Brazilian Agriculture." Paper presented to Columbia University Seminar on Brazil, February 1969.

Shows how plantations lock rural workers into a cycle of hopelessness by failing to diversify production and utilize advanced farming methods.

1136. Smith, T. Lynn. *The Race Between Population and Food Supply in Latin America*. Albuquerque: University of New Mexico Press, 1976.

Devotes much of his analysis to Brazil, whose efforts to modernize agriculture and dairy production are seen as positive steps toward socioeconomic planning.

1137. Soares, Glaúcio Ary Dillon. *A questão agrária na América Latina*. Rio de Janeiro: Zahar, 1976.

A sociologist's view of agricultural organization, attempting to show structural linkages between producing sectors within Latin American "social space."

1138. Sternberg, Hilgard O'Reilly. "O progresso têchnico e a decentralisição na paisagem agrária do nordeste do Brasil." Paper presented to the Paris Colloquium, October 1965.

Describes the agrarian reform planned by the Castelo Branco government and advocates the establishment of industry in the rural backlands as well as along the coast.

1139. Sund, Michael. *Land Tenure and Economic Performance of Agricultural Establishments in Northeast Brazil*. Madison: University of Wisconsin Land Tenure Center, 1965.

Blames the low agricultural yield of northeastern agriculture on *latifundia-minifundia* domination, the tiny proportion of land under cultivation, and the problem of an excessively large unskilled labor force.

1140. University of Wisconsin. Land Tenure Center. *Agrarian Reform in Latin America: An Annotated Bibliography*. 2 vols. Madison: University of Wisconsin Land Tenure Center, 1974.

Contains a full complement of entries on Brazil.

1141. Webb, Kempton E. "Origins and Development of a Food Economy in Central Minas Gerais." *Association of American Geographers' Annals*, 49 (1959), 409-419.

Traces food supply networks from the eighteenth century gold era through the age of the airplane, which has dramatically modified distribution patterns; even fruits, vegetables and rice are sent by air from Minas to Rio de Janeiro.

1142. Wharton, Clifton R. "A Case Study of the Economic Impact of Technical Assistance: Capital and Technology in the Agricultural Development of Minas Gerais, Brazil." Diss., University of Chicago, 1958.

B. RURAL LIFE

1143. Amorim, Deolindo. *Sertão de meu tempo*. Rio de Janeiro: n.p., 1978.

Narrates the author's experiences as a youth in the northeastern backlands before modern transportation linked the region more closely to influences from the urban coast.

1144. Bastos, Abguar. *Safra*. 2nd ed. Rio de Janeiro: Ed. Conquista, 1958.

The former socialist deputy tries his hand at fiction set in the Amazon region.

1145. Batchelor, Courtenay Malcolm. *Stories and Storytellers of Brazil*. Havana: Ucar García, 1953.

Folklore and folk tales from Brazil's rural interior.

1146. Caldeira, Clóvis. *Mutirão: formas de ajuda mutua no meio rural*. São Paulo: Companhia Editôra Nacional, 1956.

Demonstrates that sharecroppers' contracts frequently fail to specify the size of his plot, giving the upper hand to the landlord, who can make adjustments after the crop has been sown.

1147. Caldeira, Clóvis. *Menores no meio rural*. Rio de Janeiro: Instituto Nacional de Estudos Pedagôgicos, 1960.

Rural children fail to attend school because they have to work; moreover they lack shoes, uniforms, and school material even if tuition is free, and find the primary curriculum rigid and foreign.

1148. Cândido, Antônio. *Os parceiros do Rio Bonito: Estudo sôbre o caipira paulista e a transformação dos seus meios da vida*. Rio de Janeiro: José Olympio, 1964.

Constructs an economic definition of the *paulista* peasantry and shows that sharecroppers' lives have been disoriented by urban influences on rural culture.

1149. Castro, Josué de. *Death in the Northeast*. New York: Random House, 1966.

Provides a moving description of life in the squalid Northeast. DeCastro was a Recife-born physician who lived most of his life in exile in Paris.

1150. Castro, Josué de. *Documentário do nordeste*. 2nd ed. São Paulo: Ed. Brasiliense, 1959.

Surveys life and geography in the rural northeastern *agreste* and backlands.

1151. Castro, Josué de. *The Geopolitics of Hunger*. New York: Monthly Review Press, 1973.

Originally published as *The Geography of Hunger* and revised by the author in 1973. Calls hunger the "biological manifestation of underdevelopment," using examples from the Northeast and elsewhere to document his charge that hunger is man-made.

1152. Cavalcanti, Clóvis and Dirceu Pessôa. *Vale do Moxotó*. Recife: Instituto Joacquim Nabuco, 1970.

Offers a socioeconomic analysis of the rural Moxotó Valley in rural Pernambuco.

1153. Converse, James W. "Anomia and Alienation: Social Psychological Factors in the Modernization of an Isolated Area in Rural Brazil." Diss., University of Wisconsin, 1969.

1154. Cruls, Gastão Luis. *A Amazônia misteriosa, romance*. 3rd ed. São Paulo: Companhia Editôra Nacional, 1939.

A realistic novel about the Amazon.

1155. Duarte, Paulo de Queiroz. *O nordeste na II Guerra Mundial*. Rio de Janeiro: Record, 1971.

Describes the Northeast during the Second World War under the impact of what the author calls United States "occupation."

1156. Duncan, James A. *Educational and Agricultural Attitudes in a Small Brazilian Community: A Culture in Transition*. Madison: University of Wisconsin, College of Agriculture, Department of Agricultural and Extension Education, 1967.

Studies three hundred rural families in Dois Irmaõs, Rio Grande do Sul.

1157. Eckholm, Erik. *Losing Ground*. New York: W.W. Norton, 1976.

Examines the adverse effect of deforestation on the Amazon and predicts failure of colonization schemes unless provisions are made to change the traditional, unecological way of dealing with the land.

1158. Farhat, Emil. *Cangerão*. Rio de Janeiro: José Olympio, 1939.

An unusual fictionalized account of the lives of victimized children in the mining regions of Minas Gerais.

1159. Forman, Shepard. *The Brazilian Peasantry.* New York: Columbia University Press, 1975.

Stresses the ways Brazilian peasants--mostly subsistence sharecroppers and fishermen--are tied to larger regional, national and international networks. The focus is on the Northeast where the author did most of his fieldwork.

1160. Forman, Shepard. *The Raft Fisherman: Tradition and Change in the Brazilian Peasant Economy.* Bloomington: Indiana University Press, 1970.

Argues that peasants will accept innovation and change if shown an effective way to improve their lives.

1161. Harris, Marvin. *Town and Country in Brazil.* 2nd ed. New York: W.W. Norton, 1971.

An indispensable study of social relations and class structure in Minas Velhas, Bahia. Harris shows that small town sub-culture shares more in common with large urban centers than with nearby rural villages, which are truly isolated.

1162. Herkenhoff, João Baptista. *A função judiciaria no interior.* São Paulo: Resenha Universitária, 1977.

Shows that in the small towns of the interior the local judge plays the role of "poder moderador," the traditional "moderating power" function exercised by the Emperor in the previous century.

1163. Herrman, Lucília. "Evolução da estrutura social de Guaratinguetá num período de trezentos anos." *Revista de Administração* (São Paulo), 2 (March-June 1948), 3-326.

A book-length article on the social transformation of a *paulista* community, Guaratinguetá. Based on field work and primary sources.

1164. Hutchinson, Harry W. *Village and Plantation Life in Northeastern Brazil.* Seattle: University of Washington Press, 1957.

Affirms that race phenotype is a badge of social rank but can be outweighed by class considerations.

1165. Johnson, Allen W. *Sharecroppers of the Sertão: Economics and Dependence on a Brazilian Plantation.* Stanford: Stanford University Press, 1971.

Individuals at Boa Ventura, a plantation in Ceará's backlands, find themselves forced by their poverty and insecurity to seek protection against a hostile environment. At the same time, they are resourceful, independent, and able to adapt their family units to changing needs.

1166. Johnson, Allen W. and Joyce F. Riegelhaupt. "Peasants, Integration, and Modernization in Brazil." Paper presented to Columbia University Seminar on Brazil, April 1969.

Finds that peasants, rather than being "inherently conservative," have their behavior largely determined by the conditions under which they live.

1167. Julião, Francisco. *Cambão: The Yoke. The Hidden Face of Brazil.* Harmondsworth, England: Penguin Books, 1972.

Julião, the exiled former leader of the Northeast's Peasant Leagues, describes the misery of life in his afflicted region.

1168. Leal, Victor Nunes. *Coronelismo, enxada e voto: o município e o regime representativo no Brasil.* Rio de Janeiro: Ed. Forense, 1948.

A classic study of *coronelismo* as a structural process and a residual byproduct of the decadence of the rural landholding system and sanctioned as a form of local social control. Revised edition published in 1978.

1169. Leão, Sylvia. *White Shores of Olinda.* New York: The Vanguard Press, 1943.

A novel written in English about fishermen sailing from Olinda, Pernambuco's old capital.

1170. Lyra Filho, João. *O sertão social; ensaio de psicologia coletiva.* São Paulo: Companhia Editôra Nacional, 1933.

Attributes the backwardness of the Northeast in part to deficiencies in the structure of education as well as to economic hardship.

1171. Malloy, James M. "Authoritarianism and the Extension of Social Security Protection to the Rural Sector in Brazil." *Luso-Brazilian Review*, 14 (Winter 1977), 195-210.

Argues that rural workers have been forced to pay a

high price in terms of personal and group autonomy. Social security in Brazil, he concludes, has largely amounted to a "mirage."

1172. Martins, Francisco. *Estrêla do pastor*. Fortaleza: Ed. Clã, 1942.

A novel comprising short stories woven together about life in the northeastern *sertão*.

1173. Meggers, Betty J. *Amazônia: Man and Culture in a Counterfeit Paradise*. Chicago: Aldine, Atherton, 1971.

An anthropologist examines Amazonian life and culture on the eve of the opening of the region to development.

1174. Menezes, Djacir. *O outro nordeste*. 2nd ed. Rio de Janeiro: Ed. Artenova, 1970.

Blames the feudal basis of society and land use for the woes afflicting the "other Northeast," the region of the poor.

1175. Mitchell, Simon, ed. *The Logic of Poverty: The Stagnation of North East Brazil*. London: Routledge & Kegan Paul, 1977.

Collected articles by David Goodman, Jaime Reis, Mitchell, Bainbridge Cowell, Jr., and others on the region's economy and social structure.

1176. Paim, Alina. *Simão Dias*. Rio de Janeiro: Casa do Estudante do Brasil, 1949.

A short novel about women in the rural small towns of the backlands.

1177. Palhano, Lauro. *Paracoera*. Rio de Janeiro: Schmidt Editôra, c. 1930.

One of the first proletarian novels in Brazilian literature, set in the Amazon.

1178. Pierson, Donald. *Cruz das Almas: A Brazilian Village*. Westport, Conn.: Greenwood Press, 1973.

A classical anthropological field study first published in 1948.

1179. Queiroz, Rachel de. *The Three Marias*. Tr. Fred P. Ellison. Austin: University of Texas Press, 1963.

The major novel of the regionalist writer who, in 1976, became the first woman to be elected to the Brazilian Academy of Letters.

1180. Ramos, Graciliano. *Infância.* Rio de Janeiro: José Olympio, 1945.

Childhood reminiscences by the Northeast's leading socially-conscious novelist.

1181. Rêgo, José Lins do. *Bangûe.* 2nd ed. Rio de Janeiro: José Olympio, 1943.

First published in 1934, a major regionalist novel describing life on the northeastern sugar plantations.

1182. Rêgo, José Lins do. *Fôgo morto, romance.* Rio de Janeiro: José Olympio, 1944.

Another novel set in the rural Northeast.

1183. Rêgo, José Lins do. *Menino de engenho.* Rio de Janeiro: José Olympio, 1932.

The first volume in the *Cíclo de cana de açucar* (Sugar Cane Cycle) and the most well-known. Tells the story of a young boy on a sugar plantation.

1184. Rêgo, José Lins do. *O moleque Ricardo.* Rio de Janeiro: José Olympio, 1935

The fourth (and least known) volume of the Sugar Cane Cycle.

1185. Riegelhaupt, Joyce F. and Shepard Forman. "Bodo Was Never Brazilian: Economic Integration and Rural Development among a Contemporary Peasantry." *Journal of Economic History*, 30 (March 1970), 100-116.

Argues that Brazil's agrarian problems cannot be blamed on the heritage of feudalism. The Brazilian peasant is closely linked to the commercial system, and is displaced by technological advances. Brazilian peasants find themselves hostages of the modern world.

1186. Rocha, Glauber, director. "Barravento." b/w film. 76 min. New Yorker Films, 1962.

In English, "Turning Wind." The film portrays the stubborn, tradition-bound attitudes of the inhabitants of a coastal fishing village in Bahia and calls for social change.

1187. Rosa, João Guimarães. *The Devil to Pay in the Backlands*. Tr. James L. Taylor and Harriet de Onis. New York: Alfred A. Knopf, 1963.

Relates the memoirs of an old man in the backlands of northern Minas Gerais. The language is extremely colorful and occasionally obscure, but the novel portrays regional life with brilliance.

1188. Ross, Eric B. "The Evolution of the Amazon Peasantry." *Journal of Latin American Studies*, 10 (November 1978), 193-218.

Shows that centuries of commercial domination have produced a way of life in the Amazon valley in which the relatively isolated nuclear family has proven to be the most adaptive unit of production in a tropical extractive ecostructure.

1189. Sá, M. Auxiliadora Ferraz de. *Dos velhos aos novos coronéis*. Recife: PIMES, 1974.

Examines the evolution of *coronelismo* from its crude origins as a form of violent local boss rule to more subtle modern forms. Includes a detailed bibliography.

1190. Salgado, Plínio. *O cavalheiro de Itararé*. São Paulo: Ed. Unitas, 1933.

A novel about *paulista* life by the head of the fascist Integralists, influenced by the modernistic movement of the 1920's.

1191. Shirley, Robert W. *The End of a Tradition? Culture Change and Development in the Municipio of Cunha, São Paulo, Brazil*. New York: Columbia University Press, 1971.

Returns to study the site of the first community study, by Willems in 1945, of an archetypical isolated Brazilian town. Finds that nearby industrial expansion has profoundly affected social organization; the traditions of the past are fast disappearing.

1192. Silva, Celson José da. *Marchas e contramarchas do mandonismo local*. Belo Horizonte: Universidade de Minas Gerais, 1975.

Studies local elites in a small mining community of Minas Gerais and shows that the *coronel* model is not universally applicable.

1193. Smith, T. Lynn. "Some Aspects of Rural Community Development in Brazil." *Luso-Brazilian Review*, 10 (June 1973), 3-18.

Enumerates the questions which must be resolved if community development is to succeed: the nature and extent of the commitment to change; the choice of goals; and relationships with official agencies.

1194. Somarriba, M. das M.G. "Public Health in the Countryside of Brazil." Diss., University of Sussex, Great Britain, 1979.

A case study of a government pilot program in the Jequitinhonha Valley.

1195. Sternberg, Hilgard O'Reilly. *The Amazon River of Brazil*. Wiesbaden: Erklund, Wissen, 1975.

A leading geographer looks at the human and ecological environment of the Amazon region.

1196. Toop, Walter R. "Organized Religious Groups in a Village of Northeastern Brazil." *Luso-Brazilian Review*, 9 (December 1972), 58-77.

Focuses on Ceará. Suggests that change is sweeping the Northeast and that rural isolation is rapidly disappearing.

1197. Turner, Doris J. "The Poor and Social Symbolism: An Examination of Three Novels of Jorge Amado." Diss., St. Louis University, 1967.

1198. Verissimo, Érico. *Time and the Wind*. Tr. L.L. Barrett. New York: Alfred A. Knopf, 1951.

Verissimo's major work, a searing historical novel set in the 1930's, echoing the regional color of Rio Grande do Sul.

1199. Villaça, Marcos and Roberto Cavalcanti de Albuquarque. *Coronel, coronéis*. Rio de Janeiro: Tempo Brasileiro, 1965.

Finds that the penetration of capitalism into the backlands has reduced the power of the traditional local bosses, although many of them, threatened by loss of power, become innovative and adapt to the times, substituting economic pressure for crude violence.

1200. Webb, Kempton E. *The Changing Face of Northeast Brazil*. New York: Columbia University Press, 1974.

Portrays the Northeast as a region in transition as men adjust slowly to change in land ownership, technical innovations, and fluctuations in agricultural prices.

1201. Willems, Emílio. *Cunha: tradição e transição em uma cultura regional no Brasil*. São Paulo: Secretária de Agriculture, 1947.

A classic sociological study of life in a small town, Cunha, in São Paulo state.

1202. Willems, Emílio. *Uma vila brasileira*. São Paulo: DIFEL, 1961.

A study of an interior *paulista* town which, the author notes, finds itself transformed by an increasing necessity to deal with the outside world.

1203. Willems, Emílio. "The Rise of a Rural Middle Class in a Frontier Society." *Brazil in the Sixties* (item 423), pp. 325-344.

Contends that patterns of economic and social mobility in the case of northern Paraná were far more flexible than the rigid system which dominated the Northeast.

C. SOCIAL MOVEMENTS

1204. Anselmo, Otacílio. *Padre Cícero: mito e realidade*. Rio de Janeiro: Civilização Brasileira, 1968.

Reconstructs the events surrounding the rise of Padre Cícero as regional *coronel* in the Cearense *sertão*. Considers Joaseiro to have been much more deeply rooted in social issues than Canudos.

1205. Barreto, Leda. *Julião, Nordeste, Revolução*. Rio de Janeiro: Civilização Brasileira, 1963.

Predicts social revolution, to be led by Francisco Julião in the North, Lionel Brizola in the South, and Miguel Arraes as national leader.

1206. Borges, Fragman Carlos. "O movimento camponês no nordeste." *Estudos Sociais*, 14 (1962), 248-60.

Shows how the leader of the Peasant Leagues, Francisco Julião, although called a Communist by his enemies, was attacked by the Party for being bourgeois and for emphasizing work in cities rather than in the countryside.

1207. Callado, Antonio. "Les Ligues paysannes du Nord-Est bresilien." *Les Temps Modernes* (Paris), 23 (October 1967), 751-60.

Describes Francisco Julião's Peasant Leagues, organized among dissident agrarian workers in the Northeast in the late 1950's until 1964.

1208. Carvalho, Rodrigues de. *Lampião e a sociologia do cangaço*. Rio de Janeiro: n.p., 1976.

Calls the rural bandit a "tragic product" of a country in need of heroes, despite the fact that the *cangaceiros* allied with landowners and other exploiters of the backlands peasantry.

1209. Chandler, Billy Jaynes. *The Bandit King: Lampião of Brazil*. College Station: Texas A & M Press, 1978.

A biography of the most notorious *cangaceiro* in the Brazilian Northeast, Virgolino Ferreiro da Silva, or Lampião.

1210. Cunha, Euclides da. *Os sertões*. 14th ed. Rio de Janeiro: Livraria Francisco Alves, 1938.

Although first published in 1901, this classic fictionalized account of the 1897 Canudos rebellion profoundly influenced Brazilians' view of themselves in subsequent decades.

1211. Daus, Ronald. *Der Epische Zyklus der Cangaceiros in der Volkspoesie Nordost-Brasiliens*. Berlin: Colloquium Verlag, 1969.

Studies the genesis of the image and symbol of the *cangeceiro* of the Northeast by analyzing the verse narrative of the region's folk literature.

1212. Della Cava, Ralph. "Brazilian Messianism and National Institutions: A Reappraisal of Canudos and Jaoseiro." *Hispanic American Historical Review*, 48 (August 1968), 402-420.

Views the Canudos rebellion of Antônio Conselheiro not as isolated rural "fanaticism" but the consequence of pressures from state and federal encroachment as modernization extended the reach of the coastal government.

1213. Della Cava, Ralph. *Miracle at Joaseiro*. New York: Columbia University Press, 1970.

A multidimensional study of the regional, national and international linkages intertwined in the remarkable rural messianic religious movement led by the charismatic and politically astute Padre Cícero Romão Batista.

1214. Facó, Rui. *Cangaceiros e fanáticos*. Rio de Janeiro: Civilização Brasileira, 1963.

Emphasizes class conflict as the basis of messianic movements among the peasantry and rural banditry. Agricultural stagnation served to entrench *latifundários* and exacerbate the misery of the lower classes.

1215. Forman, Shepard. "Disunity and Discontent: A Study of Peasant Political Movements in Brazil." *Journal of Latin American Studies*, 3 (May 1971), 3-24.

Observes that as peasant organizations became more sophisticated and well-organized, especially in the early 1960's, they moved further and further from the possibility of dealing with the elite, which bridled at their radicalism.

1216. Franco, Maria Sylvia de Carvalho. "O Código do Sertão: um estudo sôbre violência no meio rural." *Dados*, 5 (1968), 22-56.

Studies rural violence and the role of the landless peasant. The poverty of local culture reinforces the vitality of institutional violence against the lower classes.

1217. Hobsbawm, Eric J. *Primitive Rebels*. New York: Norton, 1959.

A provocative examination of rural banditry in Brazil as a phenomenon of social protest. Reissued in 1969 under the title *Bandits* (Delacorte Press).

1218. Leeds, Anthony. "Brazil and the Myth of Francisco Julião." *Politics of Change in Latin America*. Ed.

Joseph Maier and Richard Weatherhead. New York: Praeger, 1964, pp. 190-204.

Discusses the false expectations raised by the organization of the militant Peasant Leagues in the pre-1964 Northeastern agricultural zone.

1219. Machado, Maria Christian Matta. *As tâticas de guerra dos cangaceiros*. 2nd ed. Saõ Paulo: Ed. Brasiliense, 1978.

Examines the tactics used by state and federal militias to subdue the *cangaco* bandits who infested the backlands of the Northeast until the late 1930's.

1220. Morton, Ann. "Religion in Juàzeiro Since the Death of Padre Cícero." Master's Thesis, Columbia University, 1966.

Provides a case study of backlands messianic activity and social mobility.

1221. Queiroz, Maria Isaura Pereira de. *Os cangaceiros*. São Paulo: Duas Cidades, 1977.

Dissects the brutal social and economic environment of the Northeast and shows how men found themselves driven to violence and banditry.

1222. Queiroz, Maria Isaura Pereira de. "Messiahs in Brazil." *Past and Present*, 31 (July 1965), 62-86.

An English-language version of the author's views on messianism in Brazil as the result of conscious efforts to reorganize rural society when traditional relationships fail. The discussion includes such recent movements as the Beata do Caldeirão (1930's) and the Bahian "Velho Pedro."

1223. Queiroz, Maria Isaura Pereira de. *O messianismo no Brasil e no mundo*. São Paulo: Universidade de São Paulo, 1965.

Discusses the social origins of the members of the messianic cults common to rural Brazil during the Old Republic (and later). Most came from the rural agricultural class: smallholders, renters, and sharecroppers, neither the most destitute elements of the peasantry nor the affluent.

1224. Ribeiro, René. "Brazilian Messianic Movements." *Millenial Dreams in Action: Essays in Comparative*

Study. Ed. Sylvia L. Thrupp. The Hague: n.p., 1962, pp. 55-69.

A Recife social psychologist offers a theoretical analysis of messianism in the context of rural Brazil.

1225. Rocha, Glauber. *Deus e o diabo na terra do sol.* Rio de Janeiro: Civilização Brasileiro, 1965.

The screenplay of the powerful Cinema Nôvo film based on the theme of backlands violence. The first part is a fictionalized account of the Canudos uprising in a more modern setting, with a black Antônio Conselheiro.

1226. Singlemann, Peter. "Political Structure and Social Banditry in Northeast Brazil." *Journal of Latin American Studies*, 7 (May 1975), 59-83.

Argues that the *cangaceiros*--called by some social bandits--survived as long as they did in the rural Northeast because of their formal links to the state political machinery.

1227. Souza, Amaury de. "O cangaço e a política da violência no nordeste brasileiro." *Dados*, 10 (1973), 97-125.

Argues that an an alienated peasant can become an entrepreneur of violence as a weapon to achieve socio-economic gain. Violence in the Northeast is a catalyst for the decay of the patriarchal order.

1228. Vilespy, François. "Juàzeiro do Norte et le Padre Cícero." *Caravelle*, 5 (1965), 61-70.

Reviews the history of the messianic cult which swept through the Ceará *sertão* in the early twentieth century and persisted into modern times.

1229. Vinhas de Queiroz, Maurício. *Messianismo no Brasil e no mundo: a guerra sertaneja do Contestado.* Rio de Janeiro: Civilização Brasileira, 1966.

Blames the economic deprivations caused by the expulsion of squatters for the rise of messianic hopes among the rural poor. Uses local sources and judicial records to reconstruct the history of the Contestado revolt.

VII.
Society

A. GENERAL STUDIES

1230. Amado, Jorge. *Capitães de areia*. São Paulo: Ed. Martins, 1937.

A novel set in the Northeast, in the fashion of proletarian literature, exploring human relations and economic linkages between the inhabitants of the region.

1231. Amado, Jorge. *Gabriela, Clove and Cinnamon*. Tr. James L. Taylor and William L Grossman. New York: Alfred A. Knopf, 1962.

A delightful novel parallel in ways to Twain's *Huckleberry Finn*, set in the booming cocoa city of Ilheus in 1925.

1232. Azevedo, Thales de. *Gaûchos, a fisionomia social do Rio Grande do Sul*. 2nd ed. Salvador: Ed. Cruzeiro, 1958.

A brief (146 pp.) essay on the social structure of life in Brazil's southernmost state.

1233. Azevedo, Thales de. *Namoro à antigua*. Salvador, Bahia: n.p., 1975.

Describes and analyzes the Brazilian custom of courtship, emphasizing patterns of social behavior derived from the perceived necessity of maintaining traditional values.

1234. Azevedo, Thales de. *Social Change in Brazil*. Gainesville: School of Inter-American Studies, University of Florida, 1962.

A brief analysis of social structure and changing values.

1235. Bastide, Roger. *Brasil, terra de contrastes.* São Paulo: DIFEL, 1959.

Introduces the reader to the contrasts and contradictions in Brazilian social organization and geographic reality.

1236. Bazzanella, Waldemiro. *Estratificação e mobilidade social no Brasil, fontes bibliográficas.* Rio de Janeiro: Centro Latino Americano de Pesquisas em Ciências Educacionais, 1956.

A bibliography on social stratification and mobility in Brazil.

1237. Berlinck, Manoel T. *Marginalidade social e relações de classes em São Paulo.* Petrópolis: Ed. Vozes, 1975.

Argues that current theories on social marginality are inadequate to understand the dynamics of capitalistic economic development and its byproducts in Brazil.

1238. "Bibliografia sôbre pesquisa social." *Boletim de Biblioteca da Sudene* (Recife), 4 (November 1965), 120-123.

A bibliography of studies on Brazilian society.

1239. Bouquet, Susana. "Peace Corps Volunteers in the São Francisco Valley." *Luso-Brazilian Review*, 4 (December 1967), 79-93.

Explores the problems raised by the sharp contrast between the cultural characteristics of the United States Volunteers and the Brazilians among whom they were assigned.

1240. Brito, José Geraldo de Lemos. *O crime e os criminosos na literatura brasileira.* Rio de Janeiro: José Olympio, 1946.

Studies crime and criminals in contemporary Brazilian fiction.

1241. Castro, Josué de. *The Geography of History.* Boston: Little, Brown, and Company, 1952.

Implores officials to redress the terrible social imbalance in the Brazilian Northeast which produces only hunger and the potential for revolution.

1242. Costa Pinto, Luiz de Aguiar. "As classes sociais no Brasil." *Revista Brasileira de Ciencias Sociais* (Belo Horizonte), 3 (March 1963), 217-247.

Discusses ideological liberalism, urbanization, bureaucratization, and inflation within the framework of contemporary Brazilian social structure.

1243. Da Matta, Roberto. *Carnavais, malandros e herôis: para uma sociologia do dilema brasileiro.* Rio de Janeiro, 1978 (typescript).

Argues that Brazilian society embodies properties of hierarchical and egalitarian societies: individualism is dominant in bourgeois ideology and in the legal system but hierarchy, patronage, and family predominate as social forms.

1244. Fernandes, Florestan, ed. *Comunidade e sociedade no Brasil.* São Paulo: Companhia Editôra Nacional, 1972.

An anthology for teaching use in university-level sociology classes, offering varied selections from the "classic" as well as "modern" schools of literature.

1245. Fernandes, Florestan. *Mudanças sociais no Brasil.* São Paulo: DIFEL, 1960.

Three studies of industrialization's impact on political integration; the urban history of São Paulo; and miscegenation.

1246. Fernandes, Florestan. *A sociologia no Brasil.* Petrôpolis: Ed. Vozes, 1977.

Discusses the need to probe more deeply beneath the social fabric in order to gain understanding of the dynamics of the existing order.

1247. Figueiredo, Vilma. "A racionalidade do empresário brasileiro: um estudo sôbre filantropia." Master's Thesis, Instituto Universitário de Pesquisas do Rio de Janeiro, 1970.

Finds that corporate philanthropy among Brazilian enterprises is based on fears about uncontrollable social change. Businesses contribute mostly to educational institutions and are less likely to donate funds for social welfare.

1248. Fitzpatrick, Richard S. "A Study of the Relationship of Social Class and Opinion in Rio de Janeiro, Brazil." Diss., The American University, 1959.

1249. Freyre, Gilberto. *O Nordeste*. Rio de Janeiro: José Olympio, 1937.

Continues Freyre's history of Northeastern life in the coastal *zona da mata* (sugar cane region).

1250. Freyre, Gilberto, et al. *Seminário de tropicologia da Universidade Federal de Pernambuco: 1969*. 2 vols. Recife: Universidade Federal, 1976.

Articles from the 1969 seminar on "tropicality," ranging from studies of fishing and regional agriculture to international affairs.

1251. Goldman, Frank Perry and Demarisse Machado Goldman. *Problemas brasileiros: alguns aspectos sobre o processo de envelhecer*. Piracicaba, São Paulo: n.p., 1977.

Studies the problem of aging in Brazilian society, a subject heretofore ignored in the literature.

1252. Gomes, Lúcia Maria Gaspar and Fernando José Leite Costa. "Contribução ao estudo da sociedade tradicional: bibliografia comentada." *Dados*, 5 (1968), pp. 167-180.

An annotated bibliography on traditional Brazilian society and social behavior, citing 54 studies of *coronelismo*, messianic movements, and local power.

1253. Guilherme, Wanderley. *Introdução ao estudo das contradições sociais no Brasil*. Rio de Janeiro: ISEB, 1963.

An influential Marxist analysis of Brazil's social problems, published before the 1964 coup, representing the thinking of many Goulart-era intellectuals.

1254. Hutchinson, Harry W. "Culture Change in Brazil: An Analytical Model." *Journal of Inter-American Studies*, 6 (July 1964), 303-312.

Argues that stability in social institutions produces new values which in turn accelerate social change.

1255. Ianni, Octávio. *Sociologia e sociedade no Brasil.* São Paulo: Ed. Alfa-Omega, 1975.

Examines modern Brazilian social structure and the role of the sociologist.

1256. Konder, Leandro. "A rebeldia, os intellectuais e a juventude." *Revista Civilização Brasileira*, 3 (September 1967), 135-145.

Expresses anxiety over prospects for intellectual mediocrity given Brazil's population distribution--more than half under twenty-one years of age--and the impact of cultural repression since 1964.

1257. Lambert, Jacques. *Le Brésil: Structure sociale et institutions politiques.* Paris: Colin, 1953.

Surveys the structure of Brazilian social and political institutions. Shows the urban lower classes to be a "rural peasantry in the city" rather than an urban proletariat in the European sense.

1258. Lambert, Jacques. *Os dois brasís.* 2nd ed. São Paulo: Companhia Editôra Nacional, 1959.

Divides Brazilian society into two distinct worlds, the modern (coastal life) and the primitive (the backlands).

1259. Leeds, Anthony. "Brazilian Careers and Social Structure; an Evolutionary Model and Case History." *American Anthropologist*, 66 (1964), 1321-1347.

Examines the *panelinha*, the informal associative network which facilitates career advancement in modern Brazilian society.

1260. Lipset, Seymour Martin and Aldo Solari, eds. *Elites in Latin America.* New York: Oxford University Press, 1967.

Articles on the middle classes, industrialists, political elites, the military, religion, culture, labor, and education.

1261. Maybury-Lewis, David. "Growth and Change in Brazil Since 1930: An Anthropological View." *Portugal and Brazil in Transition* (item 180), pp. 159-172.

Provides a theoretical structure for the analysis of Brazilian society since 1930, stressing political mobilization, urbanization, and efforts at social reform.

1262. Melo, Antônio. *The Coming Revolution in Brazil*. New York: Exposition Press, 1970.

Outlines the conditions under which social justice will prevail and a post-revolutionary society will emerge. Padre Melo is a priest in rural Pernambuco.

1263. Moraes, Pedro de. *Vivendo*. Rio de Janeiro: Atalier de Arte, 1976.

An unusual collection of black and white photographs taken since 1954 by a photographer with an eye for the anxiety of urban life and the pathos of rural Brazilian poverty.

1264. Mota, Mauro. *Votos e ex-votos: aspectos da vida social do Nordeste*. Recife: Universidade de Pernambuco, 1968.

A collection of essays on socio-cultural themes ranging from northeastern dietary habits to the life of the backlands peasantry.

1265. Oliveira, Francisco de. *Elegia para uma re(li)gião*. Rio de Janeiro: Paz e Terra, 1977.

A Pernambucano economist laments the failure of SUDENE, the regional development agency, to resolve the basic human problems of the Northeast.

1266. Pan American Union. Division of Philosophy, Letters and Science. *Materiales para el estudio de la classe media en América Latina*. 6 vols. Washington, D.C.: Pan American Union, 1950-51.

Twenty-seven short monographs and essays on the historical evolution of the middle class in Latin America, most dealing with the 1930's and 1940's.

1267. Pang, Eul-Soo and Seckinger, Ron L., "The Mandarins of Imperial Brazil." *Comparative Studies in Society and History*, 14 (March 1971), 215-44.

Offers a model of elite recruitment which offers interesting comparisons for the post-1930 period. The authors attribute the strength of the Second Empire (1840-1889) to the process which formed a national administrative elite.

1268. Ramos, Graciliano. *Anguish*. Tr. L.C. Kaplan. New York: Alfred A. Knopf, 1946.

The translation of *Angûstia*, one of Ramos's major works of fiction on the theme of human misery.

1269. Raphael, Allison. "Brazil's Wasted Generation." *Time* (September 11, 1978), 32-33.

Shows that nearly 16 million people--one-third of Brazil's youth--today are considered deprived. Street crime among children in urban centers is rising precipitously.

1270. Ribeiro, José Ubaldo. *Sargento Getúlio*. Rio de Janeiro: Civilização Brasileira, 1971.

A novel set in the 1950's about an M.P. Sergeant who comes to the Bahian city of Paulo Afonso to transport a prisoner to the coast.

1271. Rios, José Arthur. "Police and Development." *International Review of Criminal Policy*, 33 (1977), 3-10.

Suggests that Rio's police force is becoming bureaucratized but that residual traits of traditional behavior still persist. Policemen, for example, still show deference toward elites and are unusually brutal toward the poor.

1272. Serton, Petrus. *Süid-Afrika en Brasilie*. Kaapstaad, South Africa: Oxford University Press, 1960.

Compares Brazilian and South African socioeconomic and geographic conditions. Written in Afrikaans.

1273. Smith, T. Lynn. *Brazil: People and Institutions*. 4th ed. Baton Rouge: Louisiana State University Press, 1972.

A valuable text for dealing with population, demography and social institutions.

1274. Smith, T. Lynn. *Brazilian Society*. Albuquerque: University of New Mexico Press, 1975.

An overview of impressions of contemporary Brazilian society by an eminent rural sociologist in collection of essays and lectures.

1275. Smith, T. Lynn and Alexander Marchant, eds. *Brazil: Portrait of Half a Continent*. New York: Dryden Press, 1951.

Provides a detailed view of Brazilian society in the late 1940's. Contains items 913, 1045, 1520.

1276. Strickon, Arnold. "Anthropology in Latin America." *Social Science Research on Latin America*. Ed. Charles Wagley. New York: Columbia University Press, 1964, pp. 125-167.

Remarks that Brazil has received more scholarly attention than any other South American nation, and that most of the field work has focused on the region north of Rio de Janeiro. Southern Brazil is less frequently studied because it is relatively emergent as a critical economic area.

1277. Torres, João Camilo de Oliveira. *Estratificação social no Brasil*. São Paulo: DIFEL, 1965.

Emphasizes the legacy of Brazil's colonial land tenure system on present-day social structure.

1278. Vasconcelos, José Mauro de. *My Sweet-Orange Tree*. Tr. Edgar H. Miller, Jr. New York: Alfred A. Knopf, 1970.

A sentimental novel about a precocious 5-year-old impoverished boy, Zezé de Vasconcelos, which sold nearly a half-million copies in Brazil in the early 1970's.

1279. Verissimo, Érico. *Consider the Lilies of the Field*. Tr. J.N. Karnoff. New York: Macmillan, 1947.

A novel, lamenting the lack of opportunity for mobility within a society fixed by traditional values and prejudices.

1280. Wagley, Charles. "The Brazilian Revolution: Social Changes Since 1930." *Social Change in Latin America Today: Its Implications for United States Policy*. New York: Harper and Brothers, 1961, pp. 177-230.

An optimistic survey of economic change and social evolution since Vargas's rise to power. Stresses the role of the urban middle class and the "new upper class," rapidly fusing with the traditional landed gentry.

1281. Wolf, Eric R. and Edward C. Hansen. *The Human Condition in Latin America.* New York: Oxford University Press, 1972.

A provocative interpretive introduction to Latin American society with extensive treatment of Brazilian social structure, kinship, banditry, and poverty.

B. SEX ROLES AND THE FAMILY

1282. Alcantara, Aspásia B. "Estudos e pesquisas sobre família no Brasil." *Dados*, 1 (1966), 176-179.

A 54-item bibliography of studies on the Brazilian family, most by Brazilian researchers.

1283. Amado, Jorge. *Dona Flôr and Her Two Husbands.* New York: Bard/Avon, 1969.

A light and frivolous novel set in Salvador in 1940, gently mocking sexual mores and *macho* behavior.

1284. Austregesilo, Antônio. *Perfil da mulher brasileira.* Lisbon: Aillaud e Bertrand, 1923.

An early examination of the role of Brazilian women by a sympathetic psychiatrist and writer.

1285. Azevedo, Thales de. "Família, casamento e divórcio no Brasil." *Journal of Interamerican Studies*, 7 (April 1961), 213-237.

Shows how Brazilians of the affluent classes evaded legal restrictions on divorce by other informal means.

1286. Bambirra, Vânia. "Women's Liberation and the Class Struggle." *The Political Economy of Women*, 4 (July 1972), 75-85.

The author, an exiled Brazilian Marxist, offers a theoretical approach to the issue of women's rights in Latin America.

1287. Barreno, Maria Isabel, ed. *A imagem da mulher na imprensa.* Lisbon: Ministério dos Assuntos Sociais, 1976.

A short (89 pp.) collection of studies on the image of women in the Portuguese press. Useful for comparison with Brazil.

1288. Bittencourt, Adalzira. *A mulher paulista na história*. Rio de Janeiro: Livros de Portugal, 1954.

Surveys the dependent socioeconomic role of women in the state of São Paulo.

1289. Blachman, Morris J. "Eve in an Adamocracy: Women and Politics in Brazil." New York: New York University Ibero-American Language and Area Center, *Occasional Papers* No. 5 [1973].

Examines the fragile women's rights movement in Brazil and the role of Rio's Bertha Lutz, its matriarch.

1290. "A brasileira já não é mais aquela." *Manchete* (Rio de Janeiro), August 19, 1972, 50-55.

Literally, "The Brazilian Girl Isn't What She Used to Be." Claims that a poll of working women shows an unexpectedly high level of independence.

1291. Cahali, Yussef Said. *Divórcio e separação*. São Paulo: Revista dos Tribunais, 1978.

Reviews the new civil legislation permitting, for the first time, legal separation and divorce.

1292. Carlos, Manuel L. and Lois Sellers. "Family, Kinship Structure, and Modernization in Latin America." *Latin American Research Review*, 7 (Summer 1972), 95-141.

Observes that investigators in Brazil tend to focus on migration and hence extended family networks, the result of Freyre's influence.

1293. Chamberlain, Henriqueta. *Where the Sabiá Sings; a Partial Autobiography*. New York: Macmillan, 1947.

A young woman of partially North American parentage writes of her "coming of age" in Brazil, offering a rare detailed glimpse of family and school life.

1294. Chandler, Billy Jaynes. *The Feitosas and the Sertão dos Inhamuas*. Gainesville: University of Florida Press, 1972.

Narrates the history of the Feitosa clan of Ceará,

locally notorious since the 1700's for their strong-armed methods of acquiring economic and political hegemony.

1295. Costa Pinto, Luiz de Aguiar. *Lutas de famílias no Brasil.* São Paulo: Companhia Editôra Nacional, 1949.

Examines the role of the family as a labor unit, and shows how family groups in Brazil aggregate political power and become instruments of private justice.

1296. Da Silva, Léa M. "Family Size and Female Labor Force Participation in Brazil." Diss., Duke University, 1976.

1297. d'Eça, Raul. "Feminism in Brazil." *Bulletin of the Pan American Union*, 70 (December 1936), 981-982.

Lists women holding public office during the mid-Vargas era.

1298. Expilly, Charles. *Mulheres e costumes do Brasil.* São Paulo: Companhia Editôra Nacional, 1936.

A semi-scholarly treatise on women in Brazilian history, stressing their dependent roles.

1299. Farhat, Alfredo. *A mulher perante o direito.* São Paulo: Edição Universitário de Direito, 1971.

Surveys the position of Brazilian women before the law. Clearly demonstrates women's second-class citizenship.

1300. Friedan, Betty. "Go Home Yankee Lady!" *McCalls*, 94 (October 1971), 69-72.

Describes the unbridled hostility faced by the feminist writer during a Brazilian trip.

1301. Gouveia, Aparecida Joly. *Professoras de amanhã.* Rio de Janeiro: M.E.C., 1965.

Surveys the factors that encourage young women in São Paulo and Minas to be elementary school teachers. Finds that those most likely to do so come from "traditional" families with modest incomes and little education.

1302. Hahner, June E. *A mulher no Brasil.* Rio de Janeiro: Civilização Brasileira, 1978.

Illustrates women's roles in Brazil through the use of excerpts from women's writings--from the highest born to *favelada* Carolina Maria de Jesus.

1303. Hahner, June E. "Women and Work in Brazil, 1850-1920." *Essays Concerning the Socio-economic History of Brazil and Portuguese India, 1850-1920.* Eds. Dauril Alden and Warren Dean. Gainesville: University of Florida Press, 1977, pp. 87-117.

Surveys the growth of the women's work force to 1920. Useful for comparison with later periods.

1304. Hahner, June E. *Women in Latin American History. Their Lives and Views.* Los Angeles: UCLA Latin American Center, 1976.

A short (181 pp.) anthology of women's writing in Latin America. Includes several Brazilian selections.

1305. Horta, Elizabeth V. *A mulher na cultura brasileira.* Belo Horizonte: Imprensa Oficial, 1975.

Surveys the contributions of women to Brazilian culture and life.

1306. Karasch, Mary. "Black Worlds in the Tropics: Gilberto Freyre and the Woman of Color in Brazil." *Proceedings of the Pacific Coast Council on Latin American Studies*, 3 (1974), 19-30.

Takes aim at Freyre's condescending treatment of nonwhite women--principally *mulatas*--in his writings.

1307. Knaster, Meri. "Women in Latin America: The State of Research." *Latin American Research Review*, 11 (Spring 1976), 3-74.

Describes more than a dozen research projects on Brazilian women's roles.

1308. Kottack, Conrad Philip. "Kinship and Class in Brazil." *Ethnology*, 6 (1967), 427-443.

Observes that kinship ties survive beyond changing environmental conditions.

1309. Levi, Darrell E. "The Prado Family, European Culture, and the Rediscovery of Brazil, 1860-1930."

Revista de História (São Paulo), 52 (October-December 1975), 803-824.

Suggests that before 1930 Europe represented both a model and a threat to elite Brazilians interested in modernizing their country. The Prados were cultural brokers who attempted to transplant European culture to Brazil while at the same time seeking to preserve Brazilian traditions.

1310. Lewin, Linda. "Some Historical Implications of Kinship Organization for Family-Based Politics in the Brazilian Northeast." *Comparative Studies in Society and History*, 21 (April 1979), 262-292.

Examines the connection between kinship and power. In the Republic, a "given universe of kin defined the base of the wider network of political action."

1311. MacLachlan, Colin. "The Feminine Mystique in Brazil: A Middle-Class Image." *Proceedings of the Pacific Coast Council on Latin American Studies*, 2 (1973), 61-73.

Examines the image of middle class Brazilian women, caught between traditional expectations of docility and exaggerated femininity on one hand and currents of social change on the other.

1312. Maio, Salvador de. *O poder da mulher e a delinquencia*. Santa Catarina (Florianopolis?): Ed. Ipiranga, 1959.

Contends that women can help prevent delinquent behavior by asserting their family role.

1313. Mitchell, Simon. "The Influence of Kinship in the Social Organization of North East Brazilian Fishermen: A Contrast in Case Studies." *Journal of Latin American Studies*, 6 (November 1974), 301-313.

A field study of Pôrto de Galinhas, Pernambuco, which differs in its conclusions from Forman's *Raft Fishermen* (item 1160). Mitchell finds a lack of cooperative institutions and marked individualism among producers.

1314. Moraes, Tancredo. *Pela emancipação integral da mulher*. Rio de Janeiro: Irmãos Pongetti, 1971.

Argues in favor of women's rights and complete juridical emancipation.

1315. Moreira, Albertino G. "A mulher perante o direito social." *Cultura Política*, 2 (October 1942), 40-47.

Reviews the social legislation of the Estado Nôvo regime in behalf of the interests of women employees.

1316. Mourão, Maurício D. Horta. *A lei do divorcio e sua aplicação*. Rio de Janeiro: Freitas Bastos, 1978.

Comments on the newly adopted divorce law and its application.

1317. "Mulher, Trabalho e Libertação." *Movimento* (São Paulo), 64 (September 20, 1976), 8-9.

Discusses the lower salary and wage scale paid to working women, and the value of domestic services performed by women in the home. One of the first statements in the Brazilian press advocating increased women's rights.

1318. Muraro, Rose Marie. *A mulher na construção do mundo futuro*. Petrópolis: Ed. Vozes, 1969.

Argues in behalf of a just society based on a more independent role for Brazilian women.

1319. Muraro, Rose Marie. *Libertação sexual da mulher*. Petrópolis: Ed. Vozes, 1970.

Calls for sexual liberation for women in terms mild by foreign standards but radical according to Brazilian norms.

1320. Murphy, Yolanda and Robert F. *Women of the Forest*. New York: Columbia University Press, 1974.

Relates the social behavior of the Amazonian Munduricú's, where men officially dominate tribal culture but where women's domestic authority holds the upper hand.

1321. Pescatello, Ann. "The Brasileira: Images and Realities in Writings of Machado de Assis and Jorge Amado." *Female and Male in Latin America: Essays*. Pittsburgh: University of Pittsburgh Press, pp. 29-58.

Examines the image of Brazilian women in the fiction of Machado de Assis, himself a mulatto, and Jorge Amado.

1322. Pescatello, Ann. "*Dona e prostituta*: Growing up Female in Brazil." Paper presented to the American Historical Association, New York, December 1970.

Brazilian women's degree of sexual freedom far exceeds limits imposed by law and customs; old myths attempt to classify them either as pure (*dona*) or corrupt (*prostituta*).

1323. Pescatello, Ann. "The Female in Ibero-America: an Essay on Research Bibliography and Research Directions." *Latin American Research Review*, 2 (Summer 1972), 125-141.

Discusses the limited available literature on the subject at the time of publication.

1324. Pescatello, Ann M. *Power and Pawn: The Female in Iberian Families, Societies, and Cultures.* Westport, Conn.: Greenwood Press, 1976.

Examines the tension caused by women's dual role as wielders of power and as pawns of men.

1325. Rabello, Sylvio, et al. *A participação da mulher no mercado de trabahlo.* Recife: Instituto Joaquim Nabuco, 1969.

A study by a team of sociologists of the growing economic role of women in the Northeast's work force.

1326. Rachum, Ilan. "Feminism, Woman Suffrage, and National Politics in Brazil: 1922-1937." *Luso-Brazilian Review*, 14 (Summer 1977), 118-134.

Notes that the growth of feminism in Brazil has coincided with periods of national upheaval, and that feminist interests have become casualties of conservative authoritarianism.

1327. Rosen, Bernard C. and Manoel T. Berlinck. "Modernization and Family Structure in the Region of São Paulo, Brazil." *América Latina*, 2 (1968), 75-95.

Demonstrates that strong familial ties are maintained even after migration.

1328. Rosen, Bernard C. and Anita L. LaRaia. "Modernity in Women: An Index of Social Change in Brazil." *Journal of Marriage and the Family*, 34 (May 1972), 353-360.

Shows how the middle class is susceptible to models which offer guidelines for behavior in the modern world.

1329. Santos, José Luis dos. "Família e história: estudo de um caso e de uma questão." Master's Thesis, Departamento de Ciências Sociais, Universidade Estadual de Campinas, 1976.

Studies the structural mechanisms which act to hold families together over time through a case study of kinship ties in an extended family in the small city of Riberão Preto, São Paulo.

1330. Saraiva, Maria Terezinha Tourinho. *Brasil: Aspectos da participação da mulher no desenvolvimento*. Haifa, Israel: National Center for Human Resources, May-June 1970.

A study of the role of Brazilian women in economic development, presented to the Seventh International Conference on Women's Economic Role.

1331. Silva, Carmen da. *A arte de ser mulher*. Rio de Janeiro: Civilização Brasileira, 1966.

A guide to the "art of being a woman," from the woman's magazine *Cláudia*.

1332. Soihet, Rachel. "Bertha Lutz e a ascensão da mulher, 1919-1937." Master's Thesis, Universidade Federal Fluminese, Niteroi, 1974.

Relates the life and career of the first advocate of equal rights for Brazilian women, Bertha Lutz.

1333. Tavares de Sá, Irene. *A condição da mulher*. Rio de Janeiro: Ed. Agir, 1966.

Surveys the general condition of women in society.

1334. Van Steen, Edla, ed. *O conto da mulher brasileira*. São Paulo: Ed. Vertente, 1978.

Collected short stories by women authors, touching on such themes as the superficiality of social behavior, the difficulties of interpersonal communication, and the dehumanizing side of professional life.

1335. Wallis, Marie P. "Modern Women Poets of Brazil." Diss., University of New Mexico, 1947.

1336. Wilkening, E.A., João Bosco Pinto, and José Pastore. "Role of the Extended Family in Migration and Adaptation in Brazil." *Journal of Marriage and the Family*, (November 1968), 689-695.

Demonstrates that the extended family in Brazil is the most important reference point for migrants to urban as well as rural areas.

C. ETHNIC AND RACE RELATIONS

1. General Studies

1337. Azevedo, Thales de. *As elites de côr: un estudo de asenção social*. São Paulo: Companhia Editôra Nacional, 1955.

Studies of social mobility and the inhibiting factors posed by unwritten racial barriers.

1338. Azevedo, Thales de. *Democracia racial: ideologia e realidade*. Petrópolis: Ed. Vozes, 1975.

Reviews patterns of race relations in Brazil and stresses the gap between ideology and reality.

1339. Baldus, Herbert. *Bibliografia crítica de etnologia brasileira*. São Paulo: n.p., 1954.

An annotated (859 pp.) bibliography of ethnology and race relations.

1340. Bastide, Roger. "The Present Status of Afro-American Research in Latin America." *Daedalus*, 103 (Spring 1974), 111-120.

Stresses the importance of the "São Paulo school" of scholarship (Cardoso, Fernandes, Ianni) in proving erroneous "myths" about Brazil's racial democracy, especially Freyre's "luso-tropicalism."

1341. Bastide, Roger and Pierre van den Berghe. "Stereotypes, Norms, and Interracial Behavior in São Paulo,

Brazil." *American Sociological Review*, 22 (December 1957), 689-694.

Indicates that non-white status limits upward mobility independently of class factors.

1342. Bicudo, V.L. "Atitudes raciais de prêtos e mulatos em São Paulo." *Sociologia*, 3 (1947), 195-219.

An early study of racial perceptions among blacks and mulattos in São Paulo.

1343. Bilden, Rudiger. "Brazil, Laboratory of Civilization." *The Nation*, 128 (1929), 71-74.

Argues that Brazilian racial composition is becoming increasingly white, a factor which the author considers essential for a higher level of civilization.

1344. Blair, Thomas L. "The Negro Worker in Urban Brazil." *Crisis*, 61 (December 1954), 592-599.

Explores the mechanisms which restrict opportunities for upward social mobility for non-whites.

1344a. Bojunga, Claúdio. "O brasileiro negro, 90 anos depois." *Encontros com a Civilização Brasileira*. Rio de Janeiro: Civilização Brasileira, 1978, pp. 175-204.

Claims that 90 years after abolition of slavery, conditions for non-whites in Brazilian society are still poor. When a black appears at a social function, he is likely to be either a *futebol* player or a musician.

1345. Cardoso, Fernando Henrique and Otávio Ianni. *Côr e mobilidade em Florianápolis*. São Paulo: Companhia Editôra Nacional, 1960.

Finds color prejudice in the southern city of Florianápolis despite the region's reputation for tolerance.

1346. Corwin, Arthur F. "Afro-Brazilians: Myths and Realities." *Slavery and Race Relations in Latin America*. Ed. Robert Brent Toplin. Westport, Conn.: Greenwood Press, 1974, pp. 385-438.

Challenges Freyre's vision of dynamic racial and cultural mixture through a review of recent studies, noting that Brazil's racial problems have not yet been solved. An important contribution.

1347. Costa Pinto, L.A. *O negro no Rio de Janeiro: relações de raças numa sociedade em mundança.* São Paulo: Companhia Editôra Nacional, 1952.

A classic study of non-whites in the city of Rio de Janeiro. The author warns that racial pressures are building up to a possible future crisis.

1348. Coutinho, Afrânio. "Brazil, Laboratory of Civilization." *Free World*, 6 (August 1943), 172-4.

A wartime statement of the racial democracy theme by a leading Vargas-era intellectual.

1349. Crusoe, Romeu. *A maldição de Canaan.* Rio de Janeiro: Ed. Di Giorgio, 1951.

A novel describing the psychological effects of racial discrimination.

1350. Davis, David Brion. *The Problem of Slavery in Western Culture.* Ithaca, N.Y.: Cornell University Press, 1966.

Views Brazilian slavery and race relations as a harsh system in which reality overshadowed legal restrictions on exploitation.

1351. Degler, Carl. *Neither Black nor White.* New York: Macmillan, 1971.

Skillfully compares slavery and race relations in Brazil and the United States, suggesting that slavery was less humane in Brazil than Freyre and others have argued.

1352. Donald, Cleveland Junior. "Equality in Brazil: Confronting Reality." *Black World*, 22 (November 1972), 23-34.

A young black United States scholar raises questions about Brazil's mythology.

1353. Dzidzienyo, Anani. *The Position of Blacks in Brazilian Society.* London: Minority Rights Group. Report No. 7 [1970].

The author, a Ghanaian, presents evidence that Brazilian racial democracy is largely a myth.

1354. Elkins, Stanley. *Slavery, A Problem in American Institutional and Intellectual Life.* Chicago: University of Chicago Press, 1968.

Follows Tannenbaum's argument about inherent safeguards in the religious and juridical systems of Latin America against excessive mistreatment of slaves.

1355. Fernandes, Florestan. "Beyond Poverty: The Negro and the Mulatto in Brazil." *Slavery and Race Relations in Latin America*. Ed. Robert Brent Toplin. Westport, Conn.: Greenwood Press, 1974, pp. 277-298.

Argues that racial attributes were fixed by centuries of slavery, so that after abolition little changed: formal practices gave way to unwritten rules of behavior, making non-whites the victims of both class and race prejudice.

1356. Fernandes, Florestan. *A integração do negro na sociedade de classes*. 2 vols. 3rd ed. São Paulo: Ed. Ática, 1978. Translated as *The Negro in Brazilian Society* (1969).

Calls the legacy of slavery the most significant and dramatic agent of social disorientation in Brazilian history. Advocates a "second abolition" for Brazilian non-whites.

1357. Figueiredo, Ariosvaldo. *O Negro e a violência do branco*. Rio de Janeiro: José Álvaro, 1977.

Focusing on northeastern Sergipe, the author traces a pattern of economic, political and sexual violence over four centuries.

1358. Fontaine, Pierre-Michel. "Aspects of Afro-Brazilian Career Mobility in the Corporate World." Paper presented to the Symposium on Popular Dimensions of Brazil, U.C.L.A., February 1979.

Shows that non-whites are more likely to be found in positions accessible through formal examinations than in informally-filled posts, and in the public sector than the private.

1359. Frazier, E. Franklin. "A Comparison of Negro-White Relations in Brazil and the United States." *On Race Relations: Selected Writings*. Ed. G. Franklin Edwards. Chicago: University of Chicago Press, 1968, pp. 82-102.

A black North American scholar's observations first published in 1944 noting the subtle consciousness of color differences among the elite and the stronger color line in the southern states.

1360. Freyre, Gilberto. "Brazil and the International Crisis." *Journal of Negro Education*, 10 (July 1941), 510-514.

Argues that the Negro in Brazil is a full-fledged citizen, not an "African minority."

1361. [Freyre, Gilberto.] *The Gilberto Freyre Reader*. Tr. Barbara Shelby. New York: Alfred A. Knopf, 1975.

Somewhat terse selections from Freyre's writings, with some new translations of older ones. Stresses the breadth and range of his views on society, education, ethnicity, family life, politics, and literature.

1362. Freyre, Gilberto. *The Masters and the Slaves: A Study in the Development of Brazilian Civilization*. Tr. Samuel Putnam, New York: Alfred A. Knopf, 1946.

Freyre's *opus magnum*, published as *Casa grande e senzala* (1933), and the central source of his hypothesis that Brazilian slavery was relatively benign owing to the sexual liaisons which developed between Portuguese men and non-white women.

1363. Freyre, Gilberto. *New World in the Tropics: The Culture of Modern Brazil*. New York: Alfred A. Knopf, 1959.

Summarizes Freyre's views on the qualities of the Portuguese, the aborigine, the African, and the mulatto, lauding Brazil as a "Tropical China" and celebrating its racial outlook.

1364. Freyre, Gilberto. "Misconceptions of Brazil." *Foreign Affairs*, 40 (April 1962), 453-462.

Maintains that Brazil is not victimized by social or economic feudalism, as some left-oriented analysts have charged.

1365. Freyre, Gilberto. *Order and Progress; Brazil from Monarchy to Republic*. New York: Alfred A. Knopf, 1970.

A study of the legacy of the traditional plantation system and the passing of preeminence to urban Brazil.

1366. Freyre, Gilberto. *The Portuguese and the Tropics*. Tr. H.D. O'Matthew and F. de Mello Moser. Lisbon: Executive Committee for the Commemoration of the Vth Centenary of the Death of Prince Henry the Navigator, 1961.

Another version of Freyre's view of tropicality and the Portuguese genius for adaptation.

1367. Freyre, Gilberto. "Slavery, Monarchy, and Modern Brazil." *Foreign Affairs*, 33 (July 1955), 624-33.

Summarizes the author's theories on the relatively benign state of Brazilian slavery and its legacy.

1368. Genovese, Eugene D. *Roll, Jordan, Roll. The World Slaveholders Made*. New York: Random House, 1972.

Criticizes Tannenbaum and Freyre although agreeing that Catholicism did influence slaves's lives. Shows that the roots of Afro-Brazilian religious diversity lay in the slave plantations themselves.

1369. Graham, Richard. "Brazilian Slavery Re-Examined: A Review Article." *Journal of Social History*, 3 (Summer 1970), 431-453.

Contends that the fact that Brazil's poor are predominately black and that most blacks are poor is the modern legacy of alienation and dehumanization.

1370. Guerreiro Ramos, Alberto. "O problema do negro na sociedade brasileira." *Cadernos de Nosso Tempo*, 2 (1959), 203-215.

Criticizes Nina Rodrigues and Gilberto Freyre as romantics, and rejects white sociological theorizing about blacks as ethnocentrism. Constitutes the first published assault on the racial democracy hypothesis by an Afro-Brazilian.

1371. Haberley, David T. "Abolitionism in Brazil; Anti-Slavery and Anti-Slave." *Luso-Brazilian Review*, 9 (Dec. 1972), 30-46.

An important article which shows that stereotypes of Negro immorality and violence pervaded abolitionist thought, and continued to be held by intellectuals after abolition.

1372. Hanke, Lewis. *Gilberto Freyre. Vida y Obra, Bibliografia, Antologia*. New York: Instituto de las Españas, 1939.

A short (30-page) biographical appreciation of the Brazilian socio-folklorist's early work.

1373. Harris, Marvin. *Patterns of Race in the Americas.* New York: Walker, 1964.

Presents a strongly contrary view to the Freyre-Tannenbaum-Elkins position on slavery and race, based on demographic and economic considerations.

1374. Harris, Marvin. "Racial Identity in Brazil." *Luso-Brazilian Review*, 1 (December 1964), 21-28.

Identifies several hundred terms which fall within the calculus of Brazilian racial identification.

1375. Indiana University. Audio-Visual Center. "Brazil: The Vanishing Negro." b/w film, 30 min. Bloomington, Indiana, 1953.

A dated but revealing portrait of race identity and the "whitening" theme, filmed in Bahia. Includes interviews with Afro-Brazilians.

1376. Instituto Brazileiro de Geografia e Estatística. *Estudos sobre a composição de população do Brasil segundo a côr.* Rio de Janeiro: Instituto Brasileiro de Geografia e Estatística, 1950.

Documents the hypothesis that Brazil's population is "whitening." The study's data, taken from national censuses from 1872 to 1940, must be weighed in the light of changing social definitions of skin and color over time.

1377. Kalili, Narciso and Odacir de Mattos. "Existe preconceito de côr no Brasil." *Realidade* (Rio), 2 (1967), 53-55.

A journalist discusses racial discrimination in contemporary Brazil.

1378. Kottak, Conrad Phillip. "Race Relations in a Bahian Fishing Village." *Luso-Brazilian Review*, 4 (December 1967), 35-52.

Field work in Arembepe reveals a positive correlation between light skin color and wealth, yet color does not limit chances for entrepreneurial success in the local economy.

1379. Marais, Ben J. *Colour--Unsolved Problem of the West.* Capetown, South Africa: H. Timmins, 1952.

A South African's views on Brazilian race relations emphasizing the use of class rather than color as the basis for discrimination.

1380. Martin, Percy A. "Slavery and Abolition in Brazil." *Hispanic American Historical Review*, 13 (May 1933), 151-196.

Points to the presence of large numbers of free Negroes and mulattos before abolition as a factor of subsequent peaceful integration and emphasizes the role of Emperor Pedro II in creating a climate favorable to freeing Brazil's slaves.

1381. Mason, Philip. *Race Relations*. London: Oxford University Press, 1970.

Compares the human response to racial differences, crediting the Brazilians for their public commitment to the idea that racial discrimination is wrong but criticizing them for their reluctance to admit that it exists nonetheless.

1382. Metall, R.A. and M. Paranhos de Silva. "Equality of Opportunity in a Multiracial Society: Brazil." *International Labour Review*, 93 (January-June 1966), n.p.

Notes that light-skinned mulattos who have achieved economic success tend to hold the same racist views as whites towards blacks. The authors warn that increased racial tensions may rend the very fabric of Brazilian society.

1383. Montezuma de Carvalho, Joaquim. *Entrevista con Gilberto Freyre*. Mexico City: Frente de Afirmación Hispanista, 1975.

A fascinating interview with Freyre at 74 years of age about mysticism, sensuality, and his career.

1384. Mörner, Magnus. *Race Mixture in the History of the New World*. Boston: Little, Brown and Company, 1967.

Mostly about Spanish America, but offers useful commentary on the Brazilian race relations, including the theme "Brazil: hell for blacks; purgatory for whites; paradise for mulattos."

1385. Morse, Richard M. "The Negro in São Paulo, Brazil." *Journal of Negro History*, 38 (July 1953), 290-306.

Stresses the differences in quality and scope in race contact in the Center-South in comparison to Bahia and the Northeast.

1386. Nascimento, Abdias de. *O genocídio do negro brasileiro: processo de um racismo mascarado.* Rio de Janeiro: Paz e Terra, 1978.

The first published allegation of deliberate and official policies of "masked racist genocide" of Brazilian blacks. Highly controversial, the volume was called 'treasonous' by some government officials.

1387. Nascimento, Abdias do. *"Racial Democracy" in Brazil: Myth or Reality?* Ife, Nigeria: University of Ife, 1977.

Attacks Brazilian society for hypocrisy, alleging systematic efforts to obliterate Afro-Brazilians as cultural and physical beings.

1388. Odália, Nío. "O ideal de branqueamento da raça na historiografia brasileira." *Contexto*, 3 (July 1977), 127-136.

Focuses on the theme of "whitening" in the formation of a "Brazilian race." Contends that Skidmore (item 1401) fails to acknowledge the contribution of Varnhagen and other 19th-century Brazilian writers.

1389. Penn, Dorothy. "We Brazilians are Becoming One People." *Catholic World*, 163 (April 1946), 34-40.

Describes Brazil's tolerance of miscegenation and the process of racial amalgamation (and "whitening").

1390. Pierson, Donald. "The Negro in Bahia, Brazil." *American Sociological Review*, 4 (1939), 524-533.

Discusses the relationship between race and economic class in the role of blacks in Bahian society.

1391. Pierson, Donald. "Survey de Picinguaba." *Revista do Museu Paulista* (São Paulo), 1 (1947), 173-180.

An important early community study of Picinguaba, a small town near Ubatuba in the extreme eastern part of the state of São Paulo. Classifies local society according to race, ethnicity, and class.

1392. Ramos, Arthur. "Acculturation among the Brazilian Negroes." *Journal of Negro History*, 26 (April 1945), 244-250.

Assays the influence of Raimundo Nina Rodrigues and other Brazilian scholars of contact between black and white cultures, especially in Bahia.

1393. Ramos, Arthur. *A aculturação negra no Brasil*. São Paulo: Companhia Editôra Nacional, 1942.

A classical early view of racial acculturation.

1394. Reeve, Richard Penn. "Race and Social Conflict in a Brazilian Industrial Town." *Luso-Brazilian Review*, 14 (Winter 1977), 236-253.

Finds, in a study of "Vila Industrial," a pseudonymous town outside Belo Horizonte, that racial discrimination inhibits social mobility for non-whites.

1395. Rout, Leslie B., Jr. "Race Relations in Southern Brazil: the Pôrto Alegre Experience." *Proceedings of the Pacific Coast Council on Latin American Studies*, 4 (1975), 89-100.

Describes the author's experience in Brazil's southernmost major city, where he encounters significant racial discrimination as a black. Finds Afro-Brazilian students politically unsophisticated, like North American blacks a generation earlier.

1396. Rout, Leslie B., Jr. "Brazil: Study in Black, Brown, and Beige." *Negro Digest*, 19 (February 1970), 21-23; 65-73.

A personal account of the author's stay in Pôrto Alegre in 1962 and the racism he encountered as a black.

1397. Rout, Leslie B., Jr. "Race and Slavery in Brazil." *The Wilson Quarterly*, 1 (August 1976), 73-89.

Contends that the haphazard acceptance of the mulatto has been the most conspicuous aspect of race relations since the end of slavery, and that, with small signs of awareness among mulattos and blacks in urban centers, old patterns may be changing.

1398. Russell-Wood, A.J.R. "Race and Class in Brazil, 1937-1967." *Race*, 10 (October 1968), 185-191.

Finds that Salvador, thirty years after Pierson's study (item 1435), cannot be said to be typical of Brazil's racial situation and that Pierson's conclusions should not be applied to Brazil as a whole.

1399. Sanjek, Roger. "Brazilian Racial Terms: Some Aspects of Meaning and Learning." *American Anthropologist*, 73 (1971), 1126-1143.

Shows that despite ambiguities in racial categories, certain terms are used with great frequency, and therefore may be used empirically.

1400. Serton, Petrus. *Suid Afrika en Brasilie*. Capetown: Oxford University Press, 1960.

An Afrikaner scholar argues that apartheid exists in Brazil but is not legislated.

1401. Sio, Arnold. "Interpretation of Slavery: The Slave Status in the Americas." *Comparative Studies in Society and History*, 7 (1965), 289-308.

Attacks the Freyre-Elkins-Tannenbaum thesis that slavery in Brazil was less harsh than in the United States.

1402. Skidmore, Thomas E. *Black into White: Race and Nationality in Brazilian Thought*. New York: Oxford University Press, 1974.

Discusses the concept of "whitening," whereby the elite, by the late nineteenth century, came to believe that miscegenation would suppress Negroid and Amerindian racial traits within the Brazilian population.

1403. Skidmore, Thomas E. "Gilberto Freyre and the Early Brazilian Republic: Some Notes on Methodology." *Comparative Studies in Society and History*, 6 (July 1964), 490-505.

Raises serious criticisms about Freyre's use of sources while not disparaging his overall reputation as the father of modern Brazilian Studies.

1404. Skidmore, Thomas E. "Toward a Comparative Analysis of Race Relations Since Abolition in Brazil and the United States." *Journal of Latin American Studies*, 4 (May 1972), 1-28.

In Brazil, social relations developed within a multiracial system where whites stood at the top, the traditional value structure remained intact, and society saw itself as "whitening."

1405. Staley, Austin John. "Racial Democracy in Marriage: A Sociological Analysis of Negro-White Intermarriage in Brazilian Culture." Diss., University of Pittsburgh, 1959.

1406. Stein, Stanley J. "Freyre's Brazil Revisited: A Review of *New World in the Tropics: The Culture of Modern Brazil*." *Hispanic American Historical Review*, 41 (February 1961), 111-113.

One of the most direct criticisms of the shortcomings of Freyre's methodology.

1407. Tannenbaum, Frank. *Slave and Citizen: The Negro in the Americas*. New York: Alfred A. Knopf, 1947.

Suggests that Latin American slaves enjoyed relatively better conditions because Catholic societies acknowledged the captives' soul, and that free blacks and mulattos were able to attain upward mobility have been challenged by more recent scholarship.

1408. Toplin, Robert Brent. "Brazil: Racial Polarization in the Developing Giant." *Black World*, 22 (November 1972), 15-22.

Stresses the dangers inherent in Brazil's failure to confront racially-based economic and social disparities.

1409. Willems, Emílio. "Race Attitudes in Brazil." *American Journal of Sociology*, 54 (March 1949), 402-408.

Warns that investigations by scholars are beginning to find holes in the "racial democracy" argument.

2. Afro-Brazilians

1410. Álves, Henrique C. *Bibliografia Afro-brasileira: estudos sôbre o negro*. São Paulo: Edições "H.", 1976.

Lists without comment articles and books on Afro-Brazilian studies, a subject which has been dealt with somewhat timidly by Brazilian scholars but which promises to receive major attention in the coming decade.

1411. Amado, Jorge. *Jubiaba*. São Paulo: Ed. Martins, 1935.

Considered a major portrait of Afro-Brazilian life.

1412. Bastide, Roger. *African Civilization in the New World*. London: Hurst, 1971.

Predicts that the higher the Afro-Latin American (and Afro-Brazilian) is able to climb the ladder of social status, the more likely he will be to jettison his cultural heritage in favor of cultural assimilation.

1413. Bastide, Roger. *Estudos Afro-brasileiros.* São Paulo: Ed. Perspectiva, 1973.

A collection of Bastide's articles and short studies on Afro-Brazilian culture, especially *macumba*, *candomblé*, and syncretic Catholicism.

1414. Bastide, Roger. *O negro na imprensa e na literature.* São Paulo: Universidade de São Paulo, 1972.

Analyzes the stereotypical negative view of the black in the press and in literature.

1415. Borges, João Baptista Pereira. *Côr, profissão e mobilidade (o negro e o rádio em São Paulo).* São Paulo: Ed. Pionera/Universidade de São Paulo, 1967.

Shows that the radio industry fits blacks into rigid stereotypes for hiring as well as for portrayal over the airwaves.

1416. Carneiro, Edison, ed. *Antologia do negro brasileiro.* Rio de Janeiro: Tecnoprint Gráfica, 1967.

A collection of short articles and selections on the Brazilian Negro, treating slavery and abolition, resistance, Afro-Brazilian religion, folklore, and views of blacks in national literature.

1417. Cascudo, Luis da Câmara. *História da alimentação no Brasil.* 2 vols. São Paulo: Companhia Editôra Nacional, 1967.

Explores indigenous and African influences on Brazilian cooking and nutrition.

1418. Couceira, Solange Martins. *Bibliografia sôbre o negro brasileiro.* São Paulo: Escola de Comunicações e Artes, 1971.

A 66-page bibliography on the Afro-Brazilian presence, emphasizing anthropological and cultural studies.

1419. Dreller, Gerald. "The Afro-Brazilian: An Expression of Popular Culture in Selected Examples of Bahian Literature." Diss., University of Illinois at Champaign-Urbana, 1974.

1420. Dzidzienyo, Anani. "A África vista do Brasil." *Afro-Asia*, 10-11 (June-December 1970), 79-97.

Examines newspaper coverage in Salvador's *Jornal da Bahia* to illustrate continued interest in African affairs during the late 1960's.

1421. Freyre, Gilberto, comp. *Estudos Afro-brasileiros. Trabhalos apresentados ao 1° Congresso Afro-Brasileiro reunido do Recife em 1934.* Rio de Janeiro: Ariel Editôra, 1935.

Twenty-three pathbreaking essays by specialists ranging from Melville Herskovits to Arthur Ramos. Largely overlooked by scholars, this collection represents the first Brazilian effort to focus in depth on Afro-Brazilian culture.

1422. Freyre, Gilberto. "The Negro in Brazilian Culture and Society." *Quarterly Journal on Inter-American Relations* (Washington), 1 (1939), 69-75.

Briefly summarizes his major views on the Afro-Brazilian legacy in language, culture, the arts, and national personality.

1423. Freyre, Gilberto, comp. *Novos estudos Afro-brasileiros.* Rio de Janeiro: Civilização Brasileira, 1940.

The second volume of papers presented at Freyre's 1937 Congress on Afro-Brazilian studies in Bahia. Extremely valuable articles on witchcraft, mental illness, folklore, and race.

1424. Gomes, Antônio Osmar. "A vocação musical do mulato." *Revista do Brasil*, 2 (April 1939), 33-38.

Lauds the mulatto's "vocation for music" and his contributions to choral singing and popular bands.

1425. Herskovits, Melville J. *The New World Negro.* Bloomington: Indiana University Press, 1966.

Contains four essays on cult life in Brazil, including a study of *Panãn*, a rite of passage practiced by *candomblé* groups in Salvador.

1426. Joel, Miriam. *African Traditions in Latin America.* Cuernavaca: CIDOC, 1972.

Presents descriptive data on five Latin American societies, including Brazil, drawn from secondary sources.

1427. Latin American Studies Center. *Black Latin America.* Los Angeles: California State University, Los Angeles, 1977.

A bibliography. Brazil is treated in the general section and on pages 47-60.

1428. Levine, Robert M. "The First Afro-Brazilian Congress: Opportunities for the Study of Race in the Brazilian Northeast." *Race*, 15 (October 1973), 185-194.

Describes Gilberto Freyre's effort to bring together scholars from all parts of Brazil to examine Afro-Brazilian history and culture. A modest beginning, the Conference nonetheless was attacked by local conservatives.

1429. Mendonça, Renato. *A influência africana no português do Brasil.* 2nd ed. São Paulo: Companhia Editôra Nacional, 1935.

A bibliography of books and articles dealing with African influence on Portuguese culture in Brazil.

1430. Miller, Joseph C., comp. *Slavery: A Comparative Teaching Bibliography.* Waltham, Mass.: African Studies Association, Brandeis University, 1977.

Includes the major works on slavery and slave systems of interest to Brazilianists. 123 pages.

1431. *Mulatas.* Intro. Jorge Amado. 2nd ed. São Paulo: Ed. Três, 1978.

Soft-core pornography produced "for export," exemplifying the prevailing Brazilian stereotype of the mulata as a "natural" sex object.

1432. Nunes, Maria Luisa. "The Preservation of African Culture in Brazilian Literature: The Novels of Jorge Amado." *Luso-Brazilian Review*, 10 (June 1973), 86-101.

Acknowledges Amado's contribution as the foremost "curator" of African culture in Brazil, recognizing African rites as an integral part of the lives of their practitioners.

1433. Pereira, João Baptista Borges. "O negro e a comercialização da música popular brasileira." *Revista do Instituto de Estudos Brasileiros*, 8 (1970), 7-15.

Shows how popular stereotypes of "musical" blacks

helped gain acceptance for *samba* and other musical forms of Afro-Brazilian origin.

1434. Pierson, Donald. *Negroes in Brazil: A Study of Race Contact at Bahia*. Carbondale: Southern Illinois University Press, 1967.

Argues that the Brazilian white has never felt threatened by the black or the mulatto. As a result, Brazil, with its more firmly established class distinctions, lacks the atmosphere of racial tension prevalent in the United States.

1435. Pierson, Donald. *Survey of the Literature of Brazil of Sociological Significance Published up to 1940*. Cambridge: Harvard University Press, 1945.

Devotes particular attention to studies of religion, race relations, and Afro-Brazilian culture.

1436. Porter, Dorothy B., comp. *Afro-Braziliana: A Working Bibliography*. Boston: G.K. Hall, 1978.

Spans 5,233 entries, half of them individual writing of Afro-Brazilian authors (or writers on Afro-

Brazilian themes). Topics include social conditions, medicine and health, history, traveller's accounts, and folklore. Partially annotated.

1437. Rabassa, Gregory. "The Negro in Brazilian Fiction Since 1888." Diss., Columbia University, 1954.

A useful study by the master translator of Jorge Amado and other Latin American novelists.

1438. Ramos, Arthur. *Introdução à antropologia brasileira*. 2 vols. Rio de Janeiro: Edições da Coleção Estudos Brasileiros, 1943-47.

A major text concentrating on social interrelationships and the Afro-Brazilian presence.

1439. Rust, Frances. "Wilson Antônio Rosa: An Afro-Brazilian Pen Portrait." *Contemporary Review*, 223 (1973), 318-322.

Portrays the life and personality of a gifted itinerant beach vendor. Argues that his lack of black consciousness, his poverty, and his political naiveté do not hinder his enjoyment of life.

1440. Sayers, Raymond S. *The Negro in Brazilian Literature*. New York: Hispanic Institute, 1956.

Analyzes stereotypical views of Afro-Brazilians in national writing, ranging from the comic foil (Macunaíma) to noble rebels (Zumbí).

1441. Szwed, John F. and Roger D. Abrahams. *Afro-American Folk Culture*. Vol. 2. Philadelphia: Institute for the Study of Human Issues, 1977.

An annotated bibliography designed to "shatter [the] myth [that] Afro-Americans are a decultured people, culturally stripped by the slavery experience and its aftermath."

1442. Taváres, Regina A. and Hadjine Lisbôa. *Influencias africanas en la Américа Latina*. Rio de Janeiro: CLAPCS, 1963.

An 88-page bibliographical guide to African influences on Latin American life.

1443. Turner, Doris J. "Symbols in Two Afro-Brazilian Literary Works." *Teaching Latin American Studies*. Ed. Miriam Williford. Gainesville, Fla.: LASA, 1977, pp. 41-61.

Analyzes *Jubiabá*, the Jorge Amado novel, and *Sortilégio*, a dramatic work staged in 1957 before it was banned.

1444. Turner, J. Michael. "Reversing the Trend: Afro-Brazilian Influences in West Africa." *The Thematic Conceptual Approach to West African History*. Ed. Lathardus Goggins. Dubuque, Iowa: n.p., 1979.

Studies Bahian cultural transfers to West Africa in the nineteenth century. The author feels that Benin, ex-Dahomey, clearly shows signs of Brazilian influence, especially on the coast.

3. Native Brazilians

1445. Aborigines Protection Society of London. *Tribes of the Amazon Basin in Brazil*. London: APSL, 1973.

Describes conditions among surviving tribes.

1446. Ayrosa, Plínio. *Apontamentos para a bibliografia do lingua Tupí-Guaraní.* São Paulo: Faculdade de Filosofia, Ciências e Letras, 1943.

A bibliography of studies on Tupí-Guaraní language and culture.

1447. Beltrão, Luiz. *Indio, um mito brasileiro.* Petrópolis: Ed. Vozes, 1979.

Seeks to strip away the "myths" which have been built around Brazil's indigenous population. Defends the government's efforts to deal with the tribal groups.

1448. Bodard, Lucien. *Green Hell. Massacre of the Brazilian Indians.* Tr. Jennifer Monaghan. New York: Outerbridge and Dienstfrey, 1971.

A lurid, probably overstated account by a French journalist.

1449. Bonilla, Victor Daniel. *Servants of God or Masters of Men? The Story of a Capuchin Mission in Amazonia.* Tr. Rosemary Sheed. Baltimore: Penguin Books, 1972.

Blames priests for displacing the Indian as landowner as a result of their efforts to bring native tribes into contact with outside culture.

1450. Brooks, Edwin. "The Brazilian Road to Ethnicide." *Contemporary Review*, 224 (May 1974), 2-8.

Argues for a halt to government policies lest total ethnic disorder occur.

1451. Brooks, Edwin. "Frontiers of Ethnic Conflict in the Brazilian Amazon." *International Journal of Environmental Studies*, 7 (1974), 63-74.

Continues the line of argument against the destructive aspects of the government's Indian policy.

1452. Brooks, Edwin. "Twilight of Brazilian Tribes." *Geographical Magazine*, 45 (1973), 304-310.

Warns of the impending destruction of Brazil's aboriginal peoples as the interior is opened to development.

1453. Chiappino, Jean. *The Brazilian Indigenous Problem and Policy: The Aripunã Park.* Copenhagen: IWGIA, 1974.

Criticizes the military regime for inhumane policies toward native tribes. Seeks to discredit official Brazilian claims that resettlement causes no irreparable harm.

1454. Coutinho, Edilberto. *Rondón: O civilizador da última fronteira*. Rio de Janeiro: Civilização Brasileira, 1975.

Chronicles the life and career of Cândido Rondón, responsible for the Indian policy of the Brazilian government since the turn of the century. Notes the influence of Euclides da Cunha and other positivists on the young army officer.

1455. Cowell, Adrian. *The Tribe that Hides from Man*. London: Bodley Head, 1974.

Accounts the tragic consequences of contact with outside "civilization."

1456. Davis, Shelton H. *Victims of the Miracle: Development and the Indians of Brazil*. Cambridge, Eng.: Cambridge University Press, 1977.

Maintains that the decimation of indigenous tribes in the Amazon region has been a conscious official act. Includes a concise history of Indian policy since colonial times.

1457. Fuerst, René. "Bibliography on Brazilian Amazonian Indians." Copenhagen: International Workshop on Indigenous Affairs, 1972.

Emphasizes recent studies attesting to deteriorating conditions as a direct result of official Brazilian policies.

1458. Gregor, Thomas. *Mehinaku: The Drama of Daily Life in a Brazilian Indian Village*. Chicago: University of Chicago Press, 1978.

An illuminating study of the Mehinaku tribe.

1459. Hanbury-Tenison, Robin. *A Question of Survival for the Indians of Brazil*. New York: Charles Scribner's Sons, 1973.

Charges that Brazilian authorities have ignored the recommendations of the International Red Cross and, in consequence, have doomed the future of most of the remaining tribes in the jungle interior.

1460. Hemming, John. *Red Gold: The Conquest of the Brazilian Indians*. Cambridge, Mass.: Harvard University Press, 1978.

Although focusing on the colonial period, the author's account provides a valuable context for examining policies developed later.

1461. Kando, Ata. *Slave or Dead*. Holland: n.p., 1971.

A poignant photographic essay by a Dutch journalist documenting the life of the Piaroa and Yanomamo people, whom the author claims are being exterminated.

1462. Kiemen, Mathias C. "The Status of the Indians in Brazil after 1820." *The Americas*, 21 (January 1965), 263-273.

Provides a general analysis of the disastrous and muddled attempts in the 19th century to solve Brazil's Indian problem, as well as the Rondón reforms.

1463. Kietzman, Dale W. "Indian Survival in Brazil." Diss., University of Southern California, 1972.

One of the first studies of the impact of encroaching "civilization" upon the indigenous population.

1464. Lamb, F. Bruce. *Wizard of the Upper Amazon*. Boston: Houghton Mifflin, 1974.

Describes life in a jungle tribe at the beginning of the century on the Peruvian-Brazilian frontier widely using drugs to enhance consciousness and imagination.

1465. Lessa, Origenes. *O Índio côr-de-rosa*. Rio de Janeiro: Editôra Codecri, 1978.

A sympathetic biography of Noël Nutels, an immigrant from post-revolutionary Russia who, until his death in 1973, dedicated his life to the protection of Brazil's indigenous population.

1466. Levi-Strauss, Claude. *Tristes Tropiques*. Tr. J. Russell. New York: Atheneum, 1963.

A spellbinding, autobiographically-oriented portrait of Brazil's interior. A classic anthropological work first published in France in 1955.

1467. Maybury-Lewis, David. *The Savage and the Innocent*. Boston: Beacon, 1965.

Provides a memorable account of an anthropologist's personal efforts to gain the confidence of members of two indigenous Brazilian tribes, the Shavante and the Sherente.

1468. Primitive People's Fund. *Report of a Visit to the Indians of Brazil.* London: Primitive People's Fund, 1971.

Summarizes the dangers ahead for indigenous tribes and the harm done to date by contact with outsiders.

1469. Ribeiro, Darcy. *Os indios e a civilização.* Rio de Janeiro: Civilização Brasileira, 1970.

Surveys the history of relations between Indians and whites, concentrating on the difficulties of indigenous survivals.

1470. Rondón, Cândido M. de S. *Índios do Brasil.* 3 vols. Rio de Janeiro: Conselho Nacional de Proteção aos Índios, 1946.

An illustrated source book about tribal life, organized by geographic region.

1471. Seeger, Anthony and Eduardo Viveiros de Castro. "Pontos de vista sôbre os índios brasileiros: um ensaio bibliográfico." *Dados*, 17 (1977), 11-35.

A review article on writing about indigenous culture, contact and social change, religion, and social organization. Asks that anthropologists work to raise public consciousness so that the problem may be confronted.

1472. *The Situation of the Indian in South America.* New York: World Council of Churches, 1972.

Displays alarm at worsening conditions in Brazil.

1473. Steward, Julian H., ed. *Handbook of South American Indians.* New York: Cooper Square Press, 1963-

Provides extensive information on the indigenous population of the Amazon and Mato Grosso.

1474. Vidal, Lux Boelitz. *Morta e vida de uma sociedade indígena brasileira.* São Paulo: HUCITEC, 1977.

Examines the so-far successful efforts of the Kayapo-Xilcrin peoples of the Catetê River Valley to survive.

1475. Villas-Boas, Orlando and Cláudio. "Saving Brazil's Stone Age Tribes from Extinction." *National Geographic*, 134 (September 1968), 424-444.

Brazil's leading Indian experts argue in favor of government plans to protect indigenous tribes.

1476. Villas-Boas, Orlando and Cláudio. *Xingú: The Indians, Their Myths*. Tr. Susana H. Rudge. Ed. Kenneth S. Brecher. New York: Farrar, Straus and Giroux, 1973.

Thirty-one myths of the Juruna, Kuikurú, and Kamaiwa, set down by two renowned Indianists who lived in their midst for several decades.

1477. Von Puttkamer, W. Jesco. "Brazil's Kreen-Akakores: Requiem for a Tribe?" *National Geographic*, 147 (February 1975), 254-268.

Offers a sad view of the fate of one tribe affected by the opening of the Amazon.

1478. Wagley, Charles. *Amazon Town: A Study of Man in the Tropics*. New York: Columbia University Press, 1964.

A classic study of the Amazon region, its way of life, and the fusion of Portuguese and Indian cultures, focusing on "Itá," a fictitious name for the lower Amazon town in which the author first lived in 1939.

1479. Wagley, Charles. *Welcome of Tears: The Tapirapé Indians of Central Brazil*. London: Oxford University Press, 1977.

Examines the Brazilian tribe which Wagley first visited in 1939, whose social practices include self-imposed population control to keep the tribe in harmony with its environment.

1480. Wagley, Charles and Marvin Harris. *Minorities in the New World: Six Case Studies*. New York: Columbia University Press, 1958.

Finds that the rate of assimilation in the Brazilian interior may be sufficiently slow to preserve tribal customs, a conclusion proven overly optimistic by the early 1970's.

1481. Wycliffe Bible Translators. *Brazil's Tribes*. Campinas: Summer Institute of Linguistics, 1967.

A working directory of Brazil's tribal groups, compiled

by the major training center in native languages in Brazil.

4. Other Ethnic Groups

1482. Albersheim, Ursula. *Uma comunidade teuto-brasileiro.* Rio de Janeiro: CBPE, 1962.

A study of family life in a German-Brazilian community in South Brazil.

1483. Almeida, Tavares de. *Oeste paulista: a experiencia etnográfica e cultural.* Rio de Janeiro: Ed. Alba, 1943.

An early anthropological study of Japanese settlement in Western São Paulo.

1484. Bartolotti, Domenico. *Il Brasile meriodionale.* Rome: A. Stock, 1930.

A fascist writer points out the areas of contact between Italy and Brazil, commenting on Italian agricultural settlements, Italian religious missions, and Italo-Brazilian trade.

1485. "Bibliografia de Stefan Sweig" [sic]. *Autores e Livros* (Rio de Janeiro), 2 (1942), 97.

Lists writings on and by the Austrian-Jewish author, Stefan Zweig, who lived in Brazil as a refugee from Nazism until his suicide in 1942.

1486. Borges Pereira, João Baptista. *Italianos no mundo rural paulista.* São Paulo: Universidade de São Paulo, 1974.

Examines the Alto Sorocaba town of Pedrinhas, a rural district in the State of São Paulo heavily settled by Italian *colonos.*

1487. Cardoso, Ruth. "Associações de 'Nissei' in São Paulo." *Pesquisa e Planejamento*, 3 (1959), 154-157.

Discusses youth associations among Nisei youths in São Paulo and their role in influencing group social values.

1488. Castaldi, Carlos. "Fatores culturais que influenciam o processo educacional dos descendentes de um grupo de imigrantes italianos na cidade de São Paulo." *Educação e Ciencias Sociais*, 2 (1957), 323-342.

Interviews first and second generation Italian immigrants to São Paulo. Finds the second generation less status-oriented and more "functional" in its outlook.

1489. Chéradama, André. *Defense of the Americas*. Tr. George S. Chatties. Garden City, N.Y.: Doubleday, Doran, 1941.

Warns of the likely disloyalty of the large German ethnic community in Brazil, which has been wooed by Nazi propagandists.

1490. Correia de Souza, João Gilherme. *Um comunidade teuto-brasileira*. Pôrto Alegre: Universidade Federal do Rio Grande do Sul, 1963.

Isolates elements of Germanic cultural survival in a community in Rio Grande do Sul originally established by German immigrants.

1491. Della Cava, Ralph. "The Italian Immigrant Experience: Views of a Latin-Americanist." *Perspectives in Italian Immigration and Ethnicity*. Ed. S.M. Tomasi, New York: Center for Migration Studies, pp. 187-206.

Speculates on the differences and similarities in the immigration experience in North and Latin America.

1492. Diegues Júnior, Manuel. "Dois grupos étnico-culturais no Brasil." *Aspectos da formação e evolução no Brasil*. Rio de Janeiro: CLAPCS, 1953, pp. 185-211.

A study of acculturation of two ethnic immigrant groups: Syrian-Lebanese Arabs, and Italians.

1493. Diffie, Bailey W. "Some Foreign Influences in Contemporary Brazilian Politics." *Hispanic American Historical Review*, 20 (1940), 402-429.

Discusses European fascist influence in Brazil, especially the Integralists, but also Japanese and Italian nationalist groups.

1494. Foland, Frances M. "Amazonia: The Contribution of the Japanese." New York: Institute of Current World Affairs. Publication FMF-7 [September 1967].

Describes the successful adaptation of Japanese settlers in the late 1920's to the Amazon region as farmers and producers of black pepper and jute.

1495. Fujii, Yukio and T. Lynn Smith. *The Acculturation of the Japanese Immigrants in Brazil*. Gainesville: University of Florida Press, 1959.

Surveys the full range of Japanese adaptation to Brazilian life.

1496. Hall, Michael. "The Origins of Mass Immigration in Brazil, 1871-1914." Diss., Columbia University, 1969.

Analyzes the wave of Italian immigration from Europe to the Brazilian south, changing patterns of labor and paving the way for the final abolition of slavery.

1497. Hansen, Henri. "Japanese Immigration in Brazil." *New Mexico Quarterly Review*, 12 (1942), 5-17.

A wartime warning about the potentially disruptive impact of Japanese immigration in the Amazon and the Center-South.

1498. *The Japanese Immigrant in Brazil*. Tokyo: University of Tokyo, 1964.

A study by the Japanese Commission for the Enumeration of Japanese colonial settlers.

1499. Kunder, Manfred. "Die deutsch-brasilianische Literatur und das Bodenstandigkeitsgefuhl der deutschen Volkgruppe in Brasilien." *Ibero-Amerikanischen Archiv* (Berlin), 10 (1937), 394-495.

Catalogs Brazilian sources on the *Volksdeutsche*: Brazilians of German origin residing in Brazil and considered potential loyal supporters by the Nazis.

1500. Lerner, Harold. "The Role of Poles in the Development of Latin-American Civilization." Diss., New York University, 1962.

Analyzes Polish agricultural immigration to southern Brazil, especially to the state of Paraná.

1501. Loftin, Marion T. "The Japanese in Brazil: A Study in Immigration and Acculturation." Diss., Vanderbilt University, 1952.

1502. Maack, Reinhard. "The Germans of South Brazil: A German View." *Quarterly Journal of Inter-American Relations*, 1 (July 1938), 5-23.

A Nazi scholar warns that the presence of large numbers of Germans in southern Brazil justifies Hitler's demand for more room (*Lebensraum*) for Germany's excess population.

1503. Normano, J.F. and Antonello Gerbi. *The Japanese in South America*. New York: John Day, 1943.

A wartime survey of Japanese emigration to the continent, especially to Peru and Brazil.

1504. Pisani, Salvatore. *Lo Stato de San Paulo nel Cinquantenario dell' Immigrazione*. São Paulo: Typografia Napoli, 1937.

Recounts the history of subsidized Italian immigration to the State of São Paulo through the early 1930's.

1505. Revoredo, Júlio. *Imigração*. São Paulo: Revista dos Tribunais, 1934.

A study initiated by the São Paulo Labor Department to survey the impact of immigration to that state, emphasizing the positive attributes of foreign immigrants and their contributions to socioeconomic stability and growth.

1506. Roche, Jean. *La colonization allemande et le Rio Grande do Sul*. Paris: Institut des Hautes Études de l'Amérique Latine, 1959.

The most complete study to date of German immigration and settlement in the southern state of Rio Grande do Sul. Discusses the colonists' ability to preserve part of their own culture while adapting to the rural Brazilian environment.

1507. Rohter, Larry. "South American Nazis 'Right at Home.'" *Newsday* (Garden City, N.Y.), August 7, 1978, 13.

Recounts the rising tide of evidence that between eight and ten thousand Nazis have taken refuge in South America, almost half in Brazil, and that they are linked in a network headed by Dr. Josef Mengele.

1508. Saito, Hiroshi. *O japonês no Brasil*. São Paulo: Universidade de São Paulo, 1961.

Examines mobility and settlement patterns among Japanese-Brazilians against the larger experience of international Japanese emigration.

1509. Schweig Viera, Francisca Isabel. *O japonês da frente de expansão paulista*. São Paulo, n.p., 1973.

Credits Japanese truck farmers in the region of Marília, São Paulo State, with establishing a stable economic and social system based on enduring family values.

1510. Simonson, William H. "Nazi Infiltration in South America, 1933-1945." Diss., Tufts University, 1964.

Describes Nazi efforts to recruit support among the rural German settlements in southern Brazil.

1511. Sims, Harold D. "Japanese Postwar Migration to Brazil: An Analysis of Data Presently Available." *International Migration Review*, 6 (Fall 1972), 246-266.

Follows the more frequently studied topic of prewar Japanese immigration. Most postwar Japanese immigrants came to São Paulo and Paraná.

1512. "Sociólogo gaúcho revela que Itália ajudou integralistas." *Jornal do Brasil*, (April 7, 1978), 1° caderno, p. 8.

Cites research in Italian archives proving that Mussolini's government sent at least 50 *contos* monthly to Integralist Plínio Salgado, who also sought arms and financial aid from Nazi Germany.

1513. Tigner, James L. "Sino Remmei: Japanese Nationalism in Brazil." *Hispanic American Historical Review*, 41 (November 1961), 515-532.

Surveys the nationalistic movement which surfaced in the 1930's during the Vargas regime.

D. RELIGION

1. Catholicism

1514. Álves, Márcio Moreira. "Christians, Marxists and Dictatorship in Brazil." *Christian Century* (New York), June 10, 1970, 723-27.

Discusses Dom Helder Câmara and the campaign against him by conservatives.

1515. Álves, Márcio Moreira. *O cristo do povo.* Rio de Janeiro: Ed. Sabiá, 1968.

A collection of essays and talks on the impact of changing Catholic doctrine, especially the encyclicals of John XXIII, on the Brazilian Church. Emphasizes the tension between progressive Catholics and the Castelo Branco military regime.

1516. Antoine, Charles. *Church and Power in Brazil.* Tr. Peter Nelson. Maryknoll, N.Y.: Orbis, 1973.

Narrates the events within the Brazilian Catholic Church from 1964 to 1969, when the break within the Church between the conservative hierarchy and a progressive and outspoken minority of clerics and laymen seemed to peak.

1517. Arroyo, Gonzalo, Franz Vanderschuren, Jaime Rojas, and Paulo J. Krischke. *The Church and Politics in Latin America.* Toronto: LARU, 1977.

A special issue by a research group of mostly exiled Marxists. Places Church-State relations in the context of "crisis of bourgeois hegemony in the continent."

1518. Azevedo, Thales de. *Igreja e Estado em tensão e crise.* São Paulo: Ed. Ática, 1978.

Analyzes the history of Church-State relations in the diocese of Salvador, Bahia.

1519. Azevedo, Thales de. "Popular Catholicism in Brazil." *Portugal and Brazil in Transition* (item 180), pp. 175-179.

Briefly summarizes types of Brazilian Catholicism--official and syncretic--found in Salvador, Bahia.

1520. Bastide, Roger. "Religion and the Church in Brazil." *Brazil: Portrait of Half a Continent* (item 1275), pp. 334-55.

Examines Church problems through the late 1940's, especially "romanization," which Bastide considers a form of denationalization.

1521. Boyle, Raymond M. "Dom Helder: A Prophet Besieged." *Maryknoll*, 64 (September 1970), 2-13.

Defends the controversial Dom Helder Câmara against attacks that he is a communist.

1522. Bruneau, Thomas C. *The Political Transformation of the Brazilian Catholic Church*. New York: Cambridge University Press, 1974.

Argues that the Brazilian Church has always relied on "mechanisms of power" to exert influence on society. Speculates that given the opposition of the State to its socially-conscious impulses and its lack of power, the Brazilian Church may well become revolutionary.

1523. Bruneau, Thomas C. "Power and Influence: Analysis of the Church in Latin America and the Case of Brazil." *Latin American Research Review*, 8 (Summer 1973), 25-52.

Evaluates the Church-State issue in Brazil in terms of the military government's sensitivity to criticism and its need for legitimacy.

1524. Cardozo, Manuel. "The Brazilian Church and the New Left." *Journal of Inter-American Studies*, 6 (1964), 313-321.

Examines the dialogue between the Church and social reformers and the role of Dom Helder Câmara.

1525. Carpeaux, Otto Maria. *Alceu Amoroso Lima*. Rio de Janeiro: Ed. Graal, 1978.

Portrays the conservative lay Catholic writer and spokesman (pseud. Tristão de Athayde) in a critical but appreciative manner.

1526. Dassin, Joan. "The Wisdom of Dom Paulo." *Journal of Current Social Issues* (Summer 1978), 29-30.

Provides a brief biography of Dom Paulo Evaristo Arns, the Archbishop of São Paulo and a leading champion of human rights under the military regime.

1527. De Kadt, Emanuel. *Catholic Radicals in Brazil.* London: Cambridge University Press, 1970.

Analyzes the Movement for Basic Education of the Brazilian Conference of Bishops, phased out after the 1964 coup, although many of its innovative approaches were co-opted by the government's own literacy program, MOBRAL.

1528. Della Cava, Ralph. "Catholicism and Society in Twentieth Century Brazil." *Latin American Research Review*, 11 (Summer 1976), 7-50.

Contends that future views of Church innovation must consider the powerful influence of external ecclesiastical forces on national hierarchies. The 1964 Revolution and Vatican II may have contributed jointly to the creation of a pastoral church, wrestling with social goals and political realities.

1529. Della Cava, Ralph. "Política a curto prazo e religião a longo prazo." *Encontros com a Civilização Brasileira.* Rio de Janeiro: Civilização Brasileira, 1978, pp. 242-257.

Advocates a militant partnership between Brazilian Catholics and Marxists to create a worker's party linked to the interests of the Third World.

1530. *O diálogo do nosso tempos: dez authores: cinco católicos e cinco communistas.* Rio de Janeiro: Paz e Terra, 1968.

Reproduces a debate between five communists and five Roman Catholic laymen, whose prescriptions for Brazilian social change seem remarkably similar.

1531. Ferreira de Camargo, Cândido Procópio. *Católicos, protestantes, espíritas.* Petrópolis: Ed. Vozes, 1973.

A broad survey of the three major contemporary religious traditions--Catholic, Protestant and Spiritist/Umbanda.

1532. Gabaglia, Laurita Pessôa Raja. *O Cardeal Leme, 1882-1942.* Rio de Janeiro: Documentos Brasileiros, 1962.

A laudatory biography of Rio de Janeiro's Cardinal Sebastião Leme, one of Vargas's closest confidants.

1533. Gall, Norman. "Latin America: The Church Militant." *Commentary*, 49 (April 1970), 25-37.

Summarizes the involvement of the Brazilian Church in the human rights movement.

1534. Hallinan, Tim. "Bom Jesus da Lapa: A Sertão Shrine." *Proceedings of the Pacific Coast Council on Latin American Studies*, 2 (1973), 75-89.

Explores the social role of a backlands shrine visited annually by thousands of religious pilgrims. The Bahian town is characterized by a "curious blend of stability and innovation."

1535. Ireland, Rowan. "The Catholic Church and Social Change in Brazil: An Evaluation." *Brazil in the Sixties* (item 423), pp. 345-369.

Traces the Brazilian Church from its progressive activities of the 1960's to the "Documento Pastoral de Brasília" of 1970, a conservative document "of the middle way" which brands any formula for change anti-Church and anti-Brazilian.

1536. Krischke, Paulo J. "Nationalism and the Catholic Church." *The Church and Politics in Latin America.* Toronto: LARU, 1977, pp. 62-92.

Reviews the relationship between the Catholic Church and the military regime, strained over human rights violations.

1537. Leonard, Patrick J. "Bibliography of Helder Câmara." *Latin American Research Review*, 10 (Summer 1975), 147-166.

Provides a bibliography of articles, books, and speeches by the controversial Recife Archbishop, as well as a longer list of sources about his career.

1538. Lima Vaz, Henrique C. "The Church and *Conscientização.*" *America*, 118 (April 27, 1968), 578-581.

Reports on the efforts by the Brazilian Church to raise moral and social conscience through literacy-training programs.

1539. MacEoin, Gary. "A Continent in Agony: Latin America on the Road to Fascism." *The Progressive* (March 1979), 14-19.

Emphasizes socioeconomic inequalities and the role of the Brazilian Church in attempting to raise social awareness. Praises exiled educator Paulo Freire for his efforts to awaken continental conscience.

1540. MacEoin, Gary and the Committee for the Responsible Election of the Pope. *The Inner Elite: Dossiers of Papal Candidates*. Mission, Kansas: Sheed, Andrews and McMeel, 1978.

Compiles biographical data on several *papabili*, including Brazil's Franciscan Cardinal Aloisio Lorscheider, Archbishop of Fortaleza.

1541. Mariz, Celso. *Ibiapina, um apóstolo do Nordeste*. João Pessoa, Paraíba: n.p., 1942.

A biography of the first "modern" Northeastern-born Catholic missionary, Father José Maria de Ibiapina, whose *Casas de Caridade*--schools for girls, orphans and the daughters of local landowners and merchants--offered a new channel for upward mobility in the rural backlands.

1542. Niehaus, Thomas and Brady Tyson. "The Catholic Right in Contemporary Brazil: The Case of the Society for the Defense of Tradition, Family, and Property (TPF)." Paper presented to the Southwest Council on Latin American Studies, Waco, Texas, February 1974.

Examines the ultra conservative lay TPF, active in São Paulo in the 1960's, a reaction against the Church's declared support of basic reforms, including land reform.

1543. O'Neill, Sister M. Ancilla. *Tristão de Athayde and the Catholic Social Movement in Brazil*. Washington, D.C.: Catholic University Press, 1939.

Offers an adulatory portrait of the writer (Alceu Amoroso Lima) who led Cardinal Leme's campaign for neo-orthodoxy in the 1930's.

1544. Pang, Eul-Soo. "The Changing Role of Priests in the Politics of the Northeast, 1889-1964." *The Americas*, 30 (January 1974), 341-372.

Shows that priests exercised diverse secular functions including, at times, playing the role of local boss.

1545. Pierucci, Antônio Flávio de Oliveira. *Igreja: contradições e acomodação.* São Paulo: CEBRAP, 1978.

Discusses the position of the Brazilian Church on the issue of birth control. Finds Church policy to reflect accommodation to political realities.

1546. Queiroz, Maria Isaura Pereira de. "O Catolicismo rústico no Brasil." *Revista do Instituto de Estudos Brasileiros* (São Paulo), 5 (1968), 103-126.

Examines Catholic pluralism and the evolution of "rustic Catholicism" in the rural Brazilian interior. Finds Church life centered about religious festivities and folk ritual.

1547. Segna, Egídio Vitório. *Análise crítica do Catolicismo no Brasil.* Petrópolis: Ed. Vozes, 1978.

Warns that poverty in Brazil has produced a subreligious culture, disconnected from the Church and possibly more dynamic.

1548. Shaull, Richard. "The Church and Revolutionary Change: Continuing Perspectives." *The Church and Social Change in Latin America.* Ed. Henry A. Landsberger. Notre Dame, Ind.: University of Notre Dame, 1970, pp. 77-94.

A progressive theologian and social activist criticizes Brazilian Church hierarchy for its conservatism in contrast to the social consciousness of many clergy in lower echelons.

1549. Smith, Brian H. "Religion and Social Change: Classical Theories and New Formulations in the Context of Recent Developments in Latin America." *Latin American Research Review*, 10 (Summer 1975), 3-34.

A Jesuit scholar comments on the "staying power" of the Church as an asset in the face of growing oppression in contemporary Latin America.

1550. Souza Montenegro, João Alfredo de. *Evolução de Catolicismo no Brasil.* Petrópolis: Ed. Vozes, 1972.

Chronicles the institutional history of the Brazilian Catholic Church.

1551. Todaro, Margaret. "Pastors, Prophets and Politicians: a Study of the Political Development of the Brazilian Church." Diss., Columbia University, 1971.

A prize-winning study of the twentieth-century Brazilian Church, focusing on the role of Cardinal Sebastião Leme.

1552. Tyson, Brady. "Dom Helder as a Symbolic Man." *International Documentation on the Contemporary Church*. Cuernavaca: IDOC, 1971.

Offers a sympathetic view of the charismatic archbishop of Olinda and Recife, Dom Helder Câmara.

1553. Vallier, Ivan. *Catholicism, Social Control and Modernization in Latin America*. Englewood Cliffs, N.J.: Prentice Hall, 1970.

Theorizes about the role of Catholic elites in modernizing Latin American society.

1554. Wiarda, Howard J. *The Brazilian Catholic Labor Movement: The Dilemmas of National Development*. Boston: University of Massachusetts Press, 1969.

Emphasizes the survival of paternalistic and authoritarian forms in the labor movement as it emerged, ostensibly reformed, under Vargas in the 1930's and after.

1555. Williams, Margaret Todaro. "Integralism and the Brazilian Catholic Church." *Hispanic American Historical Review*, 54 (August 1974), 431-452.

Examines the association between the Church and the native fascists as one of the means chosen by Cardinal Leme to aggrandize Church power within the context of an elitist political strategy.

1556. Williams, Margaret Todaro. "Jackson de Figueiredo, Catholic Thinker: a Psychobiographical Study." *The Americas*, 31 (October 1974), 139-163.

Calls Figueiredo a flawed, tragic figure who turned to Catholic activities as a solution to his problem of identity and aggression. In so doing, he triggered an unprecedented moral and intellectual revival among Catholics of the upper classes.

1557. Williams, Margaret Todaro. "The Politicalization of the Brazilian Catholic Church: The Catholic Electoral

League." *Journal of Inter-American Studies and World Affairs*, 16 (August 1974), 301-325.

Analyzes Cardinal Leme's mid-1930's campaign to wield political power by organizing Catholic voters in a bloc to support candidates acceptable to the Church and its conservative stand on issues.

2. Protestantism

1558. Braga, Erasmo and Kenneth Grubb. *The Republic of Brazil: A Survey of the Religious Situation*. London: World Dominion Press, 1932.

An early survey of Protestant missionary activities in Brazil, stressing successes and future prospects.

1559. Fry, Peter. "Two Religious Movements: Protestantism and Umbanda." *Manchester and São Paulo: Problems of Rapid Urban Growth* (item 1010), pp. 177-202.

Contends that *umbanda* dramatizes principles present in society as a whole; it is a metaphor reflecting social and political reality.

1560. Read, William R. and Frank A. Ineson. *Brazil 1980: The Protestant Handbook*. Monrovia, Calif.: MARC, 1973.

Summarizes demographic data for use by evangelical missionaries.

1561. Read, William. *New Patterns of Church Growth in Brazil*. Grand Rapids, Mich.: n.p., 1965.

Describes recent successful activities by Pentecostal missionary sects in Brazil.

1562. Willems, Emílio. *Followers of the New Faith: Culture Change and the Rise of Protestantism in Brazil and Chile*. Nashville: Vanderbilt University Press, 1967.

Shows how Pentecostal sects represent a break with traditional paternalistic and feudal patterns of Brazilian social behavior.

3. Judaism

1563. Barroso, Gustavo [João Dodt]. *Judaismo, maçonaria, e communismo.* Rio de Janeiro: Schmidt Editôra, 1937.

Links "Judaism, Masonry, and Communism" as the triple enemies of the Brazilian family.

1564. Barroso, Gustavo [João Dodt]. "Lixo Internacional." *Gazeta de Notícias* (Rio de Janeiro), August 21, 1940, 1-12.

Attacks Jewish refugees fleeing from Nazi Germany as "International Garbage" and urges they be barred from entering Brazil.

1565. "Booming São Paulo." *National Jewish Monthly* (May 1963), 10-11.

Describes the recent growth of the *Paulista* Jewish community, the largest in Brazil.

1566. Borchardt, Friedrich and David Glick. "Report on the Jewish Refugee Problems in Central and South America to the Joint Distribution Committee [with] Special Reports on Rio de Janeiro and São Paulo, Brazil 1939." Rhodes Collection, American Jewish Historical Society, Box No. 2249.

1567. Congregração Israelita Paulista. *O caminho de uma geração (1933-1966).* São Paulo: CIP, 1966.

Chronicles the history of São Paulo's largest Jewish center.

1568. Fried, Jacob. "Jews in Latin America." *Jewish Affairs* (New York), 3 (January 1949), 6ff.

Estimates the Jewish community in Brazil at 110,000 persons, making it the second largest in Latin America after Argentina.

1569. Institute of Jewish Affairs. *Proceedings of the Experts Conference on Latin America and the Future of its Jewish Communities, New York, 3-4 June 1972.* London: IJA, 1973.

Concentrates on Argentine and Brazilian Jewry, noting the difficulties of Jews having to face competing demands from within their own community and from the dominant classes to which they belong.

1570. Levine, Robert M. "Brazil's Jews During the Vargas Era and After." *Luso-Brazilian Review*, 6 (Summer 1968), 45-58.

Emphasizes the stress placed on the small Jewish community by the influx of European refugees in the late 1930's and the obstacles placed in the refugees' path by hostile government officials.

1571. Margulies, Marcos. *Iudaica Brasiliensis*. Rio de Janeiro: Ed. Documentário, 1974.

A 159-page bibliography, partially annotated, on Jewish life and history in Brazil from the colonial period to the present day. Includes the anti-Semitic works of the 1930's (Barroso et al.).

1572. Pinho, Clemente Segundo. "Reflexões do mundo judáico na vida de un menino brasileiro." *Comentário* (Rio), 10 (October-December 1969), 305-313.

Recounts the experiences of a Jewish youth growing up in Brazil.

1573. Pinkuss, Fritz. "Um ensaio acerca da imigração judáica no Brasil após o cataclismo de 1933 e da Segunda Guerra Mundial." *Revista de História*, 100 (1974), 599-607.

Describes Jewish immigration to Brazil from Germany after the Nazi takeover.

1574. Raizman, Isaac Z. *História dos Israelitas no Brasil*. São Paulo: n.p., 1937.

Provides a history of Brazilian Jewry to the Estado Nôvo.

1575. *Reischvertretung der Juden in Deutschland Judische Siedlung in Brasilien*. Berlin: n.p., 1937.

A 75-page report by a German study commission on German-Jewish settlements in Brazil. In YIVO Archive, New York.

1576. Reizman, Yitzhak. *Geschichte fun Yidden in Brazil*. São Paulo: Ed. "Buch und Presse," 1935.

Summarizes research on Brazilian Jews to the mid-Vargas years. In Yiddish.

1577. Resnick, Salomon. "Como viven los judíos en el Brasil." *Judáica* (Buenos Aires), 9 (July-August 1941), 42-48.

Describes Brazilian Jewish life during the tense pre-war years.

1578. Rocha, Geraldo. *Nacionalismo político e econômico*. Rio de Janeiro: Editôra ABC, 1937.

Blames foreign business interests, especially Jewish firms, for impeding Brazil's efforts to achieve national economic integration.

1579. Sable, Martin H. *Latin American Jewry: A Research Guide*. Cincinnati: Hebrew Union College Press, 1978.

An exhaustive bibliography of secondary and primary sources in English, Spanish, Portuguese, German, Hebrew, and Yiddish.

1580. Winterstein, Vojtech. "Jews of Brazil." *World Jewry* (London), 2 (May 1959), 14-15.

Summarizes conditions during the late 1950's.

1581. Wolff, Egon and Frieda. *Os judeus no Brasil imperial*. São Paulo: Centro de Estudos Judaícos, Universidade de São Paulo, 1975.

Collected biographies and biographical excerpts of Jews in Brazil during the Empire. Includes information on the Jewish communities in each province.

4. Spiritism

1582. Acquaviva, Marcus Claúdio. *Vodú: religão e mágica negra no Haiti e no Brasil*. São Paulo: Ed. Aquarius, 1977.

Shows that Afro-Brazilian *macumba* shares common roots with Haitian *voudoun*.

1583. Barretto, Maria Amália Pereira. *Os voduns do Maranhão*. São Luis: Fundação Cultural do Maranhão, 1977.

Describes syncretistic voodoo practices in the northern state of Maranhão, geographically remote from the traditional centers of *candomblé* and *macumba* on the coast from Pernambuco South.

1584. Bastide, Roger. *O candomblé da Bahia*. Tr. Maria Pereira de Queiroz. São Paulo: Companhia Editôra Nacional, 1961.

Separate studies of Afro-Brazilian culture; racial stereotypes in Brazilian literature; *candomblé*; and the Angolan cult ritual of *Axexé*.

1585. Brown, Diana D. "Umbanda: Politics of an Urban Religious Movement." Diss., Columbia University, 1974.

1586. Fernandes, Albino Gonçalves. *Xangôs do nordeste*. Rio de Janeiro: Civilização Brasileira, 1937.

A little-known study of the psychology of African fetish cults in the Northeast, primarily in the region around Recife. Focuses on the ability of practitioners to achieve trance-like mental states.

1587. Flasche, Rainer. *Geschichte und Typologie afrikanisches Religiosität in Brasilien*. Marburg: Marburger Studien zur Afrika und Asien Kunde, 1973.

Disagrees with the standard practice of applying exogenous reference systems to such unique phenomena as *macumba* and *umbanda*.

1588. Herskovits, Melville J. "African Gods and Catholic Saints in New World Negro Belief." *American Anthropologist*, 39 (1937), 635-643.

A major study of ethno-religious syncretism.

1589. Leacock, Seth and Ruth. *Spirits of the Deep: A Study of an Afro-Brazilian Cult*. Garden City, N.Y.: Doubleday, 1972.

Describes and analyzes the *batuque* cult of Belém, a local folk-religion with strong healing dimensions, not merely, as commonly believed, simply an Amazonian *Candomblé*.

1590. McGregor, Pedro. *Jesus of the Spirits*. New York: Stein and Day, 1967.

Examines Afro-Brazilian *candomblé* and spiritism.

1591. Renshaw, J. Parke. "A Sociological Analysis of Spiritism in Brazil." Diss., University of Florida, 1969.

1592. Ribeiro, René. *Cultos afro-brasileiros do Recife*. Recife: Instituto Joaquim Nabuco, 1952.

A brief but important monograph (150 p.) exploring the organizational structure of Afro-Brazilian religious cults in Recife and problems of social behavior among practitioners.

1593. Valente, Waldemar. *Sobrevivências daomeanas no grupos de culto afronordestinos*. Recife: Instituto Joaquim Nabuco, 1964.

A sociologist assesses survivals from Dahomey culture among Afro-Brazilian cults in Northeastern Brazil.

1594. Warren, Donald, Jr. "The Healing Art in the Urban Setting, 1880-1930." Paper presented to the Symposium on Popular Dimensions of Brazil, U.C.L.A., November 1979.

Shows that the spirits which emerged after 1930 as the predilect ones in folk spiritism were *caboclos* and blacks, characterized by their passivity and lives of suffering.

1595. Warren, Donald, Jr. "The Negro and Religion in Brazil." *Race*, 6 (January 1965), 199-216.

Surveys the African-spiritist influence on Catholicism in Brazil.

1596. Warren, Donald, Jr. "Portuguese Roots of Brazilian Spiritism." *Luso-Brazilian Review*, 5 (Dec. 1968), 3-34.

Shows that folk spiritism in Brazil has developed from Portuguese practices, noting what Warren calls "the fixation of all Portuguese ranks on secret Judaism and not-so-secret Sebastianism."

VIII.
Culture

A. GENERAL STUDIES

1597. Andrade, Mário de. *Macunaíma: o herói sem nenhum caráter.* 15th ed. São Paulo: Ed. Martins, 1978.

The classic "anthropophagist" novel of modernist black humor, an allegorical tale mocking Brazilian urban culture and the stereotypical views of racial miscegenation.

1598. Andrade, Mário de. *O turista aprendiz.* São Paulo: Duas Cidades, 1977.

The poet's diary from two Amazon journeys in the late 1920's, originally published in São Paulo's *Diario Nacional*, revealing the intellectual's struggle to sacrifice his preconceived notions and immerse himself in the "truly Brazilian" environment.

1599. Andrade, Oswald de. *Do pau-brasil à antropologia e às utópias.* Rio de Janeiro: Civilização Brasileira, 1972.

Traces the history of modernism from its earliest days.

1600. Azevedo, Fernando de. *Brazilian Culture.* New York: Macmillan, 1950.

A classic, panoramic view of Brazilian culture in the broadest sense of the term, emphasizing social and ethnological roots. The volume is startingly racist from today's perspective.

1601. Bishop, Elizabeth and Emanuel Brasil. *An Anthology of Twentieth Century Brazilian Poetry.* Middletown, Conn.: Wesleyan University Press, 1971.

A bi-lingual anthology of poems by 14 Brazilian writers, including Cecilia Meireles, Vinicius de Moraes, João Cabral de Melo Neto, and Oswald de Andrade.

1602. Carpeaux, Otto Maria. *Reflexo e realidade.* Rio de Janeiro: Ed. Fontana, 1978.

Collected essays on literary criticism, art, and politics, including a valuable biographical sketch of Alceu de Amoroso Lima.

1603. Cascudo, Luís da Câmara. *Mouros, francescas e judeus.* Rio de Janeiro: Ed. Letras e Artes, 1967.

A semi-scholarly examination of Arab, Jewish, and French impact on Brazilian national culture.

1604. Chacon, Vamireh. *Galileus modernos.* Rio de Janeiro: Tempo Brasileiro, 1965.

Examines Galileo Galilei as a "collective metaphor" and a model for modern iconoclasts. Criticizes Brazil for not having produced such "modern Galileos."

1605. Costa, João Cruz. *A History of Ideas in Brazil: The Development of Philosophy in Brazil and the Evolution of National History.* Tr. Suzette Macedo. Berkeley: University of California Press, 1964.

Discusses the interplay of ideas and Brazilian reality through the twentieth century, stressing the influence of positivism.

1606. Crawford, William Rex. *A Century of Latin American Thought.* Cambridge: Harvard University Press, 1944.

Discusses the Brazilian positivist school and its legacy.

1607. Cunha, Maria Emília Melo e. "Catálogo e índice de *Os Cadernos de Cultura.*" *Revista do Livro* (Rio de Janeiro), 13 (1970), 99-111.

Lists 140 publications in the Ministry of Education's series on Brazilian culture (1952-1964). Titles range from history to literature to anthropology.

1608. Dassin, Joan. *Política e poesia em Mário de Andrade.* São Paulo: Duas Cidades, 1978.

A major analysis of the work of the "utopianist" modernist writer who helped establish a genuinely Brazilian literary form.

1609. Davis, Harold. *Latin American Thought: A Historical Introduction.* New York: The Free Press, 1972.

Discusses Euclides da Cunha and Ruy Barbosa in terms of their contributions as liberal positivists.

1610. Dimmick, Ralph Edward. "The Brazilian Literary Generation of 1930." Paper presented to the Modern Language Association, New York, 1948.

Discusses the work of the remarkable generation of new authors--Jorge Amado, Marques Rebelo, José Lins do Rêgo, Carlos Drummond de Andrade, and others--who came into literary prominence between 1930 and 1935.

1611. Dourado, Autran. *Armas e coraçoēs*. São Paulo: DIFEL, 1978.

Maintains that Brazilian fictional heroes are rarely active; most play the role of passive observers. When exceptions are found they tend to be less credible.

1612. Ellison, Fred P. *Brazil's New Novel; Four Modern Masters*. Berkeley: University of California Press, 1954.

Studies four major novelists identified with the regionalist genre: José Lins do Rêgo, Jorge Amado, Rachel de Queiroz, and Graciliano Ramos.

1613. Figueiredo, Guilherme. *As excelências, ou como entrar para a academia*. Rio de Janeiro: Civilização Brasileira, 1964.

Pokes fun at the Brazilian Academy of Letters and its forty "immortal" members through brief biographical sketches and reminiscences.

1614. Fresnot, Daniel. *O pensamento político de Érico Verissimo*. Rio de Janeiro: Ed. Graal, 1977.

A short study of the political views of the *gaúcho* novelist, finding him to have turned to political themes during periods of dictatorship and repression as a form of artistic protest in favor of democracy.

1615. Freyre, Gilberto. "Brazilian National Character in the Twentieth Century." *Annals of the American Academy of Political and Social Science*, 370 (March 1967), 57-72.

Presents the Brazilian as Apollonian, à la James Bryce, emphasizing his spiritual volition, adventurousness, and political vision.

1616. Freyre, Gilberto. *Uma cultura ameaçada: a luso-brasileira.* Recife: Gabinete Português de Literatura, 1940.

Warns that Luso-Brazilian culture will disappear unless steps are taken to restore pride in local and regional tradition.

1617. Freyre, Gilberto. *Região e tradição.* Rio de Janeiro: José Olympio, 1941.

Argues that regional characteristics offer a key to understanding the uniqueness of the Brazilian environment.

1618. Heyck, Denis Lynn. "Coutinho's Controversy: the Debate Over the *Nova Crítica*." *Latin American Research Review*, 14 (1979), 99-115.

Dissects the moralistic and forceful "New Criticism" of Afrânio Coutinho, introduced in the early 1950's, an attempt to broaden the social and psychological base of Brazilian literary criticism.

1619. Jambo, Arnoldo. *Diário de Pernambuco.* Recife: Ed. *Diário de Pernambuco*, 1975.

A history of Recife's (and Brazil's) oldest daily newspaper, founded in the 1820's.

1620. Johnson, Phil Brian. "Up-Tight about Ruy: An Essay on Brazilian Cultural Nationalism and Mythology." *Journal of Inter-American Studies and World Affairs*, 2 (May 1973), 191-205.

Describes the cult that has grown up around Ruy Barbosa, a man of diminutive stature who epitomized the intellectual style of the Republic. In the late 1960's attacks on Ruy's myth provoked a literary-historical furor.

1621. Kavanagh, Thomas M. "Dialectics and the Textuality of Class Conflict." *Journal of Latin American Lore*, 4 (1978), 135-143.

Differentiates between folklore, the noninstitutionalized knowledge of the masses, and elitelore, the noninstitutionalized knowledge of the ruling elite, whose "primary function is the consolidation and justification of their status as an elite."

1622. Kellemen, Peter. *Brasil para principiantes.* 2nd ed. Rio de Janeiro: Civilização Brasileira, 1963.

Provides a humorous introduction to the culture-shock experienced by foreigners who come to Brazil as permanent residents. The author, a Hungarian immigrant, emphasizes the "unwritten laws" which govern daily behavior.

1623. Lafetá, João Luiz. "Estética e ideologia: o modernismo en 1930." *Argumento* (Rio de Janeiro), 1 (November 1973), 19-31.

Shows that the introduction of awareness of Brazil's underdevelopment with the 1930 Revolution served to dampen the "anarchistic optimism" of modernism's early stage.

1624. Lessa, Luiz Carlos. *O modernismo brasileiro e a lingua portuguesa.* 2nd ed. Rio de Janeiro: Ed. Grifo, 1977.

Claims that the study of modernism offers the key to understanding Brazilian literary language in general.

1625. Martins, Roberto. "Cultura nordestina em debate." Paper presented to the Conference on the Brazilian Northeast, Racine, Wisconsin, November 1974.

Argues that historical analyses of Northeastern backwardness are limited, typically failing to examine the region in a larger contextual sphere.

1626. Martins, Wilson. *História da inteligencia brasileira.* 3 vols. São Paulo: Ed. Cultrix, 1977.

Three volumes in projected series of seven on the history of Brazilian thought since the nineteenth century.

1627. Martins, Wilson. *The Modernist Idea: A Critical Survey of Brazilian Writing in the Twentieth Century.* Tr. Jack E. Tomlins. New York: New York University Press, 1970.

Perspectives on selected modernist authors and their works, including Jorge de Lima, Manuel Bandeira, Mário de Andrade. Carlos Drummond de Andrade's role is slighted.

1628. Mazzara, Richard A. *Graciliano Ramos*. New York: Twayne Publishers, 1974.

An excellent literary biography emphasizing the novelist's willingness to experiment and the psychological underpinnings of his writing.

1629. Michalski, Jan. "Brazilian Bizarreiros." *Censorship*, 2 (1966), 25-29.

Describes the military regime's often Kafkaesque policy of censorship of theater, music, books, and the media.

1630. Mota, Carlos Guilherme. *Ideologia da cultura brasileira*. São Paulo: Ed. Ática, 1977.

Studies the changing cultural climate from 1933 to the mid-1970's. Much cultural energy has had to be expended in dissent against political repression.

1631. Naro, Anthony J., E. Coseriu, and J. Mattoso Câmara. *Current Trends in the Language Sciences*. The Hague: Mouton, 1975.

Examines recent tendencies in Portuguese-Brazilian language and philology.

1632. Neves, Fernão. *A Academia Brasileira de Letras*. Rio de Janeiro: Academia Brasileira de Letras, 1940.

A history of the Brazilian Academy of Letters from 1896 to 1940, including biographies of all members as well as their respective bibliographies.

1633. Neves, Luiz Felipe Baeta. *O combate dos soldados de Cristo na terra dos papagaios*. Rio de Janeiro: Forense-Universitária, 1978.

An anthropological analysis of the conflict generated by the arrival of the "Soldiers of Christ in the land of the Parrots"--the first Jesuits, in 1570. Raises questions of epistemology as well as history, and of the acceptance of imposed values.

1634. Nist, John. *The Modernist Movement in Brazil*. Austin: University of Texas Press, 1965.

Chronicles the explosion of cultural nationalism celebrated in the Modern Art Week Exhibit in São Paulo in February 1922 and traces its impact through the regionalist manifestations of the Vargas era.

1635. Nunes, Cassiano. "História da poesia brasileira." *Boletim Bibliográfico* (São Paulo), 2 (April-June 1953), 59-78.

One of the best surveys of Brazilian poetry available. Includes a useful bibliography.

1636. Pedreira, Fernando. *A liberdade e a ostra*. 2nd ed. Rio de Janeiro: Ed. Nova Fronteira, 1977.

Analyzes the role of public expression in an authoritarian society.

1637. Prowess, M. Cavalcade, Tony Frank and Harry O'Fields. *McLuhanaima, The Solid Gold Hero, or, O herói com bastante caráter (uma fuga)*. Hiawatha, Ontarisota: mimeographed, 1976.

Explores the inner dimensions of Brazilian mythopoetic confrontations through the prism of the Terra dos Papagaios. Richard M. Morse should be held responsible.

1638. Putnam, Samuel. *Adeus ao Brasil. Jornal de bordo*. São Paulo: Departamento Estadual de Informações, 1947.

A brief (31 pp.) "shipboard diary" written on Putnam's departure from Brazil, comparing Brazilian and United States cultural life.

1639. Putnam, Samuel. *Marvelous Journey: A Survey of Four Centuries of Brazilian Writing*. New York: Alfred A. Knopf, 1931.

Emphasizes the evolution of Brazilian fiction into new and original forms of national expression sensitive to racial, cultural, and regional issues.

1640. Rachum, Ilan. "Antropofagia Against Verdamarelo." *Latin American Literary Review*, 4 (Spring-Summer 1976), 67-81.

Chronicles the debate between warring modernist groups of the 1920's--the nationalist "green and yellows," led by Cassiano Ricardo, and Oswald de Andrade's free-spirit "antropofagists," or "cannibals." In the end, the conservative nationalists prevailed.

1641. Rodman, Selden, comp. *Tongues of Fallen Angels*. New York: New Directions, 1974.

Translations of Latin American Poetry, including Chico Buarque de Holanda's *Construção*.

1642. Rodrigues, José Honório. *The Brazilians: Their Character and Aspirations.* Tr. Ralph Edward Dimmick. Austin: University of Texas, 1967.

Accepts Freyre's view of a uniquely Brazilian cultural synthesis but warns that it constantly is threatened by social change. This requires that Brazilian institutions need constantly to be reexamined lest they become ossified.

1643. Rodríguez, Ricardo Vélez. "A filosofia política de inspiração positivista no Brasil." *Convivium* (São Paulo), 16 (March-April 1977), 107-131.

Examines the impact of Castilhista thought--the gaúcho brand of scientific positivism linked to Júlio de Castilhos--upon non-representative, authoritarian government in Brazil. Unlike Comte, Castilhos stressed political reform as the prerequisite for social change.

1644. Sissón, Roberto. *O gênio nacional da história do Brasil.* Rio de Janeiro: Ed. Unidade, 1966.

Searches for Brazilian "national genius" in the form of epic poetry with a Marxist flavor.

1645. Sobrinho, Barbosa Lima. *A lingua portuguesa e a unidade do Brasil.* 2nd ed. Rio de Janeiro: José Olympio, 1978.

Affirms that the most complete understanding of Brazilian language will come from recognizing regional variations without permitting them to overshadow the national language.

1646. Sodré, Nelson Werneck. *História da literatura brasileira. Seus fundamentos econômicos.* Rio de Janeiro: José Olympio, 1938.

Analyzes the history of Brazilian literature from the perspective of such economic issues as agricultural cycles and regionalism.

1647. Souto Maior, Mário. *Nomes próprios pouco comuns.* Recife: São Jose, 1974.

Compiles dozens of fascinating proper names, sociologically verified, of Northeasterners. For example: A.E. Cacique de New York, Índio do Brasil Astiaga Lima; Gylwalraydy Silva Brasileiro.

1648. "O terrorismo cultural." *Revista Civilização Brasileira*, 1 (1965), 239-298.

An eloquent editorial statement appealing for intellectual freedom, protesting against the military regime's campaign of "cultural terrorism" in the form of censorship and arrests of writers, scholars, journalists and students.

1649. Tobias, José Antônio. *História das idéias estéticas no Brasil*. São Paulo: Ed. Grijalbo, 1967.

Surveys the legacy of modernism in the evolution of Brazilian thought.

1650. Veríssimo, Érico. *Brazilian Literature, an Outline*. 2nd ed. New York: Greenwood Press, 1969.

A leading regionalist novelist, a native of Pôrto Alegre, offers a brief and modest summary of his country's literature. Originally a series of public lectures delivered in 1944 at the University of California, Berkeley.

1651. Vita, Luis Washington. "Tentativa de esquematização da filosofia atual no Brasil." *Luso-Brazilian Review*, 3 (1966), 33-45.

Advocates reclassification of Brazilian thought into three categories: leftist-revolutionary; rightist-conservative; and conciliatory-reformist.

1652. Werneck, Humberto. "Antropofagia." *Veja* (São Paulo), 506 (May 17, 1978), 111-114.

A critical, nostalgic review of the modernist *Revista de Antropofagia* on the fiftieth anniversary of its first issue, stressing its iconoclastic search for the "real" Brazil.

B. VISUAL ARTS

1653. Banham, Reyner. *Guide to Modern Architecture*. London: Architectural Press, 1962.

Credits the Brazilians with having created the first national style of modern architecture, unashamedly Latin in temperament.

1654. Barata, Mário. "Fernando Goldgaber: uma poeta fotografica." *Revista Civilização Brasileira*, 1 (July 1965), 161-163.

A brief biography of one of Brazil's first documentary photographers (1926-), whose ability to capture spontaneity in human actions earn him the title "poet-photographer."

1655. Bardi, P.M. *The Arts in Brazil*. Milan: Edizioni del Milano, 1956.

Surveys Brazilian art through the collection of the new São Paulo museum. Interestingly, none of Portinari's depictions of blacks or mulattos are included.

1656. Bardi, P.M. *Profile of the New Brazilian Art*. Rio de Janeiro: Ed. Kosmos, 1970.

Surveys the full spectrum of Brazilian art from primitive to *avant garde*. Include's Brazil's innovative landscape architecture and advertising graphics.

1657. Bon, A., M. Gautherot and P. Verger. *Brazil in Pictures*. London: Gerald Duckworth & Co., 1958.

An above-average collection of photographs taken in the late 1940's across Brazil, showing glimpses of working-class life, religious practices, and (now) vanishing architecture.

1658. Castedo, Leopoldo. *The Baroque Prevalence in Brazilian Art*. New York: C. Frank, 1964.

Describes the originality and sophistication of Baroque art survivals in Minas Gerais and Bahia.

1659. Castedo, Leopoldo. *A History of Latin American Art and Architecture: From Pre-Columbian Times to the Present*. New York: Praeger, 1969.

Includes detailed coverage of Brazilian art, whose baroque period the author finds sophisticated, fascinating, and original. Also touches on di Cavalcanti, Segall, and Portinari.

1660. Costa, Lúcio. "Architecture and Contemporary Society." *Arts and Architecture*, 71 (October 1954), 14-15.

The principal designer of Brasília discusses his feeling that design should help mold social relations.

1661. Fuss, Peter. *Brazil*. Berlin and Zurich: Atlantis-Verlag, 1937.

A photo-essay by a German photographer.

1662. Mindlin, Henrique. *Brazilian Architecture*. Rome: Brazilian Embassy, 1961.

Lectures given at the Royal College of Art, London, by a leading architect, the designer of Rio's Edifício Central.

1663. Niemeyer, Oscar. "Considerações sôbre a arquitectura brasileira." *Módulo*, 7 (February 1957), 5-10.

Attributes the success of modern architecture in Brazil to its rapid acceptance by everyone from government officials to private citizens.

1664. Papadaki, Stamo. *The Work of Oscar Niemeyer*. New York: Reinhold, 1950.

Discusses the architectural views of one of the two designers of Brasília.

1665. Pires, Padre Heliodora. "Pesquisadores e livros de arte no Brasil." *Mensário do Jornal do Comercio*, 31 (September 1945), 655-659.

A bibliographic review of studies on Brazilian art, including commentary on the state of current research.

1666. Roiter, Fúlvio. *Brazil*. Tr. John M. Brownjohn. Rio de Janeiro: n.p., 1974.

Photographs, accompanied by cogent essays by Antônio Callado, Sérgio Buarque de Hollanda and Hugo Loetscher as well as a vapid piece on race relations by Jorge Amado.

1667. Vieira, Hermes. *Portinari: His Life and Art*. Chicago: University of Chicago Press, 1940.

Provides a complete biography of Brazil's greatest painter.

C. PERFORMING ARTS

1668. Amico, Gianni. "Trópici" [Tropics]. b/w film. 87 min. New Yorker Films, 1969.

Follows the life of a northeastern migrant family from the backlands to the slums of Recife and finally to the city of São Paulo in search of urban opportunity.

1669. Barreto, Lima. "Cangaceiro." b/w film. 92 min. Audio Brandon Films, 1954.

Portrays the life of the backlands outlaws, the *cangaceiros*, and the violence of rural society. The film was the first Brazilian production released in the United States.

1670. Bernardet, Jean-Claude. *Brasil em tempo de cinema*. Rio de Janeiro: Civilização Brasileira, 1967.

Reviews the role of the middle class as cultural consumers and the effort of Brazilian filmmakers to create a unique form of cinematic expression.

1671. Boal, Augusto and Gianfrancesco Guarneiri. *Arena conta Tiradentes*. São Paulo: Teatro Arena, 1967.

A play, utilizing the late eighteenth-century Tiradentes revolt to symbolize race relations in modern Brazil and the struggle among intellectuals to oust the military regime.

1672. Burns, E. Bradford, Fred Estevez, Peter L. Reich, Anne Fleck. "History in the Brazilian Cinema." *Luso-Brazilian Review*, 14 (Summer 1977), 49-59.

Reviews the major films of the experimental, socially-conscious *Cinema Novo* (1959-1965).

1673. Dahl, Gustavo. "Cinema Nôvo e estruturas econômicas tradicionais." *Revista Civilização Brasileira*, 1 (March 1966), 193-204.

Laments the precarious state of realistic Brazilian cinema owing to lack of public support and adequate financial resources for non-traditional art forms.

1674. Dassin, Joan. "Arte política: 50 anos de Macunaíma." *Veja*, 516 (July 26, 1978), 95-100.

Explores the dilemma of an artist--Mário de Andrade--attempting to write a popular culture "classic" for the elite Brazilian literary audience.

1675. Dassin, Joan [Molotnik, J.R.]. "Politics and Popular Culture in Brazil." *Massachusetts Review*, 7 (Autumn 1976), 507-524.

Examines the codes and innuendos used by artists, musicians, and writers in Brazil to bypass the strictures of censorship. Despite heavy restrictions and the constant threat of arrest, anti-regime "messages" permeated popular culture during the late 1960's and early 1970's.

1676. Duarte, Anselmo. "Pagador de promessas." (*The Given Word*). b/w film. 98 min. Audio Brandon Films, 1962.

Relates the story of Zé, a Bahian peasant who has vowed to make a pilgrimage to Santa Barbara. The story poignantly probes the theme of the traditional versus the secular in Brazilian life.

1677. Guerra, Rui, director. "Os deuses e os mortos." (*The Gods and the Dead*). color film. 96 min. New Yorker Films, 1971.

Shows corruption and foreign exploitation through the eyes of the inhabitants of Bahia's cocoa plantation zone.

1678. Guerra, Rui, director. "Os fuzis." (*The Rifles*). b/w film. 109 min. New Yorker Films, 1963.

Powerfully portrays the forces of armed repression and mysticism in the drought-ridden backlands.

1679. Holanda, Chico Buarque de and Paulo Pontes. *Gota d'agua*. Rio de Janeiro: Civilização Brasileira, 1975.

Speaks to the need to reopen dialogue within Brazilian society and to combat the injustices of modern life.

1680. Holanda, Chico Buarque de. *Ópera do melandro*. Rio de Janeiro: Cultura, 1978.

A Brechtian play on the corruption of Brazilian life in the 1940's under the Vargas dictatorship, based on John Gay's "Beggar's Opera."

1681. Loy, Jane and Lewis Hanke. *Latin America: Sights and Sounds.* Gainesville: University of Florida Press, 1973.

Lists and reviews 142 films, many of them Brazilian, available in the United States for rental.

1682. Lyday, L.F. and G.W. Woodyard, eds. *Dramatists in Revolt: The New Latin American Theater.* Austin: University of Texas Press, 1976.

Assesses the work of several Brazilian dramatists, especially Plínio Marcos and his exposé of lower class misery.

1683. Martins, Wilson and Seymour Menton, eds. *Teatro brasileiro contemporâneo.* New York: Appleton-Century-Crofts, 1966.

Reprints five major Brazilian plays, including Ariano Suassuna's *Auto da Compadecida.* Asserts that "modern" Brazilian plays may be dated from 1932, with the production of Joracy Camargo's revolution-minded *Deus lhe pague.*

1684. Paixão, Múcio da. *O teatro no Brasil.* Rio de Janeiro: Editôra Moderna, c. 1938.

A 606-page bibliography of Brazilian theater.

1685. Peixoto, Fernando. "Problemas do teatro no Brasil." *Revista Civilização Brasileira*, 3 (September 1967), 229-243.

Argues that self-censorship poses a worse threat than government-imposed censorship. Laments the current state of Brazilian theater.

1686. Pereira, Geraldo Santos. *Plano geral do cinema brasileira.* Rio de Janeiro: Borsoi, 1973.

Reviews the history of Brazilian filmmaking.

1687. Rêgo, José Lins do. "Menino de engenho." (*Plantation Boy*). b/w film. 85 min. New Yorker films, 1965.

Portrays the humiliating, impoverished life of a northeastern family of *caboclos* residing within the drought region.

1688. Rocha, Glauber. "Uma estêtica da fome." *Revista Civilizaçao Brasileira*, 1 (July 1965), 165-170.

Argues that the *Cinema Nôvo* movement is rooted in "the politics of hunger," and, as such, suffers from the vulnerability associated with such roots.

1689. Santos, Nelson Pereira dos, director. "How Tasty was My Little Frenchman." Color film. 97 min. New Yorker Films, 1971.

Narrates the adventures of a Portuguese sailor captured (and eaten) by coastal aborigines during the early sixteenth century. An innovative and sensitive film about cultural values.

1690. Santos, Nelson Pereira dos, director. "Vidas Secas." (*Barren Lands*). b/w film. 115 min. New Yorker Films, 1963.

Called the "key formative work" of the *Cinema Nôvo*. Tells the story of life among the drought-ridden, impoverished poor of the northeastern backlands.

1691. Schoenbach, Peter Julian. "Modern Brazilian Social Theatre: Art and Social Document." Diss., Rutgers University, 1973.

1692. Silva, Lafayette. *Histõria da teatro brasileiro*. Rio de Janeiro: Ministẽrio de Educação e Saũde, 1938.

Relates the history of Brazilian theater to 1937.

1693. Souza, Josẽ Galante de. *O Teatro no Brasil*. Rio de Janeiro: Instituto Nacional do Livro, 1960.

Lists and discusses sources for the study of the history of Brazilian theater.

1694. Thomas, Earl W. "Protest in the Novel and Theater." *Brazil in the Sixties* (item 423), pp. 397-421.

Summarizes the principles and ideas of the protest writers of the 1960's: pro-land reform; anti-repression; anti-United States; neutrality toward the Catholic Church.

D. SPORTS

1695. Adler, Larry. *Man With a Mission: Pelé*. Milwaukee: Raintree Editions, 1976.

An adulatory biography of the soccer hero emphasizing his personal traits of humility and friendliness, the basis of his carefully cultivated public image.

1696. Alencar, Edigar de, ed. *Flamengo: força e alegria do povo*. Rio de Janeiro: Ed. Conquista, 1970.

Commemorates the 75th anniversary of the Flamengo soccer club, the "people's joy."

1697. Allison, Lincoln. "Association Football and the Urban Ethos." *Manchester and São Paulo: Problems of Rapid Urban Growth* (item 1010), pp. 203-228.

Analyzes football as a dimension of urbanization, finding English and Brazilian versions to be a functional compromise between ancient emotions and modern urban stress.

1698. Azevedo, Guilherme Themistocles. *O três é brasileiro em futebol e história*. Rio de Janeiro: Ed. Rhodes, 1971.

Tries to link Brazil's soccer victories in the World Cup to the nation's international political stature.

1699. Castro, Alceu Mendes de Oliveira and José Carneiro Felippe Filho. *Seleções brasileiras através dos tempos, 1914-1960*. Rio de Janeiro: A. Schermann, 1961.

Chronicles the history of the all-star teams which have represented Brazil in international soccer competition since the first match with Argentina in 1914.

1700. Castro, Marcos de and João Máximo. *Gigantes do futebol brasileiro*. Rio de Janeiro: Lidador, 1965.

Offers thirteen chapter-length biographies of Brazil's greatest soccer heroes.

1701. Coelho Netto, Francisco. *O Fluminense na intimidade*. Rio de Janeiro: Ed. Borsoi, 1955.

A spokesman for the Fluminense soccer club (a *carioca* version of the New York Yankees) complains that players have grown ungrateful and greedy in spite of the first-class treatment afforded to them.

1702. Confederação Brasileira de Desportes. *Futebol do Brasil.* Rio de Janeiro: C.B.D., 1970.

A statistical breakdown of the national structure of Brazilian soccer.

1703. Du Plessis, I.D. *Rugby in Rio.* Cape Town: Nasionale Pers Bpk., 1941.

Describes a national rugby tour by a visiting pre-war South African team.

1704. Edwards, Harry. *The Revolt of the Black Athlete.* New York: The Free Press, 1969.

Cites recent sociological scholarship to show that no inherent connection exists between racial origin and athletic prowess, despite widespread acceptance of that view in Brazil.

1705. Filho, Mário. *O negro no futebol brasileiro.* 2nd ed. Rio de Janeiro: Civilização Brasileira, 1964.

Originally published in 1946. A journalistic analysis of the breakthrough for *mulato* and black athletes in the 1920's as amateurism yielded to professionalism under public pressure for more competitive play.

1706. Fontan, Alain. *Divin football brésilien.* Paris: Éditions de la Table Ronde, 1963.

A French journalist offers homage to Brazilian soccer prowess.

1707. Gressler, Carlos Pedro. *Futebol: empolgante espetáculo esportivo.* 2nd ed. Caxias do Sul: Ed. da Universidade, 1978.

Posits solutions for problems faced within Brazil's football club structure dealing with training, player discipline, finances, and related matters.

1708. Guedes, Simoni Lahud. "O futebol brasileiro: instituição zero." Master's Thesis. Departamento de Antropologia, Museu Nacional, Universidade Federal do Rio de Janeiro, 1977.

Argues that football's social role extends far beyond the realm of sport itself.

1709. Haskins, James. *Pelé: a Biography*. Garden City, N.Y.: Doubleday, 1976.

The standard view of Pelé as gentle, friendly, and without faults.

1710. Lever, Janet. "Soccer: Opium of the Brazilian People." *Trans-Action*, 7 (1969), 36-43.

Emphasizes the willingness of government officials in Brazil (and Latin America) to exploit soccer events for political purposes.

1711. Lever, Janet. "The Social Organization of Soccer in Brazil." Paper presented to the American Sociological Association, San Francisco, August 1975.

Claims that knowledge of soccer provides the only link to the outside world for the lower classes.

1712. Levine, Robert M. "Sport and Society: The Case of Brazilian *Futebol*." Paper presented to Symposium on Brazilian Popular Culture, U.C.L.A., February 1979.

Contends that soccer's evolution has followed changes in Brazilian social organization, notably urbanization and authoritarianism. Provides five career histories of representative players: Fausto, Gentil Cardoso, Pelé, Tostão, and Afonsinho.

1713. Nascimento, Edson Arantes do. *Eu sou Pelé*. São Paulo: Francisco Álves, 1961.

An autobiography, presumably ghost-written, emphasizing Pelé's humility and sportsmanship.

1714. Nascimento, Edson Arantes de and Robert L. Fish. *My Life and the Beautiful Game*. Garden City, N.Y.: Doubleday, 1977.

A ghost-written autobiography espousing the virtues of teamwork and patriotism. Pelé's lack of social awareness and personal conservatism shines through the book.

1715. Pontes, Joel. *Palavras luso-brasileiras do futebol*. Recife: Editôra Universitária, 1974.

Examines the Luso-Brazilian impact on soccer vocabulary, which originally (e.g. "football" "futebol") was borrowed from English terminology.

1716. Saldanha, João, ed. *Na boca do túnel*. Rio de Janeiro: Editôra Gol, 1968.

Offers selected recollections about such issues as players' reactions to enforced discipline, social class distinctions, and international play. Saldanha's views are more socially conscious than most persons associated with the sport.

1717. Sarno, Francisco José. *Futebol: a dança do diabo*. São Paulo: Ed. Souza Lopes, 1967.

Emphasizes the gritty, unglamorous side of *futebol*: fear of disabling injuries, low pay, and sudden loss of status once their playing days ended.

1718. Thébaud, François. *Pelé*. New York: Harper and Row, 1976.

A biography of the soccer hero speculating on the sport's appeal as a "universal language."

1719. "Tostão." *Folha da Eva* (Rio de Janeiro), 1 (January 27, 1972), 6-7.

Interview with the *mineiro* soccer star by five women journalists from the feminist *Folha da Eva*. Tostão reveals a faint political liberalism but remains a staunch traditionalist on such issues as divorce.

1720. Vogel, Arno. *O momento feliz: futebol e ethos nacional*. Report. Graduate Program in Social Anthropology, Museu Nacional, Rio de Janeiro [1977].

Shows how *futebol* not only facilitates patriotic identity with national symbols but links Brazil to the world order.

1721. Zamora, Pedro. *A hora e a vez de João Saldanha*. Rio de Janeiro: Editôra Gol, 1969.

Describes the career and views of the controversial and outspoken soccer coach João Saldanha.

E. POPULAR CULTURE

1722. Almeida, Renato. *Candomblê em cordel*. Salvador: Prefeitura da Cidade do Salvador, Departamento de Assuntos Culturais, Divisão de Cultura e Arte, 1978.

Discusses the links between folk spiritism and *cordel* literature, offering, as well, a portfolio of cordel art from the Northeast.

1723. Amado, Jorge. *Tereza Batista, Home from the Wars*. Tr. Barbara Shelby. New York: Alfred A. Knopf, 1975.

A novel, filled with local color and Afro-Brazilian popular culture. Tereza, a near-fatal beauty, symbolizes the medieval heroine who stands singlehandedly against injustice.

1724. Andrade, Margarette de. *Brazilian Cookery*. Rutland, Vt. and Tokyo, Japan: Charles E. Tuttle Company, 1965.

An excellent cookbook, with introductory essays on regional cooking (including Afro-Brazilian) cookery and customs.

1725. Biderman, Sol and Maria Tereza. *Catâlogo da coleção de literature do cordel*. Marîlia, São Paulo: Faculdade de Filosofia, Ciências e Letras, 1970.

A 79-page bibliography of rustic *cordel* literature.

1726. Boggs, Ralph Steele. *Bibliography of Latin American Folklore*. New York: H.W. Wilson, 1940.

Lists 643 entries, partially annotated, including studies pertinent to Brazil.

1727. Borba Filho, Hermîlio. *Espetâculos populares do Nordeste*. São Paulo: São Paulo Editôra, 1966.

A sociological study of rural popular festivities in the Northeast.

1728. Caldas, Waldenyr. *Acorde na aurora*. São Paulo: Companhia Editôra Nacional, 1977.

Analyzes the urbanization of backlands folk music, using two popular São Paulo television shows--*Canta Viola* and *Show de Viola*--as case studies.

1729. Cardoso, Abel, Junior. *Carmen Miranda*. Rio de Janeiro: n.p., 1978.

A tribute to the late singer of the 1940's and 1950's whose flamboyant style captivated the world and contributed to the Brazilian stereotype held by a generation of foreigners.

1730. Carvalho, Murilo, Hermílo Borba Filho and others. *Artistas e festas populares*. São Paulo: Ed. Brasiliense, 1977.

Reviews the current state of rural folk culture and art--broadly defined--and the threats to their survival.

1731. Cascudo, Luis da Câmara, ed. *Antologia de alimentações no Brasil*. Rio de Janeiro: Livros Técnicos e Ciêntíficos, 1977.

An iconoclastic and colorful folklorist from Rio Grande do Norte analyzes Brazilian culinary behavior, touching on such topics as the rise and fall (after 1930) of wine consumption, cannibalism, and fast food.

1732. Cascudo, Luis da Câmara. *Vaqueiros e cantadores*. 2nd ed. Rio de Janeiro: Edições de Ouro, 1967.

Provides a basic introduction to the *literatura de cordel*, the itinerant poetry of the rural backlands.

1733. Cortez, Marcius Frederico. "Relações de classes na literatura de cordel." *Revista Civilização Brasileira*, 1 (March 1966), 293-324.

Considers *cordel* folk poetry a form of reaction against the hierarchical class structure of rural society.

1734. "Dona Benta." *Comer bem*. 51st ed. São Paulo: Companhia Editôra Nacional, 1969.

One of the basic Brazilian cookbooks, with advice on menus, table settings, and recipes. Reflects the life style of the elite.

1735. Dunbar, David L. "Unique Motifs in Brazilian Science Fiction." Diss., University of Arizona, 1976.

Did Lampião come from a UFO?

1736. Eneida. *História do carnaval carioca.* Rio de Janeiro: Civilização Brasileira, 1958.

Traces the history of Rio de Janeiro's Carnival from a relatively private festival before the 1840's to its modern, spontaneous form of *Carnaval de rua* ("street carnival").

1737. "Especial: 500 semanas de Millôr." *Veja* (São Paulo), 512 (June 28, 1978), 110-114.

A reverent biography of Milton Viola Fernandes, called Millôr because of a smudged birth certificate, the freshest social-political cartoonist of post-1964 Brazil.

1738. Goiano, Chico. "Message from Lampião." *Pacific Moana Quarterly* (New Zealand), 3 (January 1978), 62-69.

Provides excerpts and comments on several *cordel* poems about Lampião, the Northeastern bandit. Emphasizes his sadistic cruelty.

1739. Goldman, Albert. *Carnival in Rio.* New York: Hawthorn Books, 1978.

A lavish photo-essay typifying the worst of foreign stereotypes. Carnival in Rio is "where forbidden sexual games and self-indulgence prepare a nation for the season of self-denial."

1740. Goldwasser, Maria Júlia. *O palácio de samba.* Rio de Janeiro: Zahar, 1975.

Traces the evolution of Rio de Janeiro's Samba Schools from the hillside *favelas* to their present-day status of clubs attractive to the upper-middle class elite.

1741. Leite, Sebastião Uchôa. "Cultura popular; esboço de uma resenha crítica." *Revista Civilização Brasileira*, 1 (September 1965), 269-289.

Praises Brazilian popular culture for seeking to find a "typically Brazilian vision."

1742. Leopoldi, José Sávio. *Escola de samba, ritual e sociedade.* Petrópolis: Ed. Vozes, 1978.

Finds the existence of tension between Samba School organizers and the general membership, reflecting the structured and commercialized role attributed to the organizations in recent times.

1743. Lessa, Origenes. *Getúlio Vargas na literatura do cordel*. Rio de Janeiro: Ed. Documentária, 1073.

Measures Vargas's attraction to "non-elite" Brazilians through a study of popular treatments of the President by self-educated *cordel* poets.

1744. Lewin, Linda. "Oral Tradition and Elite Myth: The Legend of the 'Good' Thief Antonio Silvino in Brazilian Popular Culture." Paper presented to the Symposium on Popular Dimensions of Brazil, UCLA, February 1979.

Shows how the *cangaceiro*'s image changed from that of a popular hero of both elite and masses into a national symbol of resistance and even revolution, in part owing to his attractiveness to left-wing nationalists seeking to promote class consciousness.

1745. Muniz, José, Júnior. *Sambistas imortais*. São Paulo: Impressa Ypiranga, 1978.

Biographical sketches of fifty *samba* masters, most from the *favelas* and slums of Rio de Janeiro.

1746. Rasmussen, Kenneth Welden. "Brazilian Portuguese Words and Phrases for Certain Aspects of Love and Parts of the Body." Diss., University of Wisconsin, 1971.

1747. Rodman, Selden. *Genius in the Backlands: Popular Artists of Brazil*. Old Greenwich, Conn.: Devin-Adair, 1977.

Glimpses some of the self-taught artists and sculptors whose work have suddenly gained acclaim.

1748. Slater, Candace. "Joe Bumpkin in the Wilds of Rio de Janeiro." Paper presented to the Symposium on Popular Dimensions of Brazil, UCLA, February 1979.

Reviews the southern cycle of the traditionally northeastern *literatura de cordel*, carried to southern centers by lower-class migrants.

1749. Soares, Jeronymo, et al. *Xilografias nordestinos*. Rio de Janeiro: Casa Rui Barbosa, 1977.

An illustrated history of northeastern folk lithographs, produced by mostly illiterate peasants and slowly earning the reputation of an art form.

1750. Soler, Luis. *As raizes árabes na tradição poético-musical do sertão nordestino*. Recife: Universidade Federal de Pernambuco, 1978.

Attempts to identify the "Arab roots" of the poetic-musical tradition of the backlands.

1751. Suassuna, Ariano. *The 'Rogues' Trial* [*Auto da Compadecia*]. Tr. D. Ratcliff. Berkeley: University of California Press, 1965.

A colorful play set in the northeastern backlands and featuring a black Jesus Christ.

1752. *Violão da Rua: Poemas para a liberdade*. 3 vols. Rio de Janeiro: Civilização Brasileira, 1962.

Three pocket-sized books of "street poetry" linked by a common sense of outrage at exploitation and repression.

F. MUSIC

1753. Alencar, Edigar de. *O carnaval carioca atraves da música*. Rio de Janeiro: Freitas Bastos, 1965.

Surveys the history of the popular pre-Lenten celebration through its music (*choros* and *sambas*).

1754. Alencar, Edigar de. *Nosso Sinhô do samba*. Rio de Janeiro: Civilização Brasileira, 1968.

A revisionist biographical study of the work of Sinhô, one of the major originators of *carioca samba*, but whose importance has been neglected by musicologists.

1755. Almeida, Renato. *História da música brasileira*. 2nd ed. Rio de Janeiro: F. Briguiet, 1942.

A detailed narrative history of Brazilian music from the colonial period.

1756. Andrade, Mário Raul de Moraes de. "A música e a canção populares no Brasil." *Revista do Arquivo Municipal*, 2 (January 1936), 249-262.

Bibliography of studies (and recordings) of Brazilian popular music of the twentieth century.

1757. Antônio, João. "Noël Rosa: um poeta do povo." *Revista Civilização Brasileira*, 1 (July 1966), 262-278.

A biography of Noël Rosa, the middle class "poet of the people" who abandoned a career in medicine to become the most popular composer of popular music before his death at 27 from tuberculosis in 1937.

1758. Bandeira, Manuel. *Mário de Andrade, animador da cultura musical brasileira*. Rio de Janeiro: Gráfica Tupy, 1954.

Calls the modernist poet a major influence on Brazilian music.

1759. Barbosa, Orestes. *Samba*. Rio de Janeiro: Livraria Educadora, 1933.

A history of the uniquely Brazilian *samba*, a blend of Afro-Brazilian and other musical forms, through the careers of its popularizers.

1760. Brazilian American Cultural Institute, Inc. *Heitor Villa-Lobos, 1887-1959*. Washington: BACI, 1969.

Recounts the life of Brazil's greatest composer and offers a bibliography of his recorded works.

1761. Caldas, Waldenyr. *Acorde na aurora*. São Paulo: Companhia Editôra Nacional, 1978.

Traces the road taken by *caipira* and other northeastern folk music to nation-wide popularity with the advent of a popular music market after 1930.

1762. Contier, Arnaldo Daraya. "A música brasileira contemporânea: estudo das principais tendências (1922-1965)." *Anais de Historia* (Assis, São Paulo), 7 (1975), 119-141.

Surveys the history of contemporary Brazilian music, contrasting nationalistic currents with "pure" music, rooted in local society.

1763. Corrêa de Azevedo and Luis Heitor. *150 anos de música no Brasil, 1800-1950*. Rio de Janeiro: José Olympio, 1956.

Reviews the evolution of Brazilian music since 1800. First published in 1952 by the Instituto Nacional de Livro.

1764. Coutinho, J. de Siqueira. "Brazilian Music and Musicians." *Bulletin of the Pan-American Union*, 54 (November 1930), 1119-1125.

Stresses the African contribution, notably the *batuque*, *samba*, and *maxixê*.

1765. Efegê, Jota [João Ferreira Gomes]. *Figuras e coisas da música popular brasileira*. Rio de Janeiro: Ed. Funarte, 1978.

Recalls the rich (and vanished) bohemian world of *carioca* popular music in the 1920's, the rise of the art of *samba*, and the personalities of that world.

1766. Ewen, David, comp. *Composers Since 1900: A Biographical and Critical Guide*. New York: H.W. Wilson Co., 1969.

Includes biographies of Camargo Guarneiri (pp. 254-56) and Heitor Villa-Lobos (pp. 607-11). Praises Villa-Lobos for his versatility and physical energy.

1767. Leopoldi, José Sávio. *Escola de samba, ritual e sociedade*. Petrópolis: Ed. Vozes, 1977.

An anthropologist's analysis of the rituals of Brazilian *samba* as meaningful links between the world of the poor and "outside."

1768. Lévy, Júlia Elizabeth Volpato de Almeida. "A pauta da ilusão: um estudo antropólogico da música popular brasileira." Master's Thesis. Departamento de Antropologia, Museu Nacional, Universidade Federal do Rio de Janeiro, 1977.

Analyzes the lyrics of 110 popular songs through the techniques of symbolic anthropology.

1769. Mariz, Vasco. *Heitor Villa-Lobos: Brazilian Composer*. Gainesville: University of Florida Press, 1963.

A biography by one of the musician's closest friends.

1770. Mariz, Vasco. "Música popular." *Quem é quem nas artes e nas letras do Brasil*. Rio de Janeiro: Ministério das Relações Exteriores, 1966, pp. 119-180.

A thorough bibliographic compilation of sources for the study of Brazilian popular music artists.

1771. Pereira, João Baptista Borges. "Der Neger und die brasilianische Volksmusik." *Staden-Jahrbuch*, 16 (1968), 23-31.

Surveys the Afro-Brazilian dimension of Brazilian folk music and its emergence as an element of publicly accepted popular culture.

1772. Pinto, Alexandre Gonçalves. *Reminisciencias dos chorões antigos*. Rio de Janeiro: Typ. Gloria, 1936.

Popular reminiscences about the *choroes*, the musical form which predated the *samba* and *bossa nova*.

1773. Rangel, Lúcio. *Bibliografia de música popular brasileira*. Rio de Janeiro: São José, 1976.

Lists the major sources for the study of Brazilian popular music.

1774. Regis, Flávio Eduardo de Macedo Soares. "A nova geração do samba." *Revista Civilização Brasileira*, 1 (May 1966), 364-374.

Contends that two schools have emerged out of bossa nova: one influenced by North American jazz, and a second, rooted in lower-class *samba*.

1775. Tinhorão, José Ramos. *Música popular de índios, negros e mestiços*. Petrópolis: Ed. Vozes, 1972.

A journalistic account tracing the origins of urban popular music organized along (not across) ethnic lines.

1776. Tinhorão, José Ramos. *Música popular: teatro e cinema*. Petrópolis: Ed. Vozes, 1972.

Surveys Brazilian popular music from nineteenth-century musical comedies to motion picture scores, with an entire chapter on *Carnaval* songs.

1777. Vasconcelos, Ary. *Raizes da música popular brasileira*. São Paulo and Brasília: Martins Editôra/Instituto Nacional do Livro, 1977.

Short biographies of composers who have influenced the development of Brazilian music from colonial times to the twentieth century. Many of the entries contain a bibliography; others include short excerpts of lyrics.

1778. Vasconcelos, Gilberto. *Música popular: de olho na fresta*. Rio de Janeiro: Ed. Graal, 1978.

Traces the history of Brazilian popular music from the bossa nova to the "unhappy" current period.

1779. Vassberg, David E. "African Influences on the Music of Brazil." *Luso-Brazilian Review*, 13 (Summer 1976), 35-54.

Suggests that Brazilian music is syncretized, neither European nor African, but profoundly influenced by African forms.

IX.
Education

A. GENERAL STUDIES

1780. Abreu, Jayme, ed. *Problemas brasileiros de educação*. Rio de Janeiro: Ed. Lidador, 1967.

Papers on Brazilian education, on the whole muted in their criticism in spite of their focus on educational "problems."

1781. Azevedo, Fernando, et al. "Manifesto dos pioneiros da Educação Nôva." *Revista Brasileira de Estudos Pedagógicos*, 34 (1956), 108-127.

The "Manifesto for New Education," first issued in 1932 but ignored by the right-leaning Vargas administration.

1782. Carneiro Leao, Antônio. *A sociedade rural, seus problemas e sua educação*. Rio de Janeiro: Ed. *A. Noite*, 1939.

Defends the role of education in rural areas as basic provider of social instruction: hygiene, nutrition, preventative health care, and literacy. Cites foreign examples (from the United States and Mexico) which might well be adopted to Brazilian conditions.

1783. Centro Brasileiro de Pesquisas Educacionais. *Bibliografia sôbre pesquisa educacional no Brasil*. Rio de Janeiro: C.B.P.E., 1967.

A bibliography on educational research in Brazil, listing 296 items from the fields of psychology and educational sociology.

1784. Collins, Denis E. "Two Utopians: A Comparison and Contrast of the Educational Philosophies of Paulo Freire and Theodore Brameld." Diss., University of Southern California, 1973.

1785. Faust, Augustus F. *Brazil: Education in an Expanding Economy.* Washington, D.C.: U.S. Office of Education, 1959.

Describes Brazil's educational system in the mid-1960's. Includes a discussion of technical schools.

1786. Fernandes, Florestan. "A democratização do ensino." *Revista Brazileira de Estudos Pedagógicos*, 34 (1960), 216-225.

Praises the new national educational law but argues that structural changes should be implemented before attempting large-scale educational expansion.

1787. Freire, Paulo. *O desafio comunista.* Rio de Janeiro: Imprensa Nacional, 1958.

The distinguished educator warns of the threat posed by underground communist activity.

1788. Freire, Paulo. *Pedagogy of the Oppressed.* New York: Seabury Press, 1968.

Advocates the use of *conscientização*, an adaptation of the Socratic method stressing politicization as the basic element in literacy training.

1789. Freire, Paulo. *Pedagogy in Progress.* New York: Seabury Press, 1979.

Further discussion of the *conscientização* approach to education.

1790. Garcia, Walter, ed. *Educação brasileira contemporânea: organização e funcionamento.* São Paulo: McGraw-Hill do Brasil, 1977.

Twelve articles examining various aspects of Brazilian educational organization, including university reform, curricular organization, and the legal bases for education.

1791. Geribello, Wanda Pompeu. *Anísio Teixeira, analise e sistematização de sua obra.* São Paulo: Ed. Átlas, 1977.

Examines the life and work of the leading educational reformer of the 1930-1964 period.

1792. Goertzel, Ted. "M.E.C. - U.S. A.I.D.: Ideologia de desenvolvimento americano aplicada e educação superior brasileira." *Revista Civilização Brasileira*, 3 (July 1967), 123-138.

Criticizes the effort by United States A.I.D. officials to implant North American educational values in the Brazilian educational system. These plans include greater emphasis on vocational training as well as efforts to introduce liberal arts subjects to Brazilian universities.

1793. Grande, Humberto. *A pedagogia no Estado Nôvo*. Rio de Janeiro: Gráfica Guarany, 1941.

Reviews the educational policy of the Estado Nôvo dictatorship and its stress upon civic pride, nationalism, and physical and moral preparedness.

1794. Haussman, Fay and Jerry Haar. *Education in Brazil*. Hamden, Conn.: Archon Books, 1978.

Summarizes the history of Brazilian education from the perspective of national needs. Obstacles to educational growth are emphasized.

1795. Havighurst, Robert J. and J. Roberto Moreira. *Society and Education in Brazil*. Pittsburgh: University of Pittsburgh Press, 1965.

In the best analysis to date, the authors examine the role of education against the larger background of Brazilian society.

1796. Levine, Robert M. "Socialization through Public Education in Brazil." Paper presented to the Latin American Studies Association, Houston, November 1977.

Examines the impact of *civismo*, the official program of civic and patriotic education as a tool for socialization and nationalism. The long-term impact of the *civismo* campaign is called into question: there have been recent signs that the post-1964 university generation is less docile than observers had predicted.

1797. Lima, Hermes. *Anísio Teixeira: Estadista da educação*. Rio de Janeiro: Civilização Brasileira, 1978.

Profiles Teixeira's life from his infancy in Caetité, Bahia, to his arrival as Brazil's leading educational planner but slights the constant, nagging hostility from opponents who ultimately hounded him to his death.

1798. McFadden, John P. "Consciousness and Social Change: The Pedagogy of Paulo Freire." Diss., University of California, Santa Cruz, 1975.

A friendly biography of the exiled Brazilian educator.

1799. McNeill, Malvina Rosat. *Guidelines to Problems of Education in Brazil: A Review and Selected Bibliography*. New York: Teacher's College, Columbia University, 1970.

An essay on the aristocratic tradition of Brazilian education, stressing efforts to modify and broaden the system, as well as an excellent annotated bibliography.

1800. Maier, Joseph and Richard W. Weatherhead, eds. *The Latin American University*. Albuquerque: University of New Mexico Press, 1979.

Essays by scholars writing on higher education, including Anísio Teixeira on Brazil.

1801. Morais, Deodato de. "Educação e o Estado Nôvo." *Cultura Política*, 1 (November 1941), 26-36.

Places the sanctity of the Brazilian family at the center of the *Estado Nôvo*'s educational effort.

1802. Moreira, J. Roberto. *Educação e desenvolvimento no Brasil*. Rio de Janeiro: CLAPCS, 1970.

Surveys the history of Brazilian education to 1960.

1803. Silva, Marinete dos Santos. "A educação brasileira no Estado Nôvo (1937-1945)." Master's Thesis, Universidade Federal Fluminense, 1975.

Studies educational policy at the national level during the Vargas dictatorship.

1804. Teixeira, Anísio S. *A educação e a crise brasileira*. São Paulo: Companhia Editôra Nacional, 1956.

Offers insight into the failure of the educational system to deal with social needs.

1805. Teixeira, Anísio S. "Educational Research in Countries Other than the United States-Brazil." *Review of Educational Research*, 27 (1957), 92-107.

Surveys Brazilian educational research, stressing its deficiencies.

1806. United States Agency for International Development. *Diagnóstico.* Recife: USAID, 1967.

A short (51 pp.) summary of educational needs in Northeast as perceived by USAID.

1807. Universidade Federal de Pernambuco. *Estudo de problemas brasileiros.* Recife: Universidade Federal de Pernambuco, 1971.

A compendium of mostly theoretical articles on Brazilian "problems" for a course on contemporary Brazil, ranging from agriculture to intellectual life.

1808. Wagley, Charles, and J. Roberto Moreira. "A educação e o desenvolvimento do Nordeste." *Educação e Ciências Sociais*, 2 (1957), 343-365.

Argues for educational reform in northeast Brazil which takes into account regional socio-economic needs.

1809. Werebe, Maria José Garcia. *Grandezas e misérias do ensino no Brasil.* São Paulo: DIFEL, 1968.

Reviews the state of Brazilian education from primary grades through universities. Finds vocational training inadequate and the small number of university openings shocking. Good statistical tables.

B. PRIMARY EDUCATION

1810. "Bibliografia sôbre educação primária." *Boletim de Biblioteca da Sudene* (Recife), 5 (February 1966), 49-70.

A bibliography on general themes in primary education.

1811. Commissão Nacional de Moral e Civismo. *Educação moral e civica.* Rio de Janeiro: Imprensa do Exército, 1970.

An Army Commission's prescription of moral and civic goals for all citizens: religious idealism, character, patriotism, love for the family, preservation of traditional values.

1812. Formigli, Vera Lucia A. "Ausentismo de escolares em três escolas de Salvador." Master's Thesis, Universidade Federal do Brasil, Salvador, Bahia, 1977.

Demonstrates that absenteeism is significantly higher in public schools and among children from poorer families than in private schools or among middle-class public school children.

1813. Gouveia, Aparecida Joly. "Desenvolvimento econômico e mundança na composição do magistério de nivel médio no Brasil." *Sociologia*, 26 (1964), 465-480.

Compares secondary education in 1944 and 1964, finding evidence that fewer men than ever entered secondary teaching, and that teachers tended to come from families of lower socioeconomic standing.

1814. Gouveia, Aparecida Joly. "Education and Development: Opinions of Secondary School Teachers." *Elites in Latin America*. Ed. Seymour M. Lipset and Aldo Solari. New York: Oxford University Press, 1967, pp. 484-513.

Shows that primary teachers in Brazil tend to be traditionalist, religious, and interested in education in order to teach moral values rather than to encourage social consciousness.

1815. Hermogenes, José de Andrade. *Educação moral e cívica*. Rio de Janeiro: Ed. Record, 1977.

An illustrated *civismo* textbook stressing moral law, interpersonal relations, religious faith, and patriotism. Typical of hundreds of texts of this type.

1816. Kimball, Solon T. "Primary Education in Brazil." *Comparative Education Review*, 4 (1960), 49-54.

Relates problems of social stratification and inadequate teacher training to the failure of Brazilian primary education.

1817. Leite, D.M. "Preconceito racial e patriotismo em seis livros didáticos brasileiros." *Boletim de Psicologia*, 3 (1950), 206-301.

Analyzes racial stereotypes in primary school texts. An important study.

1818. Moreira, J. Roberto. "A escola primária brasileira." *Educação e Ciências Sociais*, 2 (1957), 133-184.

A pessimistic evaluation of primary education and its failings by a leading Brazilian specialist.

1819. O'Neil, Charles Francis. "The Search for Order and Progress: Brazilian Mass Education, 1915-1935." Diss., University of Texas, 1975.

Notes the vastly different rates of progress from state to state before Vargas absorbed public education into the national administrative framework, focusing on efforts at innovation and the resistance which followed.

1820. "Reação contra a história." *Opinião*, 31 (June 4-11, 1973), 19-20.

Charges that history texts used in schools are "transforming the Brazilian past into a collection of superficial facts, incorrect analyses, and hurried answers."

1821. Silva, F. Altenfelder. "A educação em duas comunidades do São Francisco." *Sociologia*, 20 (1958), 3-17.

Blames the failure of rural schools in Xique and Marrecas on the condescending attitudes of the teachers, poor facilities, and the absence of real motivation for learning curricular material.

1822. Silva, Marinete dos Santos. "A educação brasileira no Estado Nôvo (1937-1945)." Master's Thesis, Instituto de Ciências Humanas e Filosofia, Universidade Federal Fluminense, 1975.

Traces the eclipse of progressive educational measures and the accompanying increased use of patriotic ideology as an instrument of social control during the Estado Nôvo.

1823. Teixeira, Anísio S. "Uma experiência de educação primaria integral no Brasil." *Revista Brasileira de Estudos Pedagógicos*, 38 (1962), 21-33.

Describes a "model" school in Salvador, later imitated in Brasília.

C. HIGHER EDUCATION

1824. Arruda Falcão Neto, Joaquim de. "Crise da universidade e crise do ensino jurídico." *A Universidade e seus mitos*. Recife: PIMES, 1977, pp. 91-142.

Examines curricular rigidity and overproduction of graduates in prestigious fields (for example, law). Warns of dangers inherent in stressing technical and scientific fields over humanities and social sciences.

1825. Barros, Roque Spencer Maciel de. *A ilustração brasiliera e a idéia de universidade*. São Paulo: n.p., 1959.

Traces the development of intellectual currents in the late nineteenth century which led to the debate over educational goals and the creation of modern universities in the 1930's.

1826. "Bibliografia sôbre reforma universitária no Brasil." *América Latina*, 12 (January-March 1969), 116-126.

A bibliography on university reform, stressing the tumultuous period between 1966 and 1968.

1827. Campos, Ernesto de Souza. *Educação superior no Brasil*. Rio de Janeiro: Ministério da Educação, 1940.

Reviews the structure of Brazilian higher education and the efforts in the late 1920's to create comprehensive, modern universities. Extensive bibliography.

1828. CAPES. "A situação do sistema universitário brasileiro." *Boletim*, 168 (1966), 22-27.

Lists the weaknesses of the university system, including obsolete administration, inflexible curricula, lax discipline, and excessive enrollment in overcrowded fields.

1829. Cardwell, Rosson L., et al. *USAID Programs in Higher Education in Brazil*. Rio de Janeiro: United States History, 1964.

Evaluates USAID educational projects in Brazil and suggests new directions for reform under cooperative auspices.

1830. Costa, Lia Parente and Silke Weber. "Universidade e Desenvolvimento: novas considerações sobre uma velha ilusão." *A Universidade e Seus Mitos.* Recife: PIMES, 1977, pp. 1-58.

Argues that higher education, by itself, does not produce social development. Warns against placing too much pressure on Brazilian universities seeking results while failing to increase employment opportunities for graduates in the marketplace.

1831. Cruz Costa, João. "A universidade Latino-Americana: suas possibilidades e responsibilidades." *Revista de História*, 12 (April 1961), 406-507.

Recounts the steps which led to the establishment of the University of São Paulo under state auspices in 1934.

1832. Feinsot, Aaron. "Brazilian Images of the United States--a Study of Brazilian University Students." Diss., New York University, 1965.

1833. Hendricks, Howard Craig. "Education and Maintenance of the Social Structure: The Faculdade de Direito do Recife and the Brazilian Northeast." Diss., S.U.N.Y. at Stony Brook, 1977.

Analyzes the history of Recife's Law School and the role of the *bacharel*--the professional graduate who became the prime candidate for recruitment into the administrative elite as government became more complex over time. The Law School contributed stability to a society slowly undergoing change.

1834. Labouriau, Luiz Gouvea. "Sôbre a carreira de pesquisador científico no Brasil." *Revista Civilização Brasileira*, 3 (May 1967), 209-224.

Lists various factors which impede scientific research in Brazil and plague the would-be career scientist: deficiencies in the educational structure, lack of support for promising youths, the continuing technological "brain-drain," and insufficient salaries.

1835. Levine, Robert M. "*Bacharelismo* in Pernambuco, 1889-1945." Paper presented to the Columbia University Seminar on Brazil, New York, January 1971.

Demonstrates that an extremely high percentage of the regional political elite held law degrees. Law schools only slowly revised their curricula, but showed growing awareness of their responsibility to train future administrators.

1836. Levine, Robert M. "Mudanças na estrutura universitária norteamericana." *Comentário* (Rio), 14 (January 1973), 23-31.

Compares higher education in the United States and Brazil, stressing changes in both countries.

1837. Levine, Robert M. and Craig Hendricks. "Pernambuco's Political Elite and the Recife Law School." Paper presented to the Conference of the Brazilian Northeast, Racine, Wisconsin, November 1974.

Attributes the decline of the Law School's influence to its inability to redefine its social role as other institutions of higher education challenged its former monopoly.

1838. Manor, Paul. "The Failure of the University Dream in Brazil, 1823-1934." *Special Series*, SUNY at Buffalo: Council on International Studies, No. 92 [1978].

Examines the overall lack of success of efforts to establish a strong university system.

1839. Myhr, Robert O. "The Political Role of University Students in Brazil." *Students and Politics in Developing Nations*. Ed. Donald K. Emmerson. New York: Praeger, 1968, pp. 249-85.

Surveys student political activity before the military coup; after 1964 most student organizations were suppressed.

1840. Ribeiro, Darcy. "Universities and Social Development." *Elites in Latin America*. Ed. Seymour M. Lipset and Aldo Solari. New York: Oxford University Press, pp. 343-381.

Argues for closer ties between universities and the market place, and more practical emphasis in curricula.

1841. Rodrigues, José Honório. "O ensino superior da história e a reforma universitária." *Revista Civilização Brasileira*, 4 (September-December 1968), 3-26.

Criticizes the state of history teaching in Brazilian universities. University reform must accomplish major structural change in the way education is conducted if better national leaders are to be produced.

1842. Seganfreddo, Sônia. *UNE: Instrumento de subversão.* Rio de Janeiro: Edicões GRK, 1963.

Attacks the left-oriented national student organization, UNE, as a blatant instrument of subversion and a tool of the Moscow-Cuba axis.

1843. Souza Campos, Ernesto de. *Educação superior no Brasil.* Rio de Janeiro: Ministério Superior da Educação, 1940.

Reviews the state of secondary and university educational facilities in Brazil during the Estado Nôvo.

1844. Sterns, Maurice Aaron. "Three Decades of Student Leadership in Brazil (1935-1965): A Study of the Career Lives of Former Student Leaders." Diss., University of Chicago, 1974.

1845. Terry, Leonard D. "Dominant Power Components in the Brazilian University Student Movement." *Journal of Inter-American Studies*, 7 (January 1965), 27-48.

Analyzes the role of student militants (and the national student organization, U.N.E.) in the heady days before the 1964 coup when students sought to ally with other groups on the left dedicated to nationalism and anti-imperialism.

Indexes

AUTHOR INDEX

Aartsen, J.P.V. 791
Aborigines Protection Society of London 1445
Abrahams, R.D. 1441
Abreu, J. 1780
Abreu, M. 749
Abreu, M. de P. 816
Abreu, S.F. 955
Ackerman, F. 750
Acquaviva, M.C. 1582
Adams, D.W. 1089
Adelman, J. 956
Adler, L. 1695
Alarcón, R. 533
Albersheim, U. 1482
Albuquerque, R.C. da 895, 1199
Alcantara de Cámargo, A. 534, 1282
Alencar, E. de 1696, 1753-54
Aléssio, N. 580
Alexander, R.J. 282-83, 915
Allison, L. 1697
Almeida, A.F. de 350
Almeida, C.M. de 700
Almeida, F.H.M. de 351
Almeida, H. 873
Almeida, J.A. de 433
Almeida, M. de 225
Almeida, R. 1722, 1755
Almeida, S.K. de 1048
Almeida, T. de 1483
Almeida, V.U. de 1011
Almeida Filho, H. 535
Álvaro Moises, J. 384
Álves, H. 602
Álves, H.C. 1410
Álves, M.M. 536-37, 1514-15
Alvim, J.C. 538
Amado, J. 284-86, 957, 1090-91, 1230-31, 1283, 1411, 1723
Amaral, A. 434
Amaral, L. 1092
Amazonas, J. 287
American Chamber of Commerce for Brazil 751
Ames, B. 603
Amico, G. 1668
Amman, S.B. 1049
Amnesty International 541
Amorim, D. 1143
Andrade, A. de 352
Andrade, B. de 353
Andrade, E.L. de 1012
Andrade, M. 55, 1724
Andrade, Mário de 1597-98
Andrade, M.C. de 792, 1092
Andrade, M.R. de M. 1756
Andrade, O. de 1599
Anonymous 435
Anselmo, O. 1204
Antoine, C. 1516
Antônio, J. 1757
Araujo, R.B. de 326
Arblaster, D. 958
Arnau, F. 959
Arraes, M. 288, 436
Arriaga, E. 1
Arroyo, G. 1517
Arruda, M. 752
Arruda Falcão Neto, J. de 1824

Athayde, T. de 324
Austregesilo, A. 1284
Avelar, R. de 605
Avellar, S.M. de 1013
Ávila, F.B. de 1014
Avni, H. 1094
Ayres Filho, P. 540
Ayrosa, P. 1446
Azambuja, D. 226
Azevedo, A. de 1050
Azevedo, F. de 1600, 1781
Azevedo, G.T. 1698
Azevedo, T. de 1232-34, 1285, 1337-38, 1518-19

Bacha, E. 701, 844, 1095
Baer, W. 702, 753, 845-47, 874-77
Baklanoff, E.N. 385
Bakota, C.S. 437, 1051
Balán, J. 1015-16
Baldus, H. 1339
Bambirra, V. 1286
Bandeira, Manuel 1758
Bandeira, Moniz 438
Banham, R. 1653
Baranson, J. 793
Barata, A. 290
Barata, M. 1654
Barbosa, O. 1759
Barbosa, R. de S. 960
Bardi, P.M. 1655-56
Barnet, R. 848
Barquin, R.C. 878
Barreno, M.I. 1287
Barreto, C.E. 354
Barreto, Leda 1205
Barreto, Lima 1669
Barretto, M.A.P. 1583
Barros, J.A.L. de 606
Barros, J.R.M. 849
Barros, R.S.M. de 1825
Barroso, G. 327-32, 1563-64
Bartley, R. 56
Bartolotti, D. 1484
Basbaum, L. 291, 305, 386, 703
Basseches, B. 109
Bastide, R. 1235, 1340-41, 1412-14, 1520, 1584
Bastos, A. 292, 1144
Bastos, H. 704, 879
Batchelor, C.M. 1145
Bayitch, S.A. 110
Bazzanella, W. 961, 1236
Behor, E. 26
Behrent, F. 111
Beigelman, P. 440
Bell, P.D. 654
Bello, J.M. 387
Beloch, I. 27
Beltrão, L. 1447
Bemis, G.W. 439
Benavides, P. 227
Bergsman, J. 880
Berlinck, M.T. 916, 1237
Bernardes, N. 1096
Bernardet, J.-C. 1670
Bernstein, H. 112, 388
Berson, T.M. 441
Bhatra, S.K. 705
Bicudo, V.L. 1342
Biderman, S. 1725
Bilac, E.D. 1052
Bilden, R. 1343
Bishop, E. 163, 1601
Bittencourt, A. 28, 1288
Blachman, M.J. 1289
Black, E. 755
Black, J.K. 655
Blair, T.L. 1344
Blakemore, H. 1017
Blondel, J. 389
Boal, A. 1671
Bodard, L. 1448
Boehrer, G.C. 185
Boggs, R.S. 1726
Boito Júnior, A. 442
Bojunga, C. 1344a
Bolton, R.H. 542
Bon, A.M. 1657
Bonilla, F. 443, 1099, 1449
Bopp, R. 325
Borba Filho, H. 444, 1727, 1730

Borchardt, F. 1566
Borges, F.C. 1206
Borges, J.B.P. 1414
Borges, T.P.A. 1018
Borges Pereira, J.B. 1486
Bouças, V.F. 817-19
Bougeard, R. 882
Bouquet, S. 1239
Bourne, R. 445
Boyle, R.M. 1521
Braga, C. 706
Braga, E. 1558
Brandão, O. 883
Brandão Lopes, J.R. 884, 918
Brasil, E. 1601
Brasil. Congresso. Câmara dos Deputados 29, 356, 390, 543, 756
Brasil. Conselho de Imigração e Colonização 2
Brasil. Conselho Nacional de Estatística 119
Brasil. Departamento Nacional de Estatística 3, 942
Brasil. Diretoria Geral de Estatística 4
Brasil. Diretoria Geral de Saúde Pública 5
Brasil. Instituto Brasileiro de Bibliografia e Documentação 120
Brasil. Instituto Brasileiro de Geografia e Estatística 7, 8, 9, 44, 1053
Brasil. Ministério da Fazenda 10, 11, 12
Brasil. Ministério da Justiça e Negócios Interiores 357
Brasil. Ministério das Relações Exteriores 30, 121
Brasil. Secretária de Planejamento 13
Brazil. Ministry of Foreign Affairs 14
Brazilian American Cultural Institute, Inc. 1760
Brenner, S.F. 144
Bresser Pereira, L.C. 707
Brinches, V. 31
British Chamber of Commerce, São Paulo 32
Brito, J.G. 1240
Britto, L.N. de 546
Brooks, E. 1450-52
Brossard, P. 547
Brown, D.A. 759
Brown, D.D. 1585
Broxson, E. 333
Bruneau, T.C. 1522-23
Bruno, E.S. 164
Buarque de Holanda. *See* Holanda, S.B. de
Buescu, M. 708, 794-95
Burns, E.B. 123, 186, 392-95, 656, 1672
Busey, J.L. 228
Byars, R.S. 187

Café Filho, J. 447
Cahali, Y.S. 1291
Caldas, W. 1728, 1761
Caldeira, C. 1146-47
Callado, A. 548, 1207
Calmón, P. 229, 396
Calogeras, J.P. 397
Calvert, P. 398
Câmara, J.M. 1631
Campbell, G. 852
Campos, E. de S. 1827
Campos, F. 448
Campos, R. de O. 820
Canabrava Filho, P. 760
Cândido, A. 1019, 1148
C.A.P.E.S. 125, 1828
Capuano, T.M. 549
Cardoso, A., Jr. 1729
Cardoso, F.H. 709-10, 885-87, 1345
Cardoso, R. 1054, 1487
Cardoso Júnior, A. 1729
Cardozo, M. 58, 1524
Cardwell, R.L. 1829
Carlos, M.L. 1292
Carneiro, E. 1416

Carneiro, G. 449, 607
Carneiro, J.F. 1020
Carneiro, R. 853
Carneiro Leão, A. 1782
Carone, E. 188, 450-51
Carpeaux, O.M. 1525, 1602
Carrazzoni, A. 452
Carvalho, A. de 1100
Carvalho, A.F. 59
Carvalho, D. de 657
Carvalho, G. 761
Carvalho, M. 1730
Carvalho, M. de 453
Carvalho, O. de 358-59
Carvalho, R. de 1208
Cascudo, L. da C. 1417, 1603, 1731-32
Castaldi, C. 1488
Castedo, L. 1658-59
Castello Branco, C. 550
Castello Branco Filho, M. 608
Castro, A.M. de O. 1699
Castro, E.V. 1471
Castro, J. de 1149-51, 1241
Castro, M. de 1700
Catholic University of America. Library 60
Cavalcanti, C. 1152
Cavalcanti, P.C.U. 551
Cavalcanti, T.B. 189, 230, 360
C.B.D. 1701
C.B.P.E. 1783
Cehelsky, M. 1101
Céspedes, G. 190
Chacon, V. 231-32, 1604
Chaffee, W.A. 124
Chagas Cruz, C.H.D. 191
Chalmers, D.A. 552
Chamberlain, B.J. 131
Chamberlain, H. 1293
Chandler, B.J. 1209, 1294
Charno, S. 95
Chéradama, A. 1489
Chernov, L. 294
Chevalier, F. 399
Chiappino, J. 1453
Chilcote, R.H. 400-01, 711
Cintra, A.O. 233
C.I.P. 1567
Claudin, F. 295
C.O.D.O.C. 122, 713
Coelho, E.C. 610
Coelho Netto, F. 1701
Cohn, G. 712, 888
Cole, J.P. 962
Collier, D. 889
Collins, D.E. 1784
Collitti-Pischel, E. 296
Collver, O.A. 15
Colombo, P. 297
Comissão Censitária dos Mucambos do Recife 1055
Comissão Nacional de Moral e Civismo, 1811
Committee for the Responsible Election of the Pope 1540
Committee on Latin America 61
Confederação Brasileira de Desportes 1702
Congregação Israelita Paulista 1567
Conn, S. 361
Conniff, M.L. 454-55, 611, 1056
Contier, A.D. 1762
Converse, J.W. 1153
Cony, C.H. 456, 553, 1057
Cooke, M.L. 658
Cooper, D. 963
Cooper, R.N. 854
Cordeiro, M.L. 1058
Cornelius, W.A. 964
Corrêa de Azevedo 1763
Corrêa e Silva, A. 919
Correia de Souza, J.G. 1490
Cortés Conde, R. 62
Cortés, C. 457
Cortez, M.F. 1733
Corwin, A.F. 1346
Coseriu, E. 1631
Costa, F.J. 554, 1252
Costa, J.C. 1605

Costa, Lia Parente 1830
Costa, Licurgo 659
Costa, Lúcio 1660
Costa, R.V. 714
Costa Gondolphim, W. da 1021
Costa Pinto, L. de A. 1242, 1295, 1347
Couceira, S.M. 1418
Courtin, R. 821
Coutinho, A. 33, 34, 1348
Coutinho, E. 1454
Coutinho, G. 1059
Coutinho, J. de S. 1764
Coutinho, L. 612
Couto e Silva, G. 660
Cowell, A. 1455
Cowell, B., Jr. 965
C.P.D.O.C. 609
Crawford, H.P. 362
Crawford, W.R. 1606
Cruls, G.L. 1154
Crusoe, R. 1349
Cruz Costa, J. 1831
Cunha, E. da 1210
Cunha, L.R.A. 832
Cunha, M.E.M. e 1607

Dahl, G. 1673
Daland, R.T. 363-64
Damata, G. 613, 1060
Da Matta, R. 1243
Dantas, C. de S.T. 661
Da Silva, L.M. 1296
Dassin, J. 1526, 1608, 1674-75
Daugherty, C. 528
Daus, R. 1211
Davis, D.B. 1350
Davis, H. 1609
Davis, H.B. 458, 920
Davis, H.E. 662
Davis, M.R. 920
Davis, S.H. 1456
Deal, C.W. 126
Dean, R.W. 614
Dean, W. 890
De Carli, G. 796
d'Eça, R. 1297
De Dubnic, V.R. 402
Degler, C. 1351
De Kadt, E. 1527
Dell, E. 459
Dell, S. 762
Della Cava, R. 555-56, 1212-13, 1491, 1528-29
Delpar, H. 45
Del Picchia, M. 334
De Noia, J. 63
Dias, C. 64
Dias, E. 921
Dickenson, J.P. 891
Diegues Júnior, M. 1492
Diffie, B.W. 1022, 1493
Dillon, D. 298
Dimas Filho, N. 615
Dimmick, R.E. 1610
Dines, A. 460
Dodt, J. *See* G. Barroso
Doellinger, C. von 763
"Dona Benta," 1734
Donald, C.J. 1352
Donald, C.L. 234
Doria, S. 461
Dorn, G.M. 127
Dos Passos, J. 165
Dos Santos, T. 299, 715
Dourado, A. 1611
Doxiadis Associates 966
Dreller, G. 1419
Duarte, A. 1676
Duarte, A.C. 967
Duarte, J.C. 855
Duarte, P. 462
Duarte, P. de Q. 1155
Duarte, P.O. 235
Duarte, S.G. 716
Duarte Pereira, O. 365
Dulles, J.W.F. 192, 300, 463-64, 616
Dunbar, D.L. 1735
Duncan, J.A. 1156
Duncan, J.S. 822
Du Plessis, I.D. 1703
Dupré, L.M.J. 1061
Dye, D.R. 558
Dzidzienyo, A. 1353, 1420

Eckardt, W. von 968
Eckholm, E. 1157
Edwards, H. 1704
Edwards, S.F. 247
Efegê, J. 1765
Einaudi, L.R. 647
Elkins, S. 1354
Ellis, H.S. 797, 856
Ellison, F.P. 1612
Emert, H. 559
Eneida 1736
Epstein, D.G. 969
Erickson, K.P. 922-24
Espínola, E. 366
Esquenazi-Mayo, R. 193
Estevez, F. 1672
Eulau, H. 335
Evenson, N. 970
Ewen, D. 1766
Expilly, C. 1298

Facó, R. 1214
Fairchild, L. 772
Faissol, S. 971
Faoro, R. 236
Farhat, A. 1299
Farhat, E. 1158
Faust, A.F. 1785
Faust, J.J. 465
Fausto, B. 166-67, 194, 925
Feder, E. 1102
Feinsot, A. 1832
Feldman, E. 987
Fernandes, A.G. 1586
Fernandes, F. 195, 1244-46, 1355-56, 1786
Fernandez, O. 96
Ferreira de Camargo, C.P. 1531
Fiechter, G.-A. 560
Figueiredo, A. 1357
Figueiredo, E. de 617
Figueiredo, G. 1613
Figueiredo, M. 237
Figueiredo, V. 717, 1247
Fish, R.L. 1714
Fishlow, A. 858-59
Fitzgibbon, R.H. 403
Fitzpatrick, R.S. 1248
Flasche, R. 1587
Fleck, A. 1672
Fleischer, D.V. 404
Florenzano, É. 46
Flynn, P. 196, 405, 618, 718
Foland, F.M. 972, 1494
Fontaine, P.-M. 1358
Fontaine, R.W. 663
Fontan, A. 1706
Fontes, A. 1062
Fontes, L. 238
Fontoura, J.N. da 466
Forman, S. 1159-60, 1185, 1215
Formigli, V.L. 1812
France. Centre d'Études de Géographie Tropicale 973
Francis, M.J. 664
Francis, P. 467
Franco, C. 561
Franco, M.S. de C. 1216
Frank, A.G. 719-21
Frank, T. 1637
Frazier, E.F. 1359
Freels, J.W., Jr. 239
Freire, J. 619
Freire, M. 562
Freire, P. 1787-89
Freitas, T.L.R. 773
Fresnot, D. 1614
Freyre, G. 468-69, 974-76, 1063, 1249-50, 1360-67, 1421-23, 1615-17
Fried, J. 1568
Friedan, B. 1300
Fry, P. 1559
Frye, A. 665
Fuerst, R. 1457
Fujii, Y. 1495
Fundação Getúlio Vargas 860
Furtado, C. 240, 406, 722-26, 798
Fuss, P. 1661

Gabaglia, L.P.R. 1532
Galeano, E. 764
Galey, J.H. 823
Galjart, B. 1103
Gall, N. 563, 1533
Garcia, R.C. 926
Garcia, W. 1790
Garcia-Zamor, J.-C. 367
Gardner, M. 97
Garg, R.C. 765
Gasparian, F. 892
Gauld, C.A. 766
Gauthier, H.L. 824
Geiger, P.P. 977
Gerbi, A. 1503
Geribello, W.P. 1791
Genovese, E.D. 1368
Gibson, H. 1064
Giffen, D.W. 666
Gilbert, A. 727
Gillett, T. 65
Gilliam, A.M. 1065
Giroletti, D.A. 893
Glick, D. 1566
Goertzel, T. 1792
Gões, W. de 564
Goff, F. 755
Goiano, C. 1738
Goldhamer, H. 667
Goldman, A. 1739
Goldman, D.M. 1251
Goldman, F.P. 1251
Goldwasser, M.J. 1740
Gomes, A.M. de C. 368
Gomes, A.O. 1424
Gomes, J.F. *See* J. Efegê.
Gomes, L.M.G. 565-66, 1252
Gomes, S. 767
Gonçalves, C. 16
Goodman, D.E. 894-95, 927-28
Gordon, L. 896
Gorender, J. 301
Gorham, R. 66
Goulart, J.A. 1066
Gouveia, A.J. 1301, 1813-14
Grabois, M. 287
Graham, D.H. 849, 989, 1023-25
Graham, L.S. 369
Graham, R. 407-08, 1369
Grande, H. 1793
Great Britain. Board of Trade 768
Gregor, T. 1458
Gressler, G.P. 1707
Griffen, C.C. 128
Griffin, H.M. 124
Grommers, E. 896
Gropp, A.E. 129
Gross, D.R. 1104-05
Grossmann, J. 98, 370
Grubb, K. 1558
Grunwald, J. 769
Guarneiri, G. 1671
Gudin Filho, E. 770
Guedes, S.L. 1708
Guerra, R. 1677-78
Guerreira Ramos, A. 1370
Guilherme, W. 1253
Guimarães, A. 35
Gunther, J. 409

Haar, J. 1794
Haberley, D.T. 151, 1371
Hahner, J.E. 1302-04
Hall, A.L. 1106
Hall, M. 1496
Haller, A. 939
Hallinan, T. 1534
Hambloch, E. 470
Hammond, G. 80
Hanbury-Tenison, R. 1459
Hanke, L. 1372, 1681
Hansen, E.C. 1281
Hansen, E.R. 1067
Hansen, H. 1497
Hanson, C.A. 130
Harding, T.F. 471, 929
Hardman, F.F. 930
Harmon, R.M. 131
Harms-Baltzer, K. 668
Harris, M. 1161, 1373-74, 1480
Harrison, J. 67
Harvard University. Bureau for Economic Research 132, 825

Haskins, J. 1709
Hasselmann, S. 17
Haussman, F. 1794
Havighurst, R.J. 1795
Hayes, R.A. 624
Hayter, T. 771
Heitor, L. 1763
Hemming, J. 1460
Hendricks, H.C. 1833, 1837
Henriques, A. 472
Herkenhoff, J.B. 1162
Hermogenes, J. de A. 1815
Herrmann, L. 1163
Herskovits, M.J. 1425, 1588
Heyck, D.L. 1618
Hill, L.F. 168, 669
Hilton, R. 36, 68, 169
Hilton, S.E. 336, 621, 670-71
Hime, M.A. 580
Hirschman, A.O. 826
Hispanic Foundation 47
Hispanic Society of America. Library 69
Hobsbawm, E.J. 1217
Hoffmann, H. 861, 931
Holanda, C.B. de 1679-80
Holanda, N. de 302, 672
Holanda, S.B. de 197, 241, 391
Holanda Filho, S.B. de 1025
Holford, W. 978
Holloway, T.H. 1026, 1107
Homem de Mello, F. 1108
Horowitz, I.L. 473
Horta, E.V. 1305
Humphrey, J. 932
Humphreys, R.A. 133, 410
Hutchinson, H.W. 70, 1164, 1254

Ianni, O. 567, 728-29, 897, 933, 1255, 1346
Inglésias, F. 799
Indiana University. Audio-Visual Center 1375
Ineson, F.A. 1560
Ingles, J.L. 772
Institut für Iberoamerika-Kunde 134
Institute of Jewish Affairs 1569
Institute of Latin American Studies 71, 135
Instituto Brasileiro de Geografia e Estatística 136, 1376
Instituto Brasileiro de Reforma Agrária 1109
Instituto Nacional do Livro 137
Inter-American Committee for Agricultural Development 1110
IPM 709, 622
Ireland, R. 1535

Jackman, R. 862
Jackson, W.V. 72, 73
Jacobina, A.P. 773
Jaguaribe, H. 242-45
Jambo, A. 1619
James, P. 170
Jerman, W. de 568
Jesús, C.M. de 1068
Joel, M. 1426
Jones, R.L. 1010
Johnson, A.W. 1165-66
Johnson, J.J. 246, 623
Johnson, P.B. 1620
Johnson, P.T. 569
Joslin, D. 800
Julião, F. 570, 1167

Kahil, R. 730
Kahili, N. 1377
Kahl, J. 731, 898
Kando, A. 1461
Karasch, M. 1306
Katzman, M.T. 979
Kavenagh, T.M. 1621
Keith, H.H. 247, 624
Kellemen, P. 1622
Kemper, R.V. 964
Kent, H. 980
Kerstenetzky, I. 702, 847

Kiemen, M.C. 1462
Kietzman, D.W. 1463
Kimball, S.T. 1816
Kingsbury, R.C. 411
Klapholz, K. 862
Klein, L.G. 554
Knaster, M. 1307
Knight, P.T. 1111
Konder, L. 1256
Kottack, C.P. 1308, 1378
Krieger, D. 474
Krischke, P.J. 1517, 1536
Kroetz, L.R. 827
Kunder, M. 1499

Labouriau, L.G. 1834
Lacerda, C. 412
Lacerda, F. 303
Lacerda, M. de 475
Laclau, E. 1112
Lacombe, A.J. 413
Lafer, C. 571
Lafetâ, J.L. 1623
Lago, M. 572
Lamb, F.B. 1464
Lambert, F. 371
Lambert, J. 1257-58
Landry, D.M. 673
Langguth, A.J. 573
Langoni, C. 863
Lappe, F.M. 1113
LaRaia, A.L. 1328
Latin American Study Center 1427
Lauerhass, L., Jr. 138
Leacock, R. 1589
Leacock, S. 1589
Leal, V.N. 1168
Leão, A.C. 199
Leão, S. 1169
Le Corbusier 981
Leeds, A. 982, 1069-72, 1218, 1259
Leff, N.H. 828-29
Leitão, E. 934
Leite, A. 476
Leite, D.M. 1817
Leite, S.U. 1741
Leonard, P.J. 1537
Leopoldi, J.S. 1742, 1767
Lerner, H. 1500
Leser, W. 1073
Lessa, L.C. 1624
Lessa, O. 1465, 1743
Lever, J. 1710-11
Levi, D.E. 200, 1309
Levine, R.M. 48, 75, 201-02, 304, 477-79, 574-77, 625, 864, 1027, 1428, 1570, 1712, 1795, 1835-37
Levi-Straus, C. 1466
Lévy, J.E. 1768
Lewin, L. 480, 1310, 1744
Lima, A.A. 324
Lima, H. 1797
Lima, H.F. 899
Lima Cavalcanti, A. 983
Lima Sobrinho, A.J.B. 481
Lima Vaz, H.C. 1538
Linhares, M.Y.L. 674
Link, M. 865
Linz, J. 578
Lipset, S.M. 1260
Lipson, L. 482
Lispector, C. 1074
Lobo, E.M.L. 801-02, 1075
Loeb, G.F. 900
Loewenstein, K. 483
Loftin, M.T. 1501
Lombardi, M. 99
Love, J.L. 187, 203, 414, 479, 484-85, 774, 830
Lovett, G. 49
Lowrie, S.H. 1028
Loy, J. 1681
Lucas, F. 372
Luddeman, M.K. 675
Ludwig, A.K. 984-85
Luizetto, F.V. 1029
Luz, N.V. 204, 248, 803, 901
Lyday, L.F. 1682
Lyra Filho, J. 1170
Lyra Tavares, A. de 626

Maack, R. 1502
Macaulay, N. 627
McCann, F.D. 486, 628, 676-77

MacCarthy, C. 76
MacEoin, G. 1539-40
McFadden, J.P. 1798
McGreevey, W.P. 139
McGregor, P. 1590
Machado, A. 305
Machado, C. 579
Machado, D. 1076
Machado, M.C.M. 1219
Machado, R. 986
Machado Neto, A.L. 249
Maciel, P. 37
McLachlan, C. 1311
McNeill, M.R. 1799
Magalhães, Agamemnon 250
Magalhães, Aloísio 987
Magalhães, I.M. 580
Magalhães Júnior, S.N. de 804
Maia, J. 678
Maia, J. de A., 140
Maia Neto 679
Maier, J. 1800
Maio, S. de 1312
Makler, H.M. 902-03
Malan, P. 732
Malloy, J.M. 373, 1077, 1171
Manchester, A.K. 77
Mandell, P.I. 988
Mangabeira, F. 775
Manor, P. 1838
Marais, B.J. 1379
Maram, S.L. 935
Marcadante, P. 251
Marchant, A. 1275
Marcílio, M.L. 1030
Margolis, M.L. 1114-15
Margulies, M. 1571
Marighela, C. 287, 293, 306-07
Mariz, C. 1541
Mariz, V. 1769-70
Markham, C.G. 1116
Marques, A.N. 1117
Marshall, A. 415
Martin, M. 49
Martin, P.A. 38, 374, 1380
Martins, A.P. 142
Martins, C.E. 680
Martins, F. 1172
Martins, Leônocio 733
Martins, Luciano 1118
Martins, M. 581
Martins, M.T.C. 143
Martins, P. 252
Martins, R.R. 582
Martins, Roberto 1625
Martins, Rodrigues 936
Martins, S. 583
Martins, W. 487, 1626-27, 1683
Marx, F.M. 375
Mason, P. 1381
Mass, B. 776
Mata, M. 1031
Mattos, O. 1377
Maurer, H. 584
Mauro, F. 171
Máximo, J. 1700
Maybury-Lewis, D. 1261, 1467
Mazzara, R.A. 1628
Medcalf, J.C. 1119
Medeiros, J. 337
Medina, C.A. 1078, 1120
Meehan, E.J. 1079
Meggers, B.J. 1173
Meijer, H. 1121
Mello Franco, A.A. de 253-54, 376-77, 416, 488
Melo, A. 1262
Mendes de Oliveira, G. de B. 831
Mendonça, R. 1429
Meneghello, L. 489
Menezes, A. de 255
Menezes, D. 1174
Menezes, J.B. de 78
Menton, S. 1683
Mericle, K.S. 734
Merrick, T.W. 989
Metall, R.A. 1382
Metzger, E. 777
Meyer, M.C. 193, 697
Michalski, J. 1629
Miller, J.C. 1430

Mindlin, H. 1662
Miralles, T. 378
Mitchell, S. 1175, 1313
Molotnik, J.R. *See* J. Dassin.
Momsen, R. 172
Monbeig, P. 173, 1032
Moniz, E. 585
Monteiro, J.V. 832
Monteiro, S. 778
Montezuma de Carvalho, J. 1383
Montgomery, E.G. 144
Montoro, F. 586
Moore, R.B. 256
Moraes, C. 490
Moraes, J.B.M. 629
Moraes, P. de 1263
Moraes, T. 1314
Morais, C.W. 630
Morais, D. de 1801
Morais, R.B. de 145
Moran, E.F. 1122
Morazé, C. 417
Moreira, A.G. 1315
Moreira, J.R. 1795, 1802, 1808, 1818
Morel, E. 681
Morgan, D.L. 80
Morley, S. 779, 866-67
Mörner, M. 1384
Morris, M. 682
Morse, R.M. 991-95, 1033, 1385
Mortara, G. 1034
Morton, A. 1220
Mota, A. 338
Mota, C.G. 205-06, 1630
Mota, M. 1264
Mourão, M.D.H. 1316
Muniz Júnior, J. 1745
Muraro, R.M. 1318-19
Murphy, R.F. 1320
Murphy, Y. 1320
Myhr, R.O. 1839

N.A.C.L.A. 781
Nagel, R. 81
Naro, A.J. 1631
Nascimento, A. de 1386-87
Nascimento, E.A. do 1713-14
Nascimento Brito, J. 18
Nasser, D. 491
Natal e Silva, C. 996
Ness, W.L. 868
Neuhaus, P. 833
Neves, F. 1632
Neves, L.F.B. 1633
New York Public Library 82
Nicholls, W.H. 1123
Nichols, G.A. 418-19
Niedergang, M. 174
Niehaus, T. 1542
Niemeyer, O. 997, 1663
Niemeyer, O.E. 834
Niemeyer, W. 937
Nist, J. 1634
Nobre, F. 587
Nóbrega, A.C. 39
Nogueira, O. 1080
Norman, J. 83
Normano, J.F. 780, 805, 1503
North, L. 384
Nunes, A.P. 588
Nunes, C. 1635
Nunes, G. 1081
Nunes, M.L. 1432
Nunn, F.M. 631

O, M. de 938
Odália, N. 683, 1388
O'Fields, H. 1637
Okinshevich, L. 146
Oliveira, E.R. de 632
Oliveira, Francisco de 735, 1265
Oliveira, Franklin de 258
Oliveira Torres, J.C. 259, 379
Oliveira Vianna, 260
Oliven, R. 998
O'Neil, C.F. 1819
O'Neill, M.A. 1543
Onody, O. 782, 806
Overholt, W.H. 807

Packenham, R.A. 261
Page, J.A. 492
Paim, A. 1176
Paiva, R.M. 1124
Paixão, M. da 1684
Palhano, L. 1177
Pan American Union 100, 1266
Pang, E.-S. 1267, 1544
Papadaki, S. 1664
Parahyba, M.A. 420
Parker, P.R. 684
Pastore, J. 939, 1336
Pásztor, L. 84
Patric, A. 308
Paula, E.S. de 101
Pedreira, F. 589, 1636
Pedrosa, C. 147
Peixoto, A.V. 493
Peixoto, F. 1685
Peláez, C.M. 803, 808-09, 904, 1125-26
Pendle, G. 421
Pendrell, N. 1082
Penn, D. 1389
Peppe, P.V. 924
Peralva, O. 309
Pereira, A. 310-11, 494, 685
Pereira, G.S. 1686
Pereira, J.B.B. 1433, 1771
Pereira, J.E. de C. 732
Pereira, N. 495
Pereira, P.A.P. 1127
Perlman, J. 1083
Perruci, G. 1128-29
Perry, W. 686
Pescatello, A. 1321-24
Pessôa, D. 1152
Pessôa Ramos, D.H.A. 207
Peterson, P.J. 496
Petras, J.E. 590
Phelps, D.M. 783
Pierson, D. 1178, 1390-91, 1434-35
Pierucci, A.F. de O. 1545
Pimpão, H. 497
Pinheiro, P.S. 208
Pinheiro Neto, J. 835
Pinho, C.S. 1572
Pinkuss, F. 1573
Pinsky, J. 687
Pinto, A.G. 1772
Pinto, B. 591
Pinto, J.B. 1336
Pires, H. 1665
Pires do Rio, J. 836
Pisani, S. 1504
Poblete-Troncoso, M. 940
Pokshishevsky, V.V. 736
Polícia Civil do Distrito Federal 312
Pompermayer, M.J. 262
Pontes, E. 1084
Pontes, J. 1715
Pontes, P. 1679
Poppino, R.E. 175
Porter, D.B. 1436
Prado, E. 339
Prado Júnior, C. 176, 1130
Prestes, L.C. 303, 313-20
Primitive People's Fund 1468
Prowess, M. Cavalcanti 1637
Putnam, S. 498, 1638-39
Pyle, G.F. 1000

Quadros, J. 688
Quartim, J. 321
Queiroz, M.I.P. de 1221-23, 1546
Queiroz, R. de 1179
Quirino, T.R. 905

Rabassa, G. 1437
Rabello, S. 1325
Raby, D. 384
Rachum, I. 263, 633-35, 1326, 1640
Rady, D.E. 906
Raine, P. 422
Raizman, I.Z. 1574
Ramos, A. 1392-93, 1438
Ramos, A.G. 264-65, 1370
Ramos, G. 1180, 1268
Ramos, J. 551

Rangel, I. 737
Rangel, L. 1773
Raphael, A. 1085, 1269
Rasmussen, K.W. 1746
Read, W.R. 1560-61
Reale, M. 340-41
Redmont, B.S. 322
Reeve, R.P. 1394
Regis, F.E. de M.S. 1174
Rêgo, J.L. do 1181-84, 1687
Reich, P.L. 1672
Reis, A.S. dos 148
Reizman, Y. 1576
Renshaw, J.P. 1591
Resnick, S. 1577
Revoredo, J. 1505
Ribeiro, D. 784, 1469, 1840
Ribeiro, J. da S. 40
Ribeiro, J.U. 1270
Ribeiro, R. 1224, 1592
Ribeiro de Castro, O. 323
Richardson, I.L. 380, 1001
Riegelhaupt, J.F. 1166, 1185
Rio de Janeiro. Biblioteca Nacional 86
Rio de Janeiro. Centro Estudos Sociais 149
Rio de Janeiro. Universidade. Faculdade de Filosofia 150
Rio de Janeiro. Universidade. Instituto de Ciências Sociais 1131
Rios, J.A. 1271
Rivera, J. 177
Robertazzi, C. 296
Robock, S.H. 837, 869
Rocha, E. 785
Rocha, G. 1186, 1225, 1578, 1688
Roche, J. 1506
Rodell, M.J. 1002
Rodman, S. 178, 1641, 1747
Rodrigues, A.M. 941
Rodrigues, J.H. 87-88, 103-04, 209-15, 689-90, 1642, 1841
Rodrigues, L. 381, 942
Rodríguez, R.V. 1642
Roett, R. 266, 423, 636, 786
Rogers, F.M. 151
Rohter, L. 1507
Roiter, F. 1666
Rojas, J. 1517
Rondón, C.M. de S. 1470
Rosa, J.G. 1187
Rosen, B.C. 1327-28
Rosenbaum, H.J. 691, 738, 1035
Ross, E.B. 1188
Rout, L.B., Jr. 1395-97
Rowe, J. 424, 528, 592
Rubião, M. 1086
Russell-Wood, A.J.R. 1398
Rust, F. 1439

Sá, M.A.F. de 1189
Sable, M.H. 51-52, 89, 152-53, 1003, 1579
Sahota, G.S. 810
Saito, H. 1508
Saldanha, J. 1716
Salgado, P. 326, 333, 342-46, 1190
Salles, P. 179
Sampaio, C.N. 425
Sampaio, N. de S. 267
Sampaio, Y. 943
Sanders, T.G. 907
Sanjeck, R. 1399
Santa Rosa, V. 268, 500
Santos, D.F. dos 637
Santos, J.L. dos 1329
Santos, N. P. dos 1689-90
Santos, R.G. 692
Santos, W.G. dos 269, 593
São Paulo. British Chamber of Commerce 19
São Paulo. Departamento Estadual de Estatística 20
São Paulo. Diretoria Administrativa 1036
São Paulo. Instituto de Economia Agrícola 1132
Saraiva, M.T. 1330

Sarno, F.J. 1717
Saunders, J.V.D. 501, 1037
Sayers, R.S. 180, 1440
Schilling, P.R. 1133
Schmidt, A.F. 594
Schmitter, P.C. 270-72, 638
Schneider, R.M. 273, 411, 528, 693
Schoenbach, P.J. 1691
Schröder, H.-J. 694
Schuh, G.E. 1134
Schurz, W.L. 181
Schwartzman, S. 426-27
Schweig Viera, F.I. 1509
Seckinger, R.L. 1267
Secretaria General de la O.E.A. 21
Seeger, A. 1471
Seganfreddo, S. 1842
Segna, E.V. 1547
Selcher, W.A. 695
Sellers, L. 1292
Semple, R.K. 824
Sena, J.F.F. 895
Senne, J.J. de A. 944
Serra, J. 739
Serton, P. 1272, 1400
Shapira, Y. 1094
Sharp, W.R. 502
Shaull, R. 1548
Shaw, B.A. 154
Shirley, R.W. 908, 1191
Siegel, G. 382
Silva, C. da 1331
Silva, C.J. da 428, 1192
Silva, H. 503-13, 639-40
Silva, J.T. da 1004
Silva, L. 1692
Silva, M. dos S. 1803, 1822
Silva, M.P. de 1382
Simonsen, M.H. 740, 753, 847, 870
Simonsen, R.C. 811, 838
Simonson, W.N. 1510
Sims, H.D. 1511
"Sinani," 303
Sinet, M. 595
Singer, P.I. 741, 1005
Singlemann, P. 1226
Sio, A. 1401
Sissón, R. 1644
Skidmore, T.E. 216-17, 274, 429-30, 514, 742, 839, 1402-04
Slater, C. 1748
Smith, A. 1038
Smith, B.H. 1549
Smith, C.T. 1017
Smith, G.W. 779
Smith, N. 1039
Smith, P.H. 408
Smith, P.S. 840-41
Smith, T.L. 1135-36, 1193, 1273-75, 1495
Soares, G.A.D. 275, 871, 1137
Soares, J. 1749
Soares Leite, J.S. 945
Sobrinho, B.L. 276, 946, 1645
Sobrinho, O.T.M. 1011
Sodré, N.W. 220, 277-78, 515, 641-43, 743, 787, 1087, 1646
Soihet, R. 1332
Sola, L. 516
Solari, A. 1260
Soler, L. 1750
Somarriba, M. das D.G. 1194
Souto Maior, M. 1647
Souza, A. de 218, 596, 1227
Souza, A.P.S. de 90
Souza, J.G. de 155, 1693
Souza, P. de 597
Souza Campos, E. de 1843
Souza Montenegro, J.A. de 1550
Souza e Silva, C.E. 558
Spiegel, H.W. 909
Springer, F. 947
Stacchini, J. 598
Staley, A.J. 1405
Staubli, W. 1006
Stein, S.J. 62, 219, 910, 1406

Steiner, H.J. 644
Sternberg, H. O'R. 1138, 1195
Stepan, A.C. 431, 645-47, 1040
Stepan, N. 182
Sterns, M.A. 1844
Steward, J.H. 1473
Storrs, K.L. 696
Strickon, A. 1276
Suassuna, A. 1751
S.U.D.E.N.E. 156, 872
Sund, M. 1139
Suzigan, W. 808-09, 812, 815
Swigart, J.E. 157
Syurud, D.E. 744
Szwed, J.F. 1441

Taeuber, I. 91
Tannenbaum, F. 183, 1407
Tapajós, V. 708
Távora, A. 599
Távora, J. 648
Tavares, R.A. 1442
Tavares de Sá, I. 1333
Teixeira, A.S. 1804-05, 1823
Teixera de Oliveira, J. 54
Telles, J. 948
Tendler, J. 788, 911
Tenório, O. 1041
Tereza, M. 1725
Terry, L. 1845
Thébaud, F. 1718
Thomas, E.W. 1694
Tigner, J.L. 1513
Tiller, A.Q. 517
Tinhorão, J.R. 1775-76
Tobias, J.A. 1649
Todaro, M. *See* M.T. Williams.
Toledo, C.N. de 745
Tolosa, H.C. 1007
Tommy, J.L. 1089
Toop, W.R. 1196
Topete, J.M. 158
Toplin, R.B. 1408
Torres, A. 279
Torres, J.C. de O. 1277
"Tostão" 1719
Trask, D.F. 697
Trask, R.R. 697-98
Trindade, H. 347-48
Truebeck, D.M. 644
Turner, D.J. 1197, 1443
Turner, J.M. 221, 1444
Tyler, W.G. 738, 789, 912, 1035
Tyson, B. 699, 1542, 1552

Underwood, B.A. 1105
Unger, R.M. 280
U.S.A.I.D. 1806
U.S. Army 649
U.S.-Brazil Fulbright Commission 23
U.S. Department of State 92, 159
U.S. Senate. Committee on Foreign Relations 600
Universidade Federal de Pernambuco 1807
University of Texas. Library 93
University of Wisconsin. Land Tenure Center 1140

Vaitsman, M. 42, 1008
Valente, W. 1593
Vallier, I. 1553
Van den Berghe, P. 1341
Vanderschuren, F. 1517
Van Steen, E. 1334
Vargas, G. 518-21, 746
Vasconcelos, A. 1777
Vasconcelos, G. 1778
Vasconcelos, J.M. de 1278
Vassberg, D.E. 1779
Velho, G. 1088
Velloso, J.P. dos R. 1043
Velloso, M.P. 349
Vergara, L. 522
Verger, P. 1657
Verissimo, E. 1198, 1279, 1650
Viana Filho, L. 650

Vianna, H. 222
Vianna, L.W. 949-50
Vidal, A. 523, 1044
Vidal, B. 524
Vidal, L.B. 1474
Vieira, D.T. 813, 913
Vieira, H. 1667
Vieira da Cunha, M.W. 105
Vilaça, M. 1199
Vilela, A. 814
Vilespy, F. 1228
Villas-Boas, C. 1475-76
Villas-Boas, O. 1475-76
Villas-Boas, P.L. 160
Vinhas de Queiroz, M. 1229
Vita, L.W. 1651
Viveiros de Castro, E. 1471
Vogel, A. 1720
Von Gersdorff, R. 815
Von Puttkamer, W.J. 1477

Waddell, A.S. 525
Wagley, C. 184, 1045, 1280, 1478-80, 1808
Wagner, S. 56
Wahrlich, B. 383
Wallis, M.P. 1335
Walters, V. 651
Warren, Jr., D. 223, 1594-96
Weatherhead, R.W. 1800
Weaver, J.L. 161
Webb, K.E. 1141, 1200
Weber, S. 1830
Weffort, F.C. 281, 526-27, 951-53
Weil, T. 24
Wells, H. 528
Wells, J. 747
Welsh, D.V. 94
Werebe, M.J. 1809
Werneck, H. 1652
Wharton, C.R. 1142
Whitaker, M. de A. 790
Wiarda, H.J. 1554
Wilhelm, J. 1009
Wilkening, E.A. 1336
Willems, E. 1046-47, 1201-03, 1409, 1562
Williams, M.T. 224, 1551, 1555-57
Winpenny, J.T. 914
Winterstein, V. 1580
Wirth, J.D. 128, 157, 479, 529, 652, 842, 1010
Wish, J.R. 748
Wolf, E.R. 1281
Wolff, E. 1581
Wolff, F. 1581
Woodyard, G.W. 1682
Worcester, D. 432
Worsnop, F.L. 530
Wycliffe Bible Translators 1481
Wycoff, T. 531
Wyer, J. 954
Wythe, G. 843

Young, J.M. 532, 653

Zamora, P. 1721
Zimmerman, I. 106, 162
Zubatsky, D. 107

SUBJECT INDEX

Abertura. *See* Liberalization, post-1964
Academy of Letters, Brazilian 1613, 1632
Acão Integralista Brasileira. *See* Integralism
Acculturation 1046. *See also* Immigration; Ethnic groups
Africa, Black, relations with 221, 674, 688-89, 695, 1420, 1444, 1593, 1764. *See also* South Africa
Afro-Brazilian studies 1337-1444, 1600, 1655; bibliography 1410, 1418, 1427, 1430, 1436, 1442, 1764, 1775, 1779; historiography 221
Agriculture 1032, 1089-1142, 1175, 1181, 1185; bibliography 1097, 1131, 1140; commodities 904, 1095, 1105, 1107, 1111, 1125-26, 1128-29. *See also* Land tenure; Minifundia; Rural life
Alagôas. *See* Northeast
Amapá 117
Amazônia 1173, 1195, 1320, 1478-79, 1598; bibliography 120; economic development 773, 823, 852, 1021, 1035, 1039, 1042-43, 1122, 1127, 1157; fiction 1144, 1154, 1177; guerrilla warfare 604; population 1045, 1113, 1188; religion 1589; travel in 1598. *See also* Amerindians
Amerindians 136, 1045, 1320, 1445-81, 1775; bibliography 1446, 1457; languages 136
Aranha, Oswaldo 441
ARENA 343, 417, 423, 430, 601. *See also* Political parties
Armed forces 261-62, 423, 430-31, 552, 602-53; political role of 273-74, 336, 400, 536, 702, 760; post-1964 *coup* 550, 560, 576, 761, 851, 858, 863-64, 871, 897; Superior War College (E.S.G.) 632; World War II 446, 511-12, 613, 629, 639-40, 649, 651, 658, 664-65, 677, 1061, 1155
Arns, Dom Paulo Evaristo 1526-27. *See also* Catholic Church
Arraes, Miguel 436, 1205. *See also* Pernambuco; Northeast
Authoritarianism 122, 191, 205-06, 247, 256, 262, 281, 398, 403, 414, 423, 429-32, 460-63, 536-601, 713, 848, 857, 864, 1076, 1171, 1630, 1636; historiography 196
Azevedo, Fernando de 269

Bahia 1178; bibliography 149; Church 1518-19, 1676;

Bahia (cont'd)
economics 1080, 1105; interior life 1090-91, 1164, 1231, 1270, 1534, 1658; population 1186; race and ethnicity 1065, 1083, 1161, 1164, 1378, 1390-93, 1411; urban life 957, 971, 1002, 1079, 1082, 1231, 1283, 1434
Baptista, Padre Cícero. *See* Padre Cícero
Barros, Adhemar de 435. *See also* São Paulo
Brasília 959-60, 968-70, 974-75, 978, 980, 984-85, 987, 990, 996-97, 999, 1006, 1008, 1660, 1662-64
Brazil. *Cf.* Spanish America 190, 223, 421, 924, 1569; agriculture 1136-37; economic development 739, 762; race relations 1407, 1425; urbanization 964
Brazil as world power. *See* Foreign relations
Brazilian studies 45-55, 62-66, 68-70, 73, 75, 87, 108-62, 183, 193, 195, 201, 211, 219-20, 994, 1245-46, 1274-76, 1307, 1438, 1466; "Brazilianists" 198, 207-08, 576

Café Filho, João 447
Câmara, Dom Helder 1514, 1521, 1524, 1527, 1535-37, 1552. *See also* Catholic Church
Campos, Francisco 337, 448. *See also* Estado Nôvo *under* Vargas, Getúlio, administration
Candomblé. *See* Spiritism
Cangaceiros (rural bandits) 218, 480, 1209, 1211, 1219, 1221, 1226-27, 1281, 1669; Lampião (Virgolino F. da Silva) 1209, 1735, 1785; Silvino, Antônio 1744. *See also* Rural life
Capitalism 232
Carnival 1071, 1243, 1736, 1739, 1742, 1745, 1753-54, 1759, 1765, 1767, 1774, 1776. *See also* Music; Samba
Castelo Branco, Humberto de, administration of 565, 571, 607, 650, 691, 1138, 1515; biography 616; economic policies 742; and Vernon Walters 742
Catholic Church 224, 423, 739, 1514-57, 1676; attacked 297; political role 324, 347, 349, 541, 1514-17, 1527-37, 1602, 1694; in rural areas 1196, 1546; statistics 39. *See also* Arns, Dom Paulo Evaristo; Câmara, Dom Helder; Leme, Cardinal Sebastião
Ceará 1116, 1165, 1172, 1196, 1294; Padre Cícero 1204, 1212-14, 1217, 1220, 1228. *See also* Northeast
Censorship 569, 584, 1629, 1675, 1689
Chemical industry 882, 891, 909, 914
Childhood 1147, 1158, 1278, 1312, 1812
Chile, Allende regime 590; post-Allende 924
Cícero, Padre 1220, 1222-25, 1228-29, 1252, 1678
Civil and human rights 381, 423, 429, 460, 536, 538, 568, 597, 600, 1533, 1536. *See also* Torture
Civil service 369, 382-83
Cold War 282, 298, 321, 683
Communism, bibliography 138, 152; Comintern in Brazil 295-96, 298, 308, 400-01;

Partido Comunista Brasileira (P.C.B.) 282, 284, 294, 300, 309-13, 323-24, 386, 400-01, 478, 508-09, 622, 637, 1206; theory 282-323, 386, 400-01; Trotskyism 283, 305, 386. *See also* Cold War; Prestes, Luis Carlos; Socialism; Urban guerrillas
Conscientização 1539, 1784, 1787-89, 1798
Constitutional law 226, 229, 230, 235-36, 255, 267, 269, 340, 350, 352-53, 365, 483, 1163; penal code 378
Constitution of 1934 354, 360, 362, 368, 372, 507, 1029, 1040
Constitution of 1937 351, 354, 360, 372, 509. *See also* Estado Nôvo *under* Vargas, Getúlio, administration
Constitution of 1967 357, 396
Cooking 1417, 1421, 1724, 1731, 1734
Coronéis 218, 236, 389, 423, 428, 480, 1168, 1189, 1192, 1199, 1252. *See also* Rural life
Corporatism 271-72, 279, 340-41, 423, 429, 431, 433-44, 446, 478, 509-10, 516, 527, 552, 922-23, 1022, 1484
Costa e Silva, Artur da, administration of 566, 580, 691; biography 615
Crime 1240, 1269, 1271, 1371
Cruz, Oswaldo 182, 963, 1194, 1833
Cultura Política 238, 446, 453; index 237
Cultural statistics 3, 11-12, 16-17, 23-24. *See also* Culture
Cultural values 334, 559, 1239, 1637
Culture 1597-1694; bibliography 1607

Dependency theory 243, 299, 339, 700-48, 760-61, 842, 910, 1237
Duarte, Paulo 462
Dutra, Eurico Gaspar 287

Economic statistics 6, 9-14, 16-17, 19-22, 24, 171, 187, 768, 770, 794-95, 797, 804, 806, 808-09, 812-13, 858-61, 920, 934; and population growth 989, 992; price indexes 801, 803, 806, 920, 1075
Economy 166-67, 171, 175-76, 204, 762, 791-815, 821-22, 927-28, 1114; bibliography 132, 139, 147, 161, 193, 825, 1078; policy-making 32-35, 37, 829-30, 832, 846; post-1964 122, 844-72, 1095, 1098-99
Education 1780-1809; bibliography 1783, 1799; careers 1257, 1259; rural 1782, 1821; technical 1785-86. *See also* Primary schools; Secondary schools
Education, Catholic 1538
Electoral politics 389-90, 404, 415-16, 424, 434-35, 443, 454, 469, 480, 482, 499, 509, 512, 518, 528, 531, 601; 1960 elections 443
Elites, political 210, 249, 336-37, 418, 424, 430-32, 434-35, 443, 480, 482, 527, 537. *See also* Political system
Estado Nôvo. *See* Vargas, Getúlio, administration
Ethnic groups, Germans 1472, 1489-90, 1499, 1502, 1506-07, 1510; Italians 989,

Ethnic groups (cont'd) 992, 1484, 1486, 1488, 1491-93, 1496, 1504-05, 1512; Japanese 989, 992, 1483, 1487, 1493-95, 1497-98, 1501, 1503, 1508-09, 1511, 1513; Poles 1500; Syrian-Lebanese 1492, 1603. *See also* Jews
Exiles from military regime 551, 561, 579, 588

Fascism. *See* Corporatism; Integralism
Family structure and behavior 1050, 1051, 1057-59, 1061, 1067, 1069, 1078, 1088, 1156, 1158, 1233-34, 1280-81, 1308, 1310, 1329, 1405, 1600; bibliography 1282; divorce 1285, 1291, 1315; fiction 1074, 1283; laws on 366
Favelas 455, 989, 1057, 1066, 1068, 1077, 1078, 1081-84, 1740; culture of poverty 1070; rights of inhabitants 361. *See also* Mucambos; Urban slums
Federalism 164, 203, 259, 374, 416-17, 423, 425, 434, 477, 479, 483-85, 529, 546
Fernandes, Florestan 195, 269, 406, 1244-46, 1355-56, 1786
Figueiredo, João Baptista de 630
Folk medicine 1464, 1594-95, 1596. *See also* Medicine
Folklore 1145, 1423, 1441, 1476, 1656; bibliography 1726. *See also* Popular Culture
Fontoura, João Neves da 466
Foreign influence, cultural 212, 559, 595, 1622, 1639, 1832; economic 212, 595, 1079
Foreign relations 43, 67, 216, 654-99, 760; Brazil as world power 165, 172-73, 398
Freire, Paulo 1539, 1784, 1787-89, 1798
Freyre, Gilberto 468-69, 974-76, 1063, 1249-50, 1292, 1306, 1340, 1346, 1351, 1360-70, 1373, 1383, 1401-04, 1406-09, 1421, 1423, 1428, 1615-17

Geisel, Ernesto, administration 564
Geography 92, 193, 727, 891, 962, 1017, 1095, 1195, 1235, 1273; bibliography 118-19, 150; economic issues 736, 792, 824, 988, 1106, 1114, 1141, 1200; frontier 1012, 1115, 1123, 1203, 1509
Góes Monteiro, Pedro Aurélio de 605, 612
Government, local 79; biographies of officeholders 25, 29, 35, 37, 425, 1298; municipal level 44, 234, 480
Guerrilla warfare, rural 604, 620

Histories, general 163-85, 393-95, 399, 408-10, 413-14, 422, 432, 815; Old Republic (1889-1930) 387-88, 392-95, 1620, 1646, 1652
Historiography 185-224, 294-95, 392, 399, 408, 1435; economic history 62, 799, 845; Estado Nôvo 437; labor 949; 1964 *coup* 596
History, bibliography 123-24, 384, 653; general information 45-46, 180, 403
Hydroelectric power 911

Immigrants, European 169,

1045-47, 1496, 1573. *See also* Ethnic groups; Immigration
Immigration 989, 1016, 1020, 1022, 1024, 1026-28, 1036, 1046-47, 1505; anti-immigration material 1029, 1040; economic aspects 1014, 1103; pro-immigration 2. *See also* Immigrants, European
Imperialism 227-78, 401, 760-61. *See also* Foreign relations
Industrialization 621, 713, 732-33, 750, 783, 793, 811, 867, 873-914, 989, 1118, 1245; bibliography 872; capital goods 828; and urbanization 989, 991. *See also* Volta Redônda
Insurance 815
Insurrection of 1935 296, 304, 320, 400, 405, 477, 508, 514, 619. *See also* Communism
Integralism 271-72, 279, 325-26, 333, 337-38, 342-49, 444, 486, 508-10, 601, 1190; aid from Italy 1512; and Church 1525, 1539, 1551, 1555-57. *See also* Salgado, Plínio

Japanese-Brazilian Relations 667
Jews 1485, 1563-81, 1603; attacked 254, 327-32, 1563-64, 1596, 1603; bibliography 1571, 1579, 1581
Journalism 550, 553, 1067, 1619; periodical indexes 95-107, 237; and race 1414-15; and women 1287. *See also* *Cultura Política*
Julião, Francisco. *See* Social movements, rural

Kennedy, John F., death of 787
Kubitchek, Juscelino, administration of 659, 683, 820, 984

Labor 143, 495, 915-54, 989, 1344; bibliography 917, 930; and Church 1554; theoretical works on 257, 884; working force 866, 917, 929, 939, 1077, 1296, 1303, 1317, 1325, 1344
Labor, Ministry of 143, 495, 929, 1077
Lacerda, Carlos 275, 412, 501
Lampião (Virgolino F. da Silva). *See* Cangaceiros
Land tenure 277, 303, 401, 708, 719-20, 723, 725, 729, 835, 1115, 1117, 1120-21, 1130-31, 1134, 1139-40, 1275, 1277, 1365-66, 1677, 1694; and Church 1542. *See also* Agriculture
Latifúndia. *See* Land tenure
Law schools, bibliography 110; Recife Law School 477, 1833, 1836-37; Recife Law School Library 78, 85. *See also* Universities
Left, the. *See* Communism
Leme, Cardinal Sebastião 1532, 1551. *See also* Catholic Church
Liberalization, post-1974 547, 555, 562-63, 575, 577, 584, 586-87, 767
Literature 1437, 1440, 1443, 1597, 1609-12, 1637, 1646, 1649-50; bibliography 158. *See also* Poetry
Living Conditions 5, 23-24, 458, 989, 1075, 1084. *See also* Rural life; Urban life
Lusardo, João Baptista 449
Lutz, Bertha 1288, 1332. *See also* feminism *under* Women

Magalhães, Agamemnon 495. *See also* Northeast; Pernambuco
Maranhão 1583
Mato Grosso 1038, 1473. *See also* Amerindians
Médici, Garrastazú, administration 554
Medicine 90, 140, 179, 963, 1194; mental illness 1423. *See also* Folk medicine
Melo, Padre Antônio 1262. *See also* Social movements, rural
Mental illness. *See* Medicine
Messianism 1220, 1222-25, 1228-29, 1252, 1678. *See also* Padre Cícero
Middle sectors 1051, 1058, 1067, 1266, 1328-29; political role 246, 249, 369, 402, 429, 1052
Migration 989, 993, 1013, 1018, 1023-24, 1030-31, 1073, 1336, 1668. *See also* Population data
Military coup (1964), defended 583, 591, 598-99
Minas Gerais 359, 404, 893, 918, 952, 1025, 1158; agriculture 1141-42, 1192; fiction 1187; race relations 1394; urban life 956, 1005; women 1301
Minifúndia 1109. *See also* Land tenure
Mucambos 1055, 1063, 1071
Municípios. *See* Government, local
Music 1750, 1753-79; bibliography 1770, 1773; and race 1424, 1433. *See also* Carnival; Samba

Names 1647
Nascimento, Edson Arantes de (Pelé) 1695, 1697-98, 1700, 1705-06, 1709-10, 1713-14, 1716, 1718
Nationalism 200, 213-14, 241-44, 251-54, 263, 265, 276, 280, 334, 362, 394-95, 1537, 1640; after 1964, 574; economic 700, 743, 746, 766-67, 879
Nina Rodrígues, Raimundo 1370, 1392
Northeast 490, 1149-51, 1167, 1174-75, 1200-27, 1249-50, 1325, 1385, 1545; agricultural development 754, 786, 791, 796, 824, 826, 837, 872-73, 894-95, 902-03, 928-29, 943, 1004, 1040, 1093, 1096-99, 1104, 1106, 1116, 1129, 1139, 1170, 1172, 1264-65, 1806, 1808; bibliography 156, 754; culture 1625, 1727, 1748-49; fiction 1179-84, 1230-31, 1687, 1690, 1751; surplus population 1043-44; urban life 1062; World War II 1155
Nutrition 1417, 1421, 1724, 1731, 1734

Old Republic. *See* Histories, general
Oligarchies, political role 188, 272, 480, 1168

Paraíba 480; politics 389, 480, 523
Paraná 1511; coffee frontier 1114-15, 1123, 1203
Pelé. *See* Nascimento, Edson Arantes de
Performing arts 1668-94; bibliography 1684
Pernambuco 477, 479, 495, 902, 1169; religious cults 1592; rural life 1152, 1262, 1313, 1668; urban life 853, 958, 971-72, 976, 1005, 1055, 1169, 1619. *See also* Northeast

Petroleum 712, 746, 775, 840-42, 883. *See also* Nationalism
Philanthropy 1247
Piauí 608. *See also* Northeast
Poetry 325, 1601, 1608, 1634-35, 1641, 1644, 1752, 1758; women's 1335
Political ideas 229, 239-40, 244-45, 247, 266-69, 272, 275, 337, 376-77, 401, 414, 497
Political parties 227-48, 376-77, 401, 414, 418-20, 423, 425-26, 469, 472, 496, 499, 528-29, 531, 571, 591-93
Political system 225-281, 412, 414-17, 423-26, 430-35, 443, 446, 451-52, 454, 467-72, 480, 483, 502-12, 526-28, 591-93. *See also* Political parties
Politics, 1945-1954 318, 392-95, 400, 405, 407, 414, 429-30, 432, 440, 442, 456, 459-60, 472-73, 482, 501, 512, 515, 531, 745, 832, 984, 1270
Politics, 1954-1964 301, 392, 394-95, 400, 402, 405, 407, 414, 429-32, 434-35, 438-39, 443, 460-65, 467, 471, 473-74, 487, 491-92, 494, 513, 513, 515, 567, 567, 832, 983, 1100
Politics, post-1964 273-74, 398, 401, 414-17, 423, 426, 430-32, 513, 526-27, 536-601
Popular culture 1722-52; popular names 1647
Population data 1, 4-5, 7-9, 11-12, 16-17, 19, 21, 24, 74, 91, 989, 995, 1053, 1073, 1136, 1273, 1376, 1479, 1560; census data criticized 1034. *See also* Migration
Populism 384, 416, 423, 432, 436, 438-40, 442-43, 445, 454-55, 459-62, 483, 497, 502-12, 519-21, 526-27, 922-23; and foreign policy 686, 696. *See also* Vargas, Getúlio, administration
Portuguese heritage 165, 392, 401, 1000, 1429, 1596, 1615-17, 1624, 1642, 1689
Prestes, Luis Carlos 285-86, 289, 291-92, 303, 312-20, 386, 400. *See also* Tenentismo
Primary Schools 1147, 1256, 1260, 1293, 1301, 1809-23; bibliography 1783, 1799. *See also* Education
Protestantism 1085, 1531, 1558-61
Public administration 350, 355-56, 363-65, 367, 370-71, 380
Public health 182, 963, 989, 1194, 1833

Race and race relations 184, 1049-51, 1057, 1080, 1161, 1164, 1321, 1377-1409, 1432-44; bibliography 1339, 1436; intermarriage 1405, 1435; "whitening" theme 1343, 1375, 1382, 1386-69, 1402-03. *See also* Afro-Brazilian studies; Nina Rodrígues; Racial data
Racial data 8, 11-12, 24, 45, 1053, 1055, 1066
Railways 822, 827
"Realidade Brasileira" 165, 174, 178, 181, 186, 197, 199, 210, 213-15, 241, 252-53, 257-58, 260, 264, 276-80, 339, 391, 548, 660, 1019
Regionalism 164, 203, 477, 479, 484, 485, 529; center-periphery relations 1015; economic integration 760,

Regionalism (cont'd) 824, 877, 927-28, 973, 1013, 1040, 1043; fiction and literature 1179-81, 1187, 1610, 1612, 1617, 1634
Religion. *See* Catholic Church; Jews; Protestantism; Spiritism
Research and library guides 55-94, 220, 222
Revolution of 1930 194, 204, 392-95, 400, 429, 466, 481, 500, 517, 523, 525, 532, 610, 633, 652-53, 1623, 1743. *See also* Vargas, Getúlio, administration
Right, the. *See* Corporatism; Integralism
Rio de Janeiro (federal district) 454, 455, 767, 802, 989, 1248, 1347; population 1053, 1071, 1081; urbanization 955, 963-64, 966-67, 970-71, 981-82, 986, 989, 1006, 1049, 1060, 1064; voluntary associations 1056, 1701, 1708, 1716
Rio Grande de Norte 447, 477-78
Rio Grande do Sul 466, 474, 484, 489, 524, 1020; bibliography 142, 160, 457; fiction 1198, 1614; positivism 1643; race and ethnic relations 1047, 1490; rural life 1156, 1232; urban life 971, 998, 1005, 1395-96
Rondônia 1042
Rural life 250, 289, 1105, 1143-1203, 1600; agricultural conditions 943, 945, 954, 1089-90, 1096, 1102-03, 1105, 1114-15, 1117, 1135, 1146, 1148, 1156, 1188, 1193; cost of living 934; fertility 1037, 1136; social structure 1047, 1104, 1112, 1165, 1167, 1216, 1221, 1225-27, 1240. *See also* Sertão
Salgado, Plínio 326, 333, 337, 342-49, 601, 1190; bibliography 338. *See also* Integralism
Samba 1433, 1736, 1740, 1742, 1759, 1765, 1767, 1774, 1776. *See also* Carnival; Music
Santa Catarina 827, 1005; immigration to 1020; race prejudice 1345
São Paulo (state) 435, 485, 561, 751, 908, 1309; agriculture 1032-33, 1119, 1132, 1148, 1191; economic role 485, 719, 774, 830, 890, 901, 904-06, 1011, 1080; immigration to 989, 1026, 1028, 1036, 1327; Jews in 332, 1565, 1567-68; middle classes 1051, 1067; population 916, 942, 947, 1052, 1058, 1067-68, 1073, 1237, 1668; Prado family of 1309; race relations 1081, 1340, 1342, 1385, 1391, 1415, 1483, 1486-88, 1509-10, 1580; rural life 1148, 1163, 1202, 1328-29; São Paulo City 982, 992, 1005, 1009-10, 1051-52; strikes 952; university of 1831; women in 1288-89, 1301, 1328
São Paulo School of Sociology 1340
Science 182, 1834
Secondary schools 1293, 1813. *See also* Education
Sergipe 1357
Sertão (backlands) 1143, 1165, 1172, 1176, 1210, 1216, 1228, 1264, 1541

Silvino, Antônio. *See* Cangaceiros
Simonsen, Roberto 899
Social legislation, of Vargas administration 369, 373, 378-79, 468, 940, 1078, 1171. *See also* Vargas, Getúlio, administration
Social mobility. *See* Society
Social movements, rural 490, 570, 1167, 1205-07, 1213-15, 1217-18, 1281. *See also* Melo, Padre Antônio
Social psychology 244, 1013, 1049, 1057, 1086, 1170, 1628
Social security legislation 373, 497, 519, 1077, 1171
Socialism 231, 302, 561, 921
Society 166-68, 170, 177, 180-81, 183-84, 1048-59, 1072, 1081-83, 1086, 1118, 1158, 1230-1336, 1391, 1438-39, 1600; aging 1251; bibliography 1236, 1238; mobility 1013, 1279, 1337, 1341, 1358, 1412
South Africa, comparison with 1272, 1379, 1381, 1400
Soviet Union 146, 159
Spiritism 1413, 1416, 1425, 1434, 1518-19, 1531, 1559, 1582-96, 1722
Sports, rugby 1703; soccer (*futebol*) 1344a, 1695-1702, 1704-21. *See also* Nascimento, Edson Arantes de (Pelé)
Superior War College (E.S.G.). *See* Armed forces

Távora, Juarez 648
Technical assistance, Israeli 1094. *See also* Foreign Relations
Teixeira, Anísio 1791, 1797, 1800, 1804-05, 1823. *See also* Education; Primary Schools
Tenentismo 189, 252, 269, 290, 503-04, 506-07, 606, 608-09, 611, 617-18, 627, 634-35, 641, 648, 652, 1052. *See also* Prestes, Luis Carlos
Torture, political use of 539-42, 545, 549, 556-57, 568, 573, 597, 600. *See also* Civil and human rights

Umbanda. *See* Spiritism
United States role 544, 595, 654-56, 666, 680-82, 684, 693, 699, 721, 752-53, 755-56, 758-59, 762, 764, 766, 771, 776-78, 780-81, 783, 785-89, 1079, 1142, 1792, 1806, 1829. *See also* Foreign relations
Universities 211, 1824-45; bibliography 1826-37; graduates 905, 944; theses listed 125, 140. *See also* Education; Law schools
University of São Paulo, School of Medicine 140. *See also* Medicine
Urban guerrillas 293, 306-07, 401. *See also* Communism
Urban life 5, 17, 19-20, 24, 41, 91, 455, 458, 698, 930, 989, 993, 1048-88, 1280-81, 1344, 1439, 1594, 1600; cost of living 801-03, 904-06, 926; the poor 716, 930, 941-42, 947, 1057, 1075, 1237, 1257, 1263, 1269, 1547, 1682
Urban slums 989, 1049, 1050, 1082. *See also* Favelas
Urbanization 925, 955-1010, 1697; bibliography 961, 986, 1003. *See also* Brasília; Rio de Janeiro

Vargas, Getúlio 192, 437, 445, 452-53, 455-56, 463,

Vargas (cont'd)
468, 470, 472, 477, 483, 488, 493, 501, 503-12, 516, 519-22, 524-25, 746
Vargas, Getúlio, administration (1930-1945) 205, 252, 263, 295-96, 386, 400, 405, 414, 430-32, 434, 440-41, 447, 449, 451, 454, 475, 481, 483-84, 486, 495, 502-12, 523, 525, 605, 610, 922-23, 937, 1040, 1261, 1267, 1280, 1297, 1347, 1513, 1532, 1554, 1556-57, 1570, 1576, 1757, 1781, 1819; economic policies 728, 749, 770, 790, 816-19, 831-33, 950, 1125-26; Estado Nôvo 260, 348-49, 374, 400, 405, 437, 447-48, 450, 464, 475, 477, 483, 495, 501, 516, 605, 1040, 1055, 1315, 1570, 1574, 1680, 1793, 1801, 1803, 1822, 1843; historiography 202, 205-06, 405; 1932 Revolution 476, 505. *See also* Insurrection of 1935; Social legislation
Verz Cruz 980. *See also* Brasília
Vianna, Oliveira 191, 260, 337; bibliography 108
Visual arts 1653-67, 1728; bibliography 1665, 1681
Volta Redônda 842, 874, 906. *See also* Industrialization

Walters, Gen. Vernon 651, 655
Women, biographies 28; courtship 1233; feminism 1287, 1300, 1304, 1311, 1314, 1318-19, 1326, 1332; in Northeast 1176; role of 1059, 1282-1336, 1600; in work force 917, 1296, 1303, 1317, 1325

Zweig, Stefan 1485